CULTURAL METAPHORS

TO MY MANY FRIENDS AND COLLEAGUES, UNIVERSITY OF MARYLAND AT COLLEGE PARK

Mike Royko, in his classic book about Mayor Daley of Chicago, acknowledged the help of others in the following way:

"I am grateful for the help of many knowledgeable Chicagoans in putting this book together. I won't name them, so they can unpack their bags and stay in town."

Similarly, I will not identify all of my many friends and colleagues at the Smith School of Business and other units of the University of Maryland, College Park, but in this instance the main reason is that the list would be excessively long. Suffice it to say that all of them have helped to enrich my life during the past 32 years; have provided support and encouragement for projects, many of which in retrospect were of questionable value and promise; and have helped to make life both intellectually stimulating and socially enjoyable.

See Mike Royko, Acknowledgements, in *Boss: Richard J. Daley of Chicago* (New York: E. P. Dutton, 1971).

Cultural Metaphors

Readings, Research Translations,
and Commentary

Martin J. Gannon

Sage Publications, Inc.
International Educational and Professional Publisher
Thousand Oaks ■ London ■ New Delhi

For information:

Sage Publications, Inc.
2455 Teller Road
Thousand Oaks, California 91320
E-mail: order@sagepub.com

Sage Publications Ltd.
6 Bonhill Street
London EC2A 4PU
United Kingdom

Sage Publications India Pvt. Ltd.
M-32 Market
Greater Kailash I
New Delhi 110 048 India

Printed in the United States of America

Library of Congress Cataloging-in-Publication Data

Main entry under title:
    Cultural metaphors: Readings, research translations, and
commentary / edited by Martin J. Gannon.
      p. cm.
    Includes bibliographical references and index.
    ISBN 0-7619-1336-X (cloth: alk. paper)
    ISBN 0-7619-1337-8 (pbk.: alk. paper)
    1. Culture—Philosophy. 2. Metaphor—Cross-cultural studies.
3. Cross-cultural orientation. 4. Social psychology. I. Gannon,
Martin J. II. Title.
    HM621 .C87 2000
    306'.01—dc21   00-008948

01 02 03 04 05 06 7 6 5 4 3 2 1

Acquiring Editor:	Marquita Flemming
Editorial Assistant:	MaryAnn Vail
Production Editor:	Diana E. Axelsen
Editorial Assistant:	Cindy Bear
Typesetter/Designer:	Lynn Miyata
Indexer:	Mary Mortensen
Cover Designer:	Michelle Lee

Contents

Preface and Acknowledgments   ix

PART I: Metaphors as Critical and Necessary   1

1. **Metaphors We Live By**   3
   George Lakoff and Mark Johnson

   Chapter 1: Concepts We Live By   3
   Chapter 2: The Systematicity of Metaphorical Concepts   5

2. **Why Metaphors Are Necessary and Not Just Nice**   9
   Andrew Ortony

   The Compactness Thesis   12
   The Inexpressibility Thesis   14
   The Vividness Thesis   16

PART II: Conceptual Frameworks for Cultural Metaphors   23

3. **Edward Hall's Multiple Metaphors:**   25
   Research Translation and Extension

4. **The Confucius Connection:**   **31**
   From Cultural Roots to Economic Growth
   Geert Hofstede and Michael Harris Bond

     Why East Asia?   32
     The Neo-Confucian Hypothesis   33
     Confucius and His Teachings   34
     The New Science of Culture Measurement   35
     Confucius and Economic Growth   44
     Western Minds and Eastern Minds   47
     The Quest for Global Management Synergy   49
     Selected Bibliography   50

5. **The Work of Geert Hofstede: Commentary**   **51**

6. **Basic Types of Human Relations, Collectivism,**   **55**
   and Individualism: *Research Translation*

7. **French Wine: An Illustration of**   **59**
   a Cultural Metaphor
   Martin J. Gannon, Peter Brown, and Sharon Ribas

     Pureness   60
     Classification   63
     Composition   68
     Suitability   72
     The Maturation Process   73

PART III: Winners and Losers   **81**

8. **Samuel P. Huntington's** *The Clash of Civilizations*:   **83**
   Research Translation and Commentary
   Commentary   86

9. **Powershift and the Assumed Decline of Nations:**   **89**
   Research Translation and Commentary

PART IV: Symbolism of Cultural Metaphors   **91**

10. **Football Games and Rock Concerts: The Ritual**   93
    Enactment of American Success Models
    Susan P. Montague and Robert Morais

11. **Bowling Alone: America's Declining Social Capital**   109
    Robert D. Putnam

    Whatever Happened to Civic Engagement?   111
    Countertrends   114
    Good Neighborliness and Social Trust   117
    Why Is U.S. Social Capital Eroding?   118
    What Is to Be Done?   120

12. **The Persistence of Cultural Stability: Applying the**   125
    Fiske Framework to North and South Italy:
    Research Translation

13. **The Balinese Cockfight:** *Research Translation*   129

14. **Negotiating With "Romans"**   133
    Stephen E. Weiss

    Selecting a Strategy   135
    Implementing Your Strategy   151
    Toward Cross-Cultural Negotiating Expertise   157

PART V: Metaphorical Applications   **163**

15. **Language Shock: Understanding the**   165
    Culture of Conversation
    Michael Agar

16. **Stages in Cross Cultural Collaboration**   173
    William H. Newman

Cross Cultural Field Study	174
Stage 1: Identifying and Committing to a Cross Cultural Win-win Strategy	178
Stage 2: Translating the Strategy Into Viable Action Plans	184
Stage 3: Execution: Making the Cross Cultural Collaboration Happen	187
Stage 4: Self-Initiation by the Emerging Organization	189
Executives Suited to Each Stage	192
Conclusions and Implications for Future Research	195
Appendix A	197
Appendix B	198

17. The Transferability of Leadership Training in the East Asian Context — 203

R. I. Westwood and Andrew Chan

Introduction	203
On the Culture-Boundedness of the North American Leadership Perspective	206
Headship or Leadership?	211
An East Asian Perspective on Headship/Leadership	213
Implications for Leadership Training and Development in East Asia	224
Conclusion	226
Commentary by Martin J. Gannon	231

18. Metaphors for Change: The ALPs Model of Change Management — 233

Craig L. Pearce and Charles P. Osmond

Dimensional Approaches to Culture	235
Metaphorical Approaches to Culture	236
The ALPs Model Approach	237
A Metaphor for Britain: The Traditional British House	238
Case Illustrations: How Access Leverage Points Impact the Management of Change	242
Conclusion	246
Selected Bibliography	249

Author Index	251
Subject Index	253
About the Editor	262

Preface

It seems as if only a few years have passed since business schools and other university departments expanded their curricula to emphasize globalization. Various perspectives and approaches have been developed, and some of them have been widely recognized as offering critical insight into business and nonbusiness issues. Geert Hofstede's framework (1980 and 1991) emphasizing five cross-cultural dimensions such as individualism-collectivism and desire for certainty has become particularly prominent, at least in part because other researchers have been able to use his measures to study their influence on such phenomena as entrepreneurship and innovation across nations. However, the overwhelming emphasis on accepting only cross-cultural dimensions that can be tested statistically and then related to other phenomena, although meritorious, needs to be supplemented by an in-depth, culture-specific perspective.

This book is designed to provide such a perspective. I have constructed this book and two related books, *Understanding Global Cultures: Metaphorical Journeys Through 23 Nations* (2nd. ed., Sage, 2001) and *Working Across Cultures: Applications and Exercises* (Sage, 2001) around the more expansive concept of metaphor, and particularly the cultural metaphor of a nation, which is any institution, phenomenon, or activity with which all or most citizens in a nation identify closely; ideally, it has originated in that particular nation, such as the Swedish *stuga* or unadorned summer home or the German symphony.

In Part I, we establish the importance and criticality of metaphors in general, and then in Part II, we review various conceptual frameworks that relate directly or indirectly to cultural metaphors. Our unit of analysis for cultural metaphors is the nation. In Part III, we turn our attention to a body of work that is very important but often overlooked by both professors of management and cross-cultural trainers in business, namely, the perspective of many prominent political scientists and journalists who basically conceive of the world in terms of zero-sum game theory, to the effect that some groups, such as nations, are treated as losers of power, whereas other groups, such as multinational corporations, are seen as winners. Part IV then explores the issue of the symbolism associated with cultural metaphors, and Part V describes specific uses of cultural metaphors or metaphorical applications.

Originally, I had conceived of this book as a readings book. However, as the ideas began to develop, it seemed more fitting to construct a distinctive or unique kind of book involving research translations, readings, and commentary on the research translations and readings. Also, the research translations include not only limited empirical studies in which specific hypotheses are tested, but also larger, more expansive works published as books and trendsetting articles. In part, this occurred because of the scope of the concepts used. This also occurred in part because some complex books and long articles were deemed so critical to the achievement of the book's objectives that the best, if not the only, possible way to highlight them in a readable fashion was to employ this format.

There are several people I would like to thank for providing input to this book. Michele Gelfand, Assistant Professor of Cross-Cultural and Organizational Psychology at the University of Maryland, has been particularly helpful because she has brought to my attention some perspectives that I had either overlooked or deemphasized in my 1994 book, when the concept of cultural metaphors was first introduced. Professors Severino Salvemini and Silvia Bagdadli of Bocconi University in Milan provided a collegial and comfortable environment in which a large portion of the writing occurred. As usual, my colleagues at the University of Maryland offered a supportive and intellectually stimulating environment in which the ideas for this book germinated. I wish to particularly thank Deans Howard Frank, Judy Olian, and Burte Leete. Colleagues who influenced some of the specific ideas in this book include Professors Stephen Carroll, Edwin Locke, Lee Preston, and Henry Sims in the Robert H. Smith School of Business, and Professor Michael Agar in the Anthropology Department. Professor Volker Rittberger of Tuebingen University in Germany provided insight into Samuel Huntington's influential work on culture. Two doctoral students, Sharyn Gardner and Abhishek Srivastava, ably assisted in the preparation of the manuscript. Needless to say, I bear responsibility for the final editorial judgments made and any errors or omissions, however unintentioned, that may occur.

PART I

Metaphors as Critical and Necessary

In some circles, metaphors—the use of one phenomenon and its characteristics to describe another phenomenon—have a poor reputation. Among the empirically inclined, for example, it is the systematic use of data to test hypotheses that is considered important. Metaphors are useful only to the extent that they give rise to hypotheses and theories. It is little wonder then, that metaphors have been primarily emphasized as literary devices in the formal educational system.

However, as the two classic readings in Part I cogently demonstrate, we live by metaphors, for they allow us to think about and organize chaotic reality, and thus they are necessary and not just nice. Also, it is the tension between the metaphor and the phenomenon that jars us to approach reality in a new and different way. But the readings argue the case far more persuasively than I am able to do, and I encourage you to peruse them closely and to employ metaphors in the manner that the authors suggest.

CHAPTER 1

Metaphors We Live By

GEORGE LAKOFF
MARK JOHNSON

Chapter 1: Concepts We Live By

Metaphor is for most people a device of the poetic imagination and the rhetorical flourish—a matter of extraordinary rather than ordinary language. Moreover, metaphor is typically viewed as characteristic of language alone, a matter of words rather than thought or action. For this reason, most people think they can get along perfectly well without metaphor. We have found, on the contrary, that metaphor is pervasive in everyday life, not just in language but in thought and action. Our ordinary conceptual system, in terms of which we both think and act, is fundamentally metaphorical in nature.

The concepts that govern our thought are not just matters of the intellect. They also govern our everyday functioning, down to the most mundane details. Our concepts structure what we perceive, how we get around in the world, and how we relate to other people. Our conceptual system thus plays a central role in defining our everyday realities. If we are right in suggesting that our conceptual system is largely metaphorical, then the way we think,

AUTHORS' NOTE: Originally published in G. Lakoff and M. Johnson, *Metaphors We Live By*. Chicago: University of Chicago Press, 1980. Copyright © 1980 by the University of Chicago Press. Reprinted by permission.

what we experience, and what we do every day is very much a matter of metaphor.

But our conceptual system is not something we are normally aware of. In most of the little things we do every day, we simply think and act more or less automatically along certain lines. Just what these lines are is by no means obvious. One way to find out is by looking at language. Since communication is based on the same conceptual system that we use in thinking and acting, language is an important source of evidence for what that system is like.

Primarily on the basis of linguistic evidence, we have found that most of our ordinary conceptual system is metaphorical in nature. And we have found a way to begin to identify in detail just what the metaphors are that structure how we perceive, how we think, and what we do.

To give some idea of what it could mean for a concept to be metaphorical and for such a concept to structure an everyday activity, let us start with the concept ARGUMENT and the conceptual metaphor ARGUMENT IS WAR. This metaphor is reflected in our everyday language by a wide variety of expressions:

> **ARGUMENT IS WAR**
>
> Your claims are *indefensible.*
> He *attacked every weak point* in my argument.
> His criticisms were *right on target.*
> I *demolished* his argument.
> I've never *won* an argument with him.
> You disagree? Okay, *shoot!*
> If you use that *strategy,* he'll *wipe you out.*
> He *shot down* all of my arguments.

It is important to see that we don't just *talk* about arguments in terms of war. We can actually win or lose arguments. We see the person we are arguing with as an opponent. We attack his positions and we defend our own. We gain and lose ground. We plan and use strategies. If we find a position indefensible, we can abandon it and take a new line of attack. Many of the things we *do* in arguing are partially structured by the concept of war. Though there is no physical battle, there is a verbal battle, and the structure of an argument—attack, defense, counterattack, etc.—reflects this. It is in this sense that the ARGUMENT IS WAR metaphor is one that we live by in this culture; it structures the actions we perform in arguing.

Try to imagine a culture where arguments are not viewed in terms of war, where no one wins or loses, where there is no sense of attacking or defending, gaining or losing ground. Imagine a culture where an argument is viewed as a dance, the participants are seen as performers, and the goal is to perform in a balanced and aesthetically pleasing way. In such a culture, people would view arguments differently, experience them differently, carry them out differently, and talk about them differently. But *we* would probably not view them as arguing at all: they would simply be doing something different. It would seem strange even to call what they were doing "arguing." Perhaps the most neutral way of describing this difference between their culture and ours would be to say that we have a discourse form structured in terms of battle and they have one structured in terms of dance.

This is an example of what it means for a metaphorical concept, namely, ARGUMENT IS WAR, to structure (at least in part) what we do and how we understand what we are doing when we argue. *The essence of metaphor is understanding and experiencing one kind of thing in terms of another.* It is not that arguments are a subspecies of war. Arguments and wars are different kinds of things, verbal discourse and armed conflict—and the actions performed are different kinds of actions. But ARGUMENT is partially structured, understood, performed, and talked about in terms of WAR. The concept is metaphorically structured, the activity is metaphorically structured, and, consequently, the language is metaphorically structured.

Moreover, this is the *ordinary* way of having an argument and talking about one. The normal way for us to talk about attacking a position is to use the words "attack a position." Our conventional ways of talking about arguments presuppose a metaphor we are hardly ever conscious of. The metaphor is not merely in the words we use—it is in our very concept of an argument. The language of argument is not poetic, fanciful, or rhetorical; it is literal. We talk about arguments that way because we conceive of them that way—and we act according to the way we conceive of things.

The most important claim we have made so far is that metaphor is not just a matter of language, that is, of mere words. We shall argue that, on the contrary, human *thought processes* are largely metaphorical. This is what we mean when we say that the human conceptual system is metaphorically structured and defined. Metaphors as linguistic expressions are possible precisely because there are metaphors in a person's conceptual system. Therefore, whenever in this book we speak of metaphors, such as ARGUMENT IS WAR, it should be understood that *metaphor* means *metaphorical concept.*

Chapter 2: The Systematicity of Metaphorical Concepts

Arguments usually follow patterns; that is, there are certain things we typically do and do not do in arguing. The fact that we in part conceptualize arguments in terms of battle systematically influences the shape arguments take and the way we talk about what we do in arguing. Because the metaphorical concept is systematic, the language we use to talk about that aspect of the concept is systematic.

We saw in the ARGUMENT IS WAR metaphor that expressions from the vocabulary of war, e.g., *attack a position, indefensible, strategy, new line of attack, win, gain ground,* etc., form a systematic way of talking about the battling aspects of arguing. It is no accident that these expressions mean what they mean when we use them to talk about arguments. A portion of the conceptual network of battle partially characterizes the concept of an argument, and the language follows suit. Since metaphorical expressions in our language are tied to metaphorical concepts in a systematic way, we can use metaphorical linguistic expressions to study the nature of metaphorical concepts and to gain an understanding of the metaphorical nature of our activities.

To get an idea of how metaphorical expressions in everyday language can give us insight into the metaphorical nature of the concepts that structure our everyday activities, let us consider the metaphorical concept TIME IS MONEY as it is reflected in contemporary English.

TIME IS MONEY

You're *wasting* my time.
This gadget will *save* you hours.
I don't *have* the time to *give* you.
How do you *spend* your time these days?
That flat tire *cost* me an hour.
I've *invested* a lot of time in her.
I don't *have enough* time to *spare* for that.
You're *running out* of time.
You need to *budget* your time.
Put aside some time for ping-pong.
Is that *worth your while?*
Do you *have* much time *left?*
He's living on *borrowed* time.
You don't *use* your time *profitably.*
I *lost* a lot of time when I got sick.
Thank you for your time.

Time in our culture is a valuable commodity. It is a limited resource that we use to accomplish our goals. Because of the way that the concept of work has developed in modern Western culture, where work is typically associated with the time it takes and time is precisely quantified, it has become customary to pay people by the hour, week, or year. In our culture TIME IS

MONEY in many ways: telephone message units, hourly wages, hotel room rates, yearly budgets, interest on loans, and paying your debt to society by "serving time." These practices are relatively new in the history of the human race, and by no means do they exist in all cultures. They have arisen in modern industrialized societies and structure our basic everyday activities in a very profound way. Corresponding to the fact that we *act* as if time is a valuable commodity—a limited resource, even money—we *conceive of* time that way. Thus we understand and experience time as the kind of thing that can be spent, wasted, budgeted, invested wisely or poorly, saved, or squandered.

TIME IS MONEY, TIME IS A LIMITED RESOURCE, and TIME IS A VALUABLE COMMODITY are all metaphorical concepts. They are metaphorical since we are using our everyday experiences with money, limited resources, and valuable commodities to conceptualize time. This isn't a necessary way for human beings to conceptualize time; it is tied to our culture. There are cultures where time is none of these things.

The metaphorical concepts TIME IS MONEY, TIME IS A RESOURCE, and TIME IS A VALUABLE COMMODITY form a single system based on subcategorization, since in our society money is a limited resource and limited resources are valuable commodities. These subcategorization relationships characterize entailment relationships between the metaphors. TIME IS MONEY entails that TIME IS A LIMITED RESOURCE, which entails that TIME IS A VALUABLE COMMODITY.

We are adopting the practice of using the most specific metaphorical concept, in this case TIME IS MONEY, to characterize the entire system. Of the expressions listed under the TIME IS MONEY metaphor, some refer specifically to money (*spend, invest, budget, profitably, cost*), others to limited resources (*use, use up, have enough of, run out of*), and still others to valuable commodities (*have, give, lose, thank you for*). This is an example of the way in which metaphorical entailments can characterize a coherent system of metaphorical concepts and a corresponding coherent system of metaphorical expressions for those concepts.

Why Metaphors Are Necessary and Not Just Nice[1]

ANDREW ORTONY

A t least since the time of Aristotle metaphor has aroused the curiosity of thinkers. Yet, the questions about it are ill-formed and the answers correspondingly unhelpful. Aristotle regarded the command of metaphor as the mark of genius. By contrast, the nineteenth-century French linguist, Breal, who coined the word 'semantics,' had a low regard for metaphors. He believed that they teach us nothing new and are "like the sayings of some peasant endowed with good sense and honesty, but not without a certain rustic cunning."[2] There is fairly wide agreement that metaphor involves, or is, the transfer of meaning. Indeed, etymologically it means "transfer," being derived from the Greek *meta* (trans) + *pherein* (to carry). According to Aristotle[3] a metaphor is a means of comparing two terms and

AUTHOR'S NOTE: Originally published in *Educational Theory, 25*(1), 45-53. Copyright © 1975 by *Educational Theory*. Reprinted by permission.

this view is shared by Richards[4] who classified the two terms and the relationship between them as the "tenor" (today often called the "topic"), of which something is being asserted, the "vehicle," the term being used metaphorically to form the basis of the comparison, and the "ground," namely that which the two have in common. The dissimilarity between the two terms being compared determines what is called the "tension."

The view that metaphors are essentially comparisons is perhaps the nearest that we have to an accepted theory of metaphor. It does explain their intelligibility compared with anomaly but does not well explain the tension. Nor does it account for the important pedagogic value of metaphor. The purpose of this paper is to propose a view of metaphor which does account for these aspects: a view which while perhaps still not a theory has the comparative nature of metaphor as a consequence rather than an explanation. The view I shall put forward comprises three theses—the compactness thesis, the inexpressibility thesis and the vividness thesis. While all three are intimately related I believe them to be distinguishable.

Metaphors, and their close relatives, similes and analogies, have been used as teaching devices since the earliest writings of civilized man. The dialogues of Plato are full of them: there is the simile of the sails in *Parmenides* used to explain the nature of the relationship between Platonic Forms and the particular objects partaking of them, or there is the cave metaphor in *The Republic* designed to illuminate various levels of knowledge. The Bible is another good source of metaphor, and, of course, metaphor is the stock-in-trade of poets and writers. The widespread use of metaphor in even the earliest "teaching texts" however, suggests that Breal is wrong and that metaphor is more than just a literary stylistic device. We shall argue here that metaphor is an essential ingredient of communication and consequently of great educational value.

Regardless of one's philosophical persuasions one aspect of human experience is beyond question (although the importance that one ascribes to it depends heavily on one's philosophical persuasions). As conscious perceivers what we experience is continuous. This fact, which so dominates the thinking of the phenomenologists and is frequently a philosophical starting point for such French thinkers as Bergson, Merleau-Ponty or Sartre, seems to be largely ignored by the bulk of British and American empiricists and, perhaps consequently, psychologists. Experience does not arrive in little discrete packets, but flows, leading us imperceptibly from one state to another. It is as though our very nature liked and needed it that way. Even in cases where one might wish to believe that there is or should be an experienceable "digital leap" rather than a smooth analog conversion, even then we often find ourselves forced into an artificial flow. Thus, when suddenly awakened by a hostile alarm clock or telephone bell we frequently feel that the noise was part of a dream—as though our (un)consciousness had constructed a bridge to take us more smoothly from one state to another. We do not experience an instant of waking up or falling asleep: as Wittgenstein put it in the *Tractatus,* "Death is not an event of life," although it must be acknowledged, in a rather different context.

The continuity of experience is not purely a question of temporal flow. It has ramifications for memory. Memory for what has been perceived incorporates some of this continuity. It has long been acknowledged by philosophers and more recently by psychologists and linguists that words do not have distinct, sharply delineated meanings. Wittgenstein in the *Investigations* expounds at length on this problem with respect to the single word "game." A recent study by the linguist Labov[5] demonstrates the foxiness of the word "cup" and a few enlightened cognitive psychologists are currently investigating what they call "semantic flexibility." A moment's thought about a paradigmatic example of reference reveals that the range of applicability of a word is fuzzy. While there is fairly universal agreement as to what is a prototypical red, it is obvious that its limits are indeterminate. The concern of idealist philosophers with "concrete universals" is another indication of a similar point—one might phrase the question as: How much can one change an object before it ceases to be the object it was? Presumably, only when it ceases to be what it was do we finally (hopefully) cease to call it what we did.

The purpose of considering this kind of continuity for word meanings is to suggest that words have to be sufficiently flexible to cover the range of possible applications. It is the objects, events and experiences that continuously vary: words have to follow suit *when they are used.* Words partition experiences but the experiences they partition are not identical: consequently words have to be sufficiently flexible to enable the most varied members of the set partitioned to be referenced by them. If there is any sense in maintaining that words have fixed meanings, it can only be that independent of context they relate to their prototypical non-linguistic counterparts. The continuity of experience, therefore, is not just a temporal continuity; it is, as it were, a continuity in "referential" space and it is the total continuity of experience which at once underlies and necessitates the use of metaphor in linguistic communication. Language and logic are discrete symbol systems. Thus, the task we have to perform in communication is to convey what is usually some kind of continuum by using discrete symbols. It would not be surprising if a discrete symbol system were incapable of literally capturing every conceivable aspect of an object, event or experience that one might wish to describe. A thesis of this paper is that this deficiency is filled by metaphor.

The Compactness Thesis

The compactness thesis hinges on a "reconstructionist" view of language comprehension. Such a view regards language production as being analytic and language comprehension as being synthetic. Few philosophers or psychologists dispute that language comprehension is intimately connected with one's knowledge of the world. The problem arises when one tries to characterize the manner in which this knowledge is involved in the comprehension process. Suppose that I read in a newspaper that a man swam the English Channel in mid-winter. The reconstructionist view would suggest that in the process of comprehending the statement I in some sense "reconstruct" the event described and that I do so by bringing to bear a great deal of what I already know, not just about the language, but about the world. I build a representation which invokes what I know about men and their capacity to swim, about what I know or believe (or even imagine) to be some characteristics of the English Channel and so on. What I invoke is largely experiential, perceptual and cognitive, and to this extent generally similar, but probably almost never identical to what others invoke. I infer that the man was probably covered with oil, that he was strong and muscular, that the sea was likely cold and rough, that the sky was perhaps gray and gloomy. I might also invoke my knowledge of likely public reaction, a reaction of admiration, incredulity, indifference or even alleged insanity. All these things and a host of others "come to mind," or many do. Perhaps the best way to construct such a representation furnished with details not specified in the literal message is to form a "mental image." Now this process of filling in the details between the linguistic signposts present in the message I call "particularization" and I take this to be an essential component in many normal instances of successful language comprehension. It has already been demonstrated empirically[6] that this is indeed an important component in language comprehension.

The point and virtue of particularization is that it enables language comprehension to take place without the need for the message to explicitly spell out all the details. Even if this were possible, it would be too boring and time consuming for either or both the speaker or hearer in the normal course of events. But particularization serves an even more important function—it is the language comprehender's digital-to-analog converter; it takes him nearer to the continuous mode of perceived experience by taking him further away from the discrete mode of linguistic symbols. What metaphor does is to allow large "chunks" to be convened or transferred: metaphor constrains and directs particularization.

Following Aristotle we will treat similes as a variety of metaphor, a variety good for illustration. Imagine our correspondent is trying to describe the way in which the swimmer entered the water and he writes: "He dived into the icy water like a *fearless warrior.*" Let us examine what is actually being communicated. First, consider what we might assume to know about warriors. There are many characteristics peculiar to warriors, or at least to the stereotypical warrior. They include perhaps, bravery, strength, fearlessness, aggressiveness, determination and so on: all these are what one might call abstract characteristics to be distinguished from perceptual ones such as muscular, perhaps large, riding a horse, armed, and possibly even wearing armor or covered with war-paint. What we have listed are characteristics for which we have words in the language: different speakers would doubtless list different ones based on a variety of (presumably) indirect experiences of warriors. The simile is directing our attention to a subset of a subset of these characteristics.[7] The first subset is determined by *salience*. We have to select that subset of all the cognitive and perceptual features which we consider to be salient or distinctive. Thus, whereas it is a characteristic of a warrior that he, for example, has a nose, or that he breathes, such characteristics are not crucial to his being a warrior as opposed, let us say, to a cowhand. Thus the first subset is characterized by being the group of features which distinguish a warrior from a non-warrior. This we can call the "distinctive set" of characteristics. It should be noticed that this account does not require that the members of the set be itemizable. It would obviously be absurd, however, were one to suppose that the entire distinctive set should be transferred to the topic of the simile. The distinctive set comprises only the potentially transferable characteristics. In order to determine the subset of the distinctive set to be transferred, we have to invoke what we know of the topic and eliminate those characteristics which give rise to the tension, namely, those which, however limited our knowledge of the topic may be, contradict or are conceptually incompatible with what we do know of it. The second subset is thus determined by *tension elimination*. The characteristics to be transferred must be conceivably transferable. Obviously the swimmer is no more clad in armor than he is riding a horse as he dives into the water. This resulting set of characteristics we might call the "appropriate distinctive set." Thus what the simile is doing is, effectively, saying "take all those aspects you know peculiar to fearless warriors which could reasonably be applied to a diving swimmer and predicate the entire set of them to the swimmer."

It is interesting to notice that some of these aspects may themselves only be applicable metaphorically. Thus, one might include within the appropriate distinctive set characteristics which themselves have been metaphorically interpreted in the same way. For example, the inclusion of "wearing armor" might enable some of the distinctive aspects of "armor wearing" (such as "providing protection," "giving a sense of security" and so on) to be transferred to the topic, thereby relating to the presumed oil cover for the swimmer.[8] This process, while possibly iterative, is not necessarily infinitely regressive. I believe that the notion of appropriate distinctive set here set out is much more precise and accurate than Black's[9] "system of associated commonplaces."

If we take this as the rule, then what has been said in a word is something like "He dived into the icy water bravely, strongly, fearlessly, aggressively, in a determined manner, etc., being muscular, large and so on." This "chunk" of unspecified features or characteristics is what is transferred, all parceled up in the two words "fearless warrior." It is quick, concise and effective and it invites and constrains the particularization of the comprehender.

The Inexpressibility Thesis

While the compactness thesis argues that metaphor enables the predication of a chunk of characteristics in a word or two that would otherwise require a long list of characteristics individually predicated, the inexpressibility thesis argues that metaphor enables the predication by transfer of characteristics which are unnameable. Of course, *ex hypothesi,* such characteristics are difficult to give by example. Consider the following metaphor: "the thought slipped my mind like a squirrel behind a tree." If one attempts to translate such a metaphor into prosaic language one is always driven to other metaphorical expressions such as "the thought went away" or "the thought evaded me" and so on. Now thoughts only come and go and evade in a metaphorical sense—we have no literal language for talking about what thoughts do. The appropriate distinctive set that one might extract from the squirrel (slipping) behind a tree would doubtless include such characteristics as ungraspableness, suddenness, nimbleness, deceptively easy to catch, camouflage and many others. Already the difficulty of finding the appropriate words is evident, and any of these predicated of an idea would itself still be metaphorical. Thus there are cases in which it would seem that there is no possible way of literally saying what has to be said so that if it is to be said at all metaphor is essential as a vehicle for its expression.

The point is not that some things are by their nature not describable. Rather, the point is that as a matter of facts, for any given language, there are certain things which are inexpressible. For example, in English Creole there is an expression which is used to convey warm, friendly, concerned sympathy to people in distress from minor disappointments or pains. The expression is "ush ya" (originally derived from "hush you" addressed to a child). In British or American English it is simply untranslatable. There *could* be a word or expression, but there is none.

The inexpressibility thesis is not particularly surprising in itself. Locke subscribed to it nearly three hundred years ago. It is perhaps more reasonable to suppose that there are objects, ideas, events and experiences which cannot be literally described in some or all of their minutest details than to suppose that there is nothing which could not be so described. One might say "whereof one cannot speak literally, thereof one should speak metaphorically."

So we attempt to establish the inexpressibility thesis with two types of argument. The first is that the continuous nature of experience precludes the possibility of having distinctions in word meanings capable of capturing every conceivable detail that one might wish to convey; and this in spite of the flexibility of individual word meanings. The second is that it would appear more reasonable to hold the inexpressibility view than its alternative that there is nothing that cannot be conveyed literally in a language. Apart from anything else this latter view would entail perfect translatability between languages— something that is widely believed to be impossible.[10]

If there is a difficulty with the view, it resides in the difficulty of ultimately distinguishing between metaphorical and literal language. But short of denying that dead metaphors are metaphors and claiming that there is nothing to be learned from etymology, such an objection could not easily get started.

If one combines the inexpressibility thesis with the compactness thesis it becomes apparent that the transferred chunks of characteristics from vehicle to topic may include all kinds of aspects which are not capable of being represented by the discrete elements within the confines of a particular language. It becomes more fruitful to think of the grounds of a metaphor, the appropriate distinctive set, as being a continuum of cognitive and perceptual characteristics with a few slices removed rather than as a list of discrete attributes. We would then say that metaphor permits the transfer of abstracted, but nevertheless nondiscretized, coherent, chunks of characteristics from the vehicle to the topic. These chunks are, as it were, predicated *en masse* and they bear a special relationship to cognition and perception because they have not (themselves) been internally discretized.

Some additional support for the claims of the inexpressibility and compactness theses can be derived by consideration of the reasons for certain kinds of failure in metaphors. Suppose someone said "Oranges are the baseballs of the fruit-lover." On being asked what was meant by this extraordinarily obscure remark, imagine the proud speaker to reply "Oh—that's a metaphor; don't you see, oranges are round and so are baseballs—it's clever isn't it?" Now according to our view the function of metaphor is to express succinctly what can only be said very circuitously if, indeed, it can be said at all. Our literary giant, however, anticipates an appropriate distinctive set comprising one easily nameable characteristic (if he anticipates anything). His metaphor fails because what he wanted to say was that oranges are round, and there was nothing preventing him saying just that! The tension in the metaphor was so great that after eliminating it almost nothing was left to appropriately transfer—he was guilty of stretching metaphor to a point of no return. People simply do not use metaphors to transfer *one* characteristic, even if it is a distinctive one, when there is a ready literal way of making the point. If the size of the transferred chunk were a measure of the quality of a metaphor, the baseball metaphor would not fare well.

The Vividness Thesis

The compactness thesis and the inexpressibility thesis are largely concerned with the mechanism employed by metaphor. Together they attempt to explain what is happening in a metaphor and why. The vividness thesis is concerned with what seems to be a consequence of the view so far espoused. It relates to the distinction drawn earlier between the continuity of experience and the discreteness of symbolic systems. Earlier it was suggested that language is a means of reconstructing experience, or experience-like representations: it was also suggested that the construction of a "mental image" might be taken as paradigmatic of success. Now, if our account of metaphor is right, then it would follow that metaphor lies much closer to perceived experience than a non-metaphorical equivalent because the vehicle enables the ground to be predicated of the topic without the need for discretizing the individual characteristics and consequently, assuming the metaphor is comprehended, the process of particularization is greatly assisted. For instead of reconstructing an analog representation from totally discrete items, the vehicle has already transferred a complete band. Thus metaphors would be particularly vivid because of their proximity to, and parasitic utilization of perceived experience: by circumventing discretization they enable the communication of ideas with a richness of detail much less likely to come about in the normal course of events.

The strong emotive force of metaphors can also be accounted for by the vividness thesis. Because of a metaphor's greater proximity to perceived experience and consequently its greater vividness, the emotive as well as the sensory and cognitive aspects are more available, for they have been left intact in the transferred chunk. Metaphors are closer to emotional reality for the same reasons that they are closer to perceptual experience. To say of an unexpected event that it was a miracle is to say far more than that it was inexplicable: it is to express joy, admiration, wonder, awe and a host of other things without mentioning any of them. If emotions could not be grounds, then poetry would be lifeless.

These features of metaphor give it its great educational utility. It has been amply demonstrated that imagibility correlates very highly with learnability.[11] Richness of detail in communicative potential provides a powerful means of moving from the known to the less well-known or unknown, and this, of course, is an important pedagogic function. The vividness of metaphor is not restricted to visual aspects alone: it extends to all sensory modalities as well as to emotive power. Noises from unknown sources are often described by similes—"It sounded as if an airplane was flying through the room." How else could one say it? The inexpressibility thesis almost forces the use of a metaphorical device in such an example.

The educational power of metaphors is thus twofold. The vivid imagery arising from metaphorical comprehension encourages memorability and generates of necessity a better, more insightful, personal understanding. But also, it is a very effective device for moving from the well-known to the less well-known, from vehicle to topic. As we shall see, there are potential dangers inherent in the use of metaphor in this respect, dangers associated with the presuppositions underlying the use of any particular metaphor.

Whereas metaphor can be used to supplement knowledge about some already quite well understood topic, it can also be used to describe very unfamiliar topics. The potential problem here is that the person who uses the metaphor needs to know how much he can assume about his addressee's knowledge of the topic in advance. If he makes an incorrect judgment in this respect, a situation may arise in which his addressee cannot construct an appropriate distinctive set of characteristics because he doesn't know enough about the topic to eliminate tension-reducing ones. There can be two consequences. He may simply fail to grasp the metaphor and recognize his failure, or, worse, he may attribute inappropriate characteristics to the topic and go away misled. It may be that one of the reasons that metaphors can become quite complicated is that the author is adding information to assist the reader in constructing the grounds. This can be done by incorporating literacy applicable qualifiers and by building up larger metaphors out of smaller ones. In poetry this is nicely illustrated by the following lines from Longfellow's "The Spirit of Poetry" (1825):

... HER HAIR

Is like the summer tresses of the trees.
When twilight makes them brown, and on her cheek
Blushes the richness of an autumn sky,
With ever-shifting beauty. Then her breath
It is so like the gentle air of Spring,
As, from the morning's dewy flower, it comes
Full of their fragrance, that it is a joy
To have it round us, and her silver voice
Is the rich music of a summer bird.
Heard in the still night, with *its* passionate cadence.

It is clear that the boundaries of metaphor are but vaguely definable. At one end we have metaphorical use of individual words as qualifiers: at the other, large blocks of text "working out" a larger, more specific picture.

From an instructional point of view it becomes very important to recognize how much guidance a metaphor should contain for constructing the ground, a consideration which grows in its importance as the audience becomes larger and more heterogeneous. A metaphor used successfully can give insight and comprehension; used unsuccessfully it can generate confusion and despair.

No attempt has been made in this paper to make a sharp distinction between simile, metaphor and analogy. I have treated simile as a kind of metaphor. Since the traditional distinction between them is made in terms of the presence or absence of words such as "like" and "as," I fail to see any important cognitive difference between them. It is often said that in addition similes make explicit comparisons while metaphors make implicit ones. This view is certainly representative of comparison theorists such as Aristotle and Richards. Adherents of the iconic theory share it. The iconic view is held by Henle[12] and Alston.[13] Alston gives the following quotation from Henle, which shows how little the theory does by way of explanation, even though Alston calls it "illuminating."

First, using symbols in Peirce's sense, directions are given for finding an object or situation. This use of language is quite ordinary. Second, it is implied that any object or situation fitting the direction may serve as an icon of what one wishes to describe. The icon is never actually presented: rather, through the rule, one understands what it must be and through this understanding, what it signifies. (p. 178)

Of the difference between metaphor and simile Alston says:

> [It] is somewhat analogous to the difference between 'My son plays baseball' and 'I have a son and he plays baseball' where what is presupposed but not explicitly asserted in the first is explicitly asserted in the second. (p. 99)

The idea, however, of attempting to discriminate between metaphors and similes on the basis that similes express an explicit comparison while metaphors are implicit seems to miss the point. Neither are in fact explicit. In simile, if there is comparison at all, rather than transfer, the comparison can only be *with respect to certain characteristics*. Determining what these characteristics are is what is involved in understanding the simile. In metaphor there is an apparent claim of identity, but again, only with respect to certain characteristics. Whether there be a claim of similarity or a claim of identity is neither here nor there. Since neither claim can be taken literally, they both direct the interpreter to determine the respects which are appropriate. Only if we can discover an important difference between "x and y are identical *in certain respects*" and "x and y are similar *in certain respects*" can we claim any important difference between metaphor and simile; a difficult task indeed if one is aiming to distinguish anything other than the characteristics, which are, of course, implicit.

The distinction between metaphor and analogy is more difficult. It is tempting to think of metaphor as being concerned with the transfer of complexes of characteristics and analogy as being concerned specifically with transfer between relations, if only because the stereotypical analogy is of the form "A is to B as C is to D." This is suggestive of a simile expressing transfer from the vehicle, the relationship between C and D, to the topic, the relationship between A and B: or rather the appropriate distinctive set of characteristics of the relationship (remember they may be emotive and perceptual so we are not committed to a bizarre view of predicating attributes, in the normal sense, of relations). Analogies, however, are not necessarily metaphors because the transfer may be possible directly—it may be that in these cases there are no inappropriate members of the distinctive set, or indeed, no *distinctive* set at all. There may be no tension in a non-metaphorical analogy (consider the use of analogy in algebra or geometry). When analogies are used figuratively they tend to be used in groups—requiring longer bodies of text to convey complicated interrelations between relations.

The great pedagogic value of figurative uses of language is to be found in their potential to transfer learning and understanding from what is known to what is less well-known and to do so in a very vivid manner. To appreciate these facts may be to make better use of them and to better understand them. Metaphors are necessary as a communicative device because they allow the transfer of coherent chunks of characteristics—perceptual, cognitive, emotional and experiential—from a vehicle which is known to a topic which is less so. In so doing they circumvent the problem of specifying one by one each of the often unnameable and innumerable characteristics; they avoid discretizing the perceived continuity of experience and are thus closer to experience and consequently more vivid and memorable.

Were our language to have a discrete word for every conceivable attribute one might wish to mention, it would be no language; metaphor saves it from such embarrassment. The power of poetry leans on shared experience. If robots are to understand sonnets, they will first have to be sentient beings, for the demands made on them will indeed be great.

There can be no more fitting conclusion than the following excerpt from Coleridge. In his *Biographia Literaria* he writes:

> The poet . . . brings the whole soul of man into activity, with the subordi-nation of its faculties to each other, according to their relative worth and dignity. He diffuses a tone, a spirit of unity, that blends, and (as it were) fuses, each into each, by that synthetic and magical power, . . . imagina-tion. This power, . . . reveals itself in the balance or reconciliation of opposite or discordant qualities: of sameness, with difference; of the general, with the concrete; the idea, with the image; the individual with the representative; the sense of novelty and freshness, with old and famil-iar objects; a more than usual state of emotion, with more than usual order . . . and while it blends and harmonizes the natural and the artifi-cial, still subordinates art to nature.

Notes

1. I am grateful for help and advice from Alan Purves and Hugh Petrie.

2. M. Breal, *Semantics,* translated by Mrs. Henry Cust (New York: Dover Publications, Inc., 1964), p. 124.

3. See, for instance, *Rhetoric,* III, iv, 1-3.

4. I. A. Richards, *The Philosophy of Rhetoric* (London: Oxford University Press, 1936).

5. W. Labov, "The Boundaries of Words and Their Meanings," in C. J. Bailey and R. Shuy (eds.), *New Ways of Analyzing Variations In English* (Washington: Georgetown University Press, 1973).

6. See, for example, R. C. Anderson and A. Ortony, "On Putting Apples into Bottles—A Problem of Polysemy" (Urbana, Illinois: Training Research Laboratory,

University of Illinois, mimeo, 1973); [*Cognitive Psychology, V,* 7, 1975, in press]; or R. C. Anderson and B. McGaw, "On the Representation of Meanings of General Terms," *Journal of Experimental Psychology, V,* 101 (1973), pp. 301-306.

7. Technically the term "interval" is more appropriate than "set" since I do not wish to imply that there is a set of discrete elements. The term "interval" allows for continuously varying quantities. In the present discussion these can to some extent be discretized by language, but this discretization is subordinate to a continuous representation. The terminology of sets is less clumsy than that of intervals, but the distinction should be kept in mind.

8. I am grateful to Alan Purves for pointing this out.

9. M. Black, *Models and Metaphors* (Ithaca: Cornell University Press, 1962).

10. See, for example, W. V. O. Quine, *Word and Object* (Cambridge, Massachusetts: MIT Press, 1960).

11. See, for instance, A. Paivio, *Imagery and Verbal Processes* (New York: Holt, Rinehart & Winston, 1971).

12. P. Henle, "Metaphor," in P. Henle (ed.), *Language, Thought and Culture* (Ann Arbor, Michigan: University of Michigan Press, 1958).

13. W. P. Alston, *Philosophy of Language* (Englewood Cliffs, New Jersey: Prentice Hall, 1964), Chapter 5.

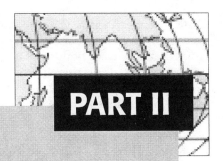

PART II

Conceptual Frameworks for Cultural Metaphors

This book is part of a three-part book series emphasizing the use of the cultural metaphor, which is a unique or distinctive activity, phenomenon, or institution that members of any group (small group, ethnic group, nation, etc.) consider to be important and with which they emotionally identify. Outsiders frequently have difficulty seeing the relationship between the cultural metaphor and the underlying values and attitudes that it represents. Once the outsiders begin to recognize the importance of the cultural metaphor, they can start to understand the culture more effectively.

In Part II, we emphasize conceptual frameworks for cultural metaphors. We begin with the well-known and very influential work of Edward Hall, which is primarily based on metaphors. We then show how Hall's work can be extended so as to understand the cultures of both ethnic groups and nations. Next, we turn our attention to the equally influential work of Geert Hofstede and Michael Bond and his associates. However, the focus is on only one aspect of it, the Confucian Ethic. Although Hofstede's work is justifiably lauded for its empirical basis, the Confucian Ethic demonstrates a significant reliance on cultural metaphors, as it is strikingly similar to Max Weber's Protestant Ethic.

We then turn our attention to the equally influential work completed independently by Alan Fiske and Harry Triandis and his associates. Underlying both sets of analysis is the metaphor of the four types of statistical data that are used to explain four generic types of human relations. We then end this section by describing France in terms of French wine to illustrate how cultural metaphors can be employed.

We emphasize that the major thrust of this part of the book is on conceptual frameworks for cultural metaphors. These frameworks are meant to be tentative and illustrative rather than definitive. We expect that other writers interested in cultural metaphors will be able to think about these conceptual frameworks and extend them in new directions.

CHAPTER 3

Edward Hall's
Multiple Metaphors

*Research Translation
and Extension*

Ｉt is difficult to write about culture without highlighting the work of
Edward Hall, who has provided many of the key ideas in the field
of intercultural communication. However, his work has not been used widely
in business schools and, more specifically, in the management area. In this
chapter, there is a description of his work, after which we demonstrate how it
can be revised so that its managerial and business implications are delineated
more clearly.

Hall's body of work can be viewed as a series of metaphors that are logically related to one another. His first major book (Hall, 1959) is titled *The
Silent Language,* and it refers to culture: From Hall's vantage point, culture is
the silent language that members of a specific ethnic, racial, or cultural group
understand, but with which outsiders have great difficulty, even when they
speak the same language. Hall makes clear his position by comparing language to music. When a listener understands the musical score—the timing,
the notes, the underlying scales, and so forth—he or she can discuss it with
others with similar understanding, enjoy it, and play it. Otherwise, the music
is gibberish. In one of the most persuasive discussions in this book, Hall
argues that the distinguished critic Lionel Trilling had taken a position that
was inaccurate when he posited that culture is a prison. For Trilling, each of
us is imprisoned by the culture in which we are engaged. Hall contends that
culture is a prison only if one does not have a system for understanding each
and every culture. Hall's entire body of work can be seen as an attempt to

construct such a system of understanding. Although Hall presents a tentative system for understanding cross-cultural differences, it was only much later that he finalized it into the influential approach explained below. However, he did make clear in this book that he views culture as a form of communication, which is the basis of his mature approach.

In this early work, Hall began to emphasize the concepts of time and space. Hall posits that Americans view time as a fixed linear quantity and emphasize the present and the future at the expense of the past, but the future extends only a few years forward. In contrast, there are some cultures that are weighed down by the past. Hall gives an incisive example involving an island that was administered by the American military for several years. One citizen excitedly rushed into the American military office to report a murder that was committed several generations ago. Also, some cultures such as the Comanche are present-oriented, even to the extent that its members will accept an offer to buy a horse that is immediately available rather than wait for one that is decidedly better at the same price.

Hall also began his exploration of space in this first book which, as suggested, is based on the metaphor that culture is a language, but a silent one. He points out that Americans like corner offices at least in part because of their emphasis on linear relations. Subordinates come to the office one at a time, and occupying this office connotes power. By contrast, the French perspective is more nonlinear and stresses that power radiates from the center. Hence an important French executive has his or her office located in the center of other offices. These contrasting emphases—linear or nonlinear/radiating— are also expressed in the manner in which American and French cities are constructed.

In 1966, Hall followed up these preliminary observations in *The Hidden Dimension*. Once again, he is using a figure of speech to emphasize his point of view. In this case, space is the hidden dimension of culture. He points out that the typical Anglo-Saxon American has four invisible circles around him: intimate (surface of the skin to 18 inches); personal (comfortable interactions reflecting friendship and closeness, 1½ to 4 feet); social (4 to 12 feet for conducting impersonal business); and public (12 feet and beyond, for recognizing others and saying hello). Such circles of distances tend to vary by culture.

Hall makes several acute observations about the use of space. For example, Germans see space as an extension of their own egos, and that is one reason why they prefer closed office doors. At one point in time—and even today in some older office buildings, in Germany and a few other Northern European nations—there was a light outside of the office controlled by its occupants that could show the colors green, red, or orange. The visitor knew immediately what to do when the light went on. One German manager went so far as to bolt the visitor's chair to the floor so that salespeople would not be able to move the chair closer to him when they were trying to close a deal.

In 1983, Hall published *The Dance of Life,* and in this instance, the metaphor is emphasized even more explicitly than in the previous works. This book analyzes time or the dance of life, and it contrasts various meanings of time: physical and metaphysical; biological and personal; synchronous and micro; and sacred and profane. The most important distinction is between monochronic and polychronic time, that is, doing one thing at a time versus doing many things simultaneously.

However, monochronic and polychronic people and cultures differ along a number of other dimensions. Monochronic people stress time commitments and adherence to deadlines and schedules, whereas polychronic people view time commitments as flexible and of low priority. These orientations occur because monochronic people are committed to the job and its completion and emphasize promptness and deadlines, whereas polychronic people are committed to people and relationships regardless of other concerns. Although Hall does not use this example, I often ask students and managerial trainees to respond to the following situation: You are walking to an important business meeting at which you are responsible for closing a $100 million dollar deal and, in the process, making a $1 million bonus for yourself when you are stopped by your best friend in the world who very emotionally tells you he needs your help immediately, and without delay. There are only two alternatives: to help your friend and miss the meeting, or to put your friend off. How do you expect monochronic and polychronic people to act? How would you act?

Hall also points out that polychronic people view time as a point, whereas monochronic people see it as a road. It is customary in polychronic cultures to say: I will see you before 1 hour, that is, it will take no longer than 1 hour to see you. This is opposed to the monochronic practice of scheduling an exact time. Also, some polychronic cultures, such as the Hopi and Sioux, do not have a word for time.

Hall's mature system is most clearly described in his book, *Beyond Culture* (1976; see also Hall & Hall, 1990). Although the book's title is not metaphorical, its thrust is clearly in this direction, because he builds a system in which culture is simply a form of communication that, if understood, allows the individual to escape the prison to which Trilling had assigned all or most humankind. He treats communication as a continuum extending from low context to high context. Hall famously states that

> a high-context (H) communication or message is one in which most of the information is either in the physical context or internalized in the

person, while very little is in the coded, explicit, transmitted part of the message. A low-context (LC) communication is just the opposite; i.e., the mass of the information is vested in the explicit code. (Hall, 1976, p. 91)

Hall points out that both methods are effective and that the same amount of information may be conveyed, but in clearly different forms. A low-context communication emphasizes the use of written and oral forms of expression: If it is not spelled out clearly, in written and/or oral form, it is not low context. Conversely, high-context messages rely on both subtle body movements and subtle use of language so that one statement really means something else in order to save face or embarrassment, such as, "That would be difficult" rather than "No, definitely not." Even the length of silence may convey a high-context message, and it is for this reason that the Japanese say that silence is communication.

There is a training video, "Crosstalk: Performance Appraising Across Cultures," that dramatically brings these two forms of communication into relief. This video, available through British Broadcasting and CRM Films, features a series of goal-setting performance interviews involving individuals from low-context (Anglo-American) and high-context (Chinese American and Korean American) cultures. The basic point is that low-context people tend to start such interviews with a conclusion: I did well during this past year, and here are the actions justifying this self-appraisal. In contrast, the high-context subordinates refuse to offer an initial conclusion and merely describe the situation during the past year and the activities they undertook in response to it; this description should be so accurate that the conclusion naturally emerges, and it is the responsibility of the superior to decide whether the performance warrants a salary increase based on this description and other facts known to him or her.

The importance of the distinction between low-context and high-context communication—and, because culture is a form of communication, low-context and high-context cultures—cannot be overestimated. The handbook accompanying "Crosstalk" describes an audiotaped situation involving American executives making business decisions. When Chinese businessmen listened to it, they considered the decision making to be illogical and even incomprehensible. However, when the American businessmen listened to an audiotape on which Chinese businessmen were making decisions, they had the same reaction. Thus, it is not only important but also critical to know if individuals are more comfortable using low-context or high-context forms of communication.

However, Hall completely overlooks the psychological or emotional component of communication. Whereas he does an excellent job of identify-

FIGURE 3.1.
Open Expression of Emotions and Feelings

		Lower	Higher
	Lower	England, Ireland, and Scotland	United States
Internalized Behavioral Rules[a]	**Higher**	China, Japan, and India	Mexico, Spain, and Italy

a. Rules are internalized, through extensive and intensive socialization within the family and associated groups, so that individuals automatically know what is expected of them. As internalized behavioral rules increase, the number of expected behaviors also rises.

ing the context of communication or the degree to which internalized behavioral rules dominate—the higher the context, the more socialized the culture and the more that behavioral rules are internalized and not explicitly expressed in oral or written form—he makes no mention of the role of emotions and feelings. As shown in Figure 3.1, nations that are similar to one another on Hofstede's dimensions, such as England and the United States, are separate in terms of degree of emotional expressiveness. Similarly, China, Japan, and India are typically classified as close to one another in terms of internalized behavioral rules, but they differ from similar high-context nations such as Mexico, Spain, and Italy in terms of emotional expressiveness. Thus, context should be considered synonymous with internalized rules, but the degree of emotional expressiveness should be stipulated.

This extension of Hall's perspective allows us to see the relationship between his approach and that of Hofstede. Also, it is possible to use this revision when examining the work of cross-cultural psychologists such as Ronen and Shenkar (1985), who emphasize the clustering of nations having similar profiles.

Additionally, it should be pointed out that it is possible for a high-context person to use a low-context style of communication, and vice versa. Hall himself points out that the high-context Japanese frequently use a low-context style of communication when dealing with Americans. However, if a visitor to another culture knows ahead of time the preferred mode, he or she can adapt to it, as Hall suggests that the Japanese do in many instances.

In sum, Hall's influential body of work can be viewed as a series of metaphors that eventually builds into a logical cross-cultural system emphasizing tion. Polychronic people tend to share space, because this allows them to learn the many subtle signals required for high-context communications. They tend to work in large, open areas in which private offices with closed doors are deemphasized. They also tend to live in a setting in which each family member has a home close to the others so that they can see one another frequently, share information, develop strong norms, and socialize the young. Such an environment tends to produce polychronic behavior. However, Hall recognizes that a low-context message can be just as effective as a high-context message, but it needs to be coded in an external form through written and oral messages. In all of these senses, Hall has emphasized communication as a metaphor for culture that has greatly strengthened our understanding of this elusive concept.

References

Crosstalk: Performance appraising across cultures [Training video]. London: British Broadcasting and CRM Films.

Hall, E. (1959). *The silent language.* Garden City, NY: Doubleday.

Hall, E. (1966). *The hidden dimension.* Garden City, NY: Doubleday.

Hall, E. (1976). *Beyond culture.* Garden City, NY: Doubleday.

Hall, E. (1983). *The dance of life.* Garden City, NY: Doubleday.

Hall, E., & Hall, M. (1990). *Understanding cultural differences.* Yarmouth, ME: Intercultural Press.

Ronen, S., & Shenkar, O. (1985). Clustering countries on attitudinal dimensions: A review and synthesis. *Academy of Management Review, 10,* 435-454.

CHAPTER 4

The Confucius Connection: From Cultural Roots to Economic Growth

GEERT HOFSTEDE
MICHAEL HARRIS BOND

In 1968, the late Nobel-prize-winning economist Gunnar Myrdal published a book entitled *Asian Drama* that described his investigations into the failure of economic development policies in South and Southeast Asia. Twenty years later, we are experiencing a very different kind of Asian drama: Japan, South Korea, Taiwan, Hong Kong, and Singapore are now outperforming the United States and Western Europe economically. Western markets are flooded with high-quality, high-technology products "made in Asia"; the production of cameras, TV sets, and domestic appliances has all but ceased in many Western countries, the automobile business has suffered severely, and President Reagan has had to violate his free-trade principles to save the U.S. microchip industry. It is true that most of the competition is from East, rather than from South or Southeast Asia; however, some

AUTHORS' NOTE: Originally published in *Organizational Dynamics, 16,* 5-21. Copyright © 1988 by Geert Hofstede. Reprinted by permission.

South and Southeast Asian countries besides Singapore, such as India, Malaysia, Thailand, and Indonesia (the very scene of Myrdal's drama), also show signs of an economic takeoff.

World Bank data on the average annual growth rate of per capita gross national product (see Exhibit 4.1) confirm the East Asian lead. The Five Dragons, as these countries are sometimes called, are heading the list, with average annual sustained-growth percentages over a 20-year period of 7.6% for Singapore, 7.2% for Taiwan, 6.6% for South Korea, 6.1% for Hong Kong, and 4.7% for Japan. These compare with rates for Western Europe of between 3.5% for Austria and 1.6% for Britain; for Latin America of between 4.3% for Brazil and –2.1% for Nicaragua; of 2.4% for Canada; and of 1.7% for the United States.

Why East Asia?

Few economists predicted the staggering economic rise of the East Asian countries, and many failed to recognize it even when it was well under way. For example, an economic forecast by Hollis B. Chenery and Alan M. Strout published in the *American Economic Review* of September 1966 did not even include Hong Kong and Singapore because they were considered insignificant in this respect. The future performances of Taiwan and Korea were heavily underrated, and those of India and Sri Lanka were overrated. Fifteen years later, Singapore with a population of 2.5 million exported more than India did with a population of 700 million.

Not only was the success of the Five Dragons unpredicted, but even after the fact economists have no explanation of why these particular countries were so successful. Why, for example, did South Korea outperform Colombia, which seemed to be in a better starting position? In 1965, Colombia's per capita income ($280) was about twice South Korea's ($150). In 1985, South Korea's per capita income ($2,150) was about one-and-a-half times Colombia's ($1,320). U.S. garment buyers, however, chose South Korea—even though Colombia is nearer—because of better selection, better quality, lower prices, and more reliable delivery times. Better management was obviously also involved, but this is too easy an explanation for two reasons. First, the quality of management depends on the qualities of the people to be managed; second, the quality-of-management explanation begs the question of how an entire nation can collectively produce better management than another nation. For the real explanation, we must turn to the domain of culture.

EXHIBIT 4.1. Economic Growth for Selected Countries and Gross National Product (GNP) per Capita

	1965-'85 Ave. Annual GNP/capita Growth Rate (%)	1965 GNP/ capita U.S. $ and (Rank)	1985 GNP/ capita U.S. $ and (Rank)
Singapore	7.6	550 (12)	7420 (10)
Taiwan	7.2	220 (16)	3600 (12)
South Korea	6.6	150 (17)	2150 (13)
Hong Kong	6.1	590 (11)	6230 (11)
Japan	4.7	780 (10)	11300 (5)
Brazil	4.3	240 (15)	1640 (15)
Austria	3.5	1180 (8)	9120 (8)
Colombia	2.9	280 (14)	1320 (16)
West Germany	2.7	1810 (5)	10940 (6)
Canada	2.4	2260 (3)	13680 (3)
Netherlands	2.0	1520 (7)	9290 (7)
Sweden	1.8	2160 (4)	11890 (4)
India	1.7	90 (18)	270 (18)
United States	1.7	3420 (1)	16690 (1)
Great Britain	1.6	1580 (6)	8460 (9)
Poland	1.5	840 (9)	2050 (14)
Switzerland	1.4	2310 (2)	16370 (2)
Nicaragua	−2.1	330 (13)	770 (17)

Source: World Development Report 1987 and other statistics.

The Neo-Confucian Hypothesis

Futurologist Herman Kahn has labeled the cultures of the East Asian countries "neo-Confucian," that is, rooted in the teachings of Confucius. Kahn saw himself as a "culturist": He, like the authors of this article, held the belief that specific nations have specific cultural traits that are "rather sticky and difficult to change in any basic fashion, although they can often be modified." The authors like to define culture as "the collective programming of the mind that distinguishes the members of one category of people from those of another." This definition applies to national as well as to corporate cultures, but we will stay at the national level. Kahn's neo-Confucian hypothesis is that the countries of East Asia have common cultural roots going far back into history, and that under the world-market conditions of the past 30 years this cultural inheritance has constituted a competitive advantage for successful business activity.

Cultural inheritances are not genetically transferred; they can in principle be acquired by any human being who is at the right place at the right time. We begin to acquire the mental programming we call culture from the day we are born, and the process continues throughout our life in a particular society. Cross-cultural developmental psychologists who have studied the behavior of children in different societies have shown that a child learns patterns of cultural behavior very early in its life. For example, Japanese male infants of 3 to 4 months are noisier than Japanese female infants of the same age, whereas in the United States the opposite is true. Sex roles are only one aspect of our cultural programming; thus from generation to generation, all kinds of cultural traits are transferred. With this in mind, let us begin to look at the teachings of Confucius.

Confucius and His Teachings

Kong Fu Ze, whom the Jesuit missionaries renamed Confucius, was a high civil servant in China around the time of 500 B.C. Known for his wisdom, he was always surrounded by a host of disciples who recorded what we know of his teachings. He thus held a position very similar to that of the Greek philosopher Socrates, who lived just 80 years later. Confucius' teachings are lessons in practical ethics without any religious content; Confucianism is not a religion but a set of pragmatic rules for daily life, derived from what Confucius saw as the lessons of Chinese history. The following are the key principles of Confucian teaching:

1. *The stability of society is based on unequal relationships between people.* The "wu Lun," or five basic relationships, are ruler/subject, father/son, older brother/younger brother, husband/wife, and older friend/younger friend. These relationships are based on mutual, complementary obligations: The junior partner owes the senior respect and obedience; the senior owes the junior partner protection and consideration.

2. *The family is the prototype of all social organizations.* A person is not primarily an individual; rather, he or she is a member of a family. Children

should learn to restrain themselves, to overcome their individuality so as to maintain the harmony in the family (if only on the surface); one's thoughts, however, remain free. Harmony is found in the maintenance of an individual's "face," meaning one's dignity, self-respect, and prestige. The use of our own word "face" in this sense was actually derived from the Chinese: Losing one's dignity, in the Chinese tradition, is equivalent to losing one's eyes, nose, and mouth. Social relations should be conducted in such a way that everybody's face is maintained. Paying respect to someone else is called "giving face."

   3. *Virtuous behavior toward others consists of treating others as one would like to be treated oneself: a basic human benevolence—which, however, does not extend as far as the Christian injunction to love thy enemies.* As Confucius said, if one should love one's enemies, what would remain for one's friends?

   4. *Virtue with regard to one's tasks in life consists of trying to acquire skills and education, working hard, not spending more than necessary, being patient, and persevering.* Conspicuous consumption is taboo, as is losing one's temper. Moderation is enjoined in all things.

The New Science of Culture Measurement

If culture is as important in determining the fate of nations as Kahn and others assume it to be, how then do we learn about culture? Mere description will not do; we need an approach that allows comparisons between countries—that is, an identification of cultural variations.
   Cultural differences can be measured indirectly; that is, they can be inferred from data about collective behavior, such as the way a country's national wealth is distributed over its population; the mobility from one social class to another; or the frequency of political violence or labor conflicts, traffic accidents, or suicides. All of these can tell us something about a country's culture, but it is not always clear how they should be interpreted.
   We can avoid this problem by taking direct measures of culture through asking well-designed questions about people's values or beliefs. For this type of measurement, we should have access to *matched* samples of respondents from a number of different countries (the more the better, but preferably at least 15). "Matching samples" means that the respondents should be people who are as similar as possible in all aspects of their lives except for their nationality. For example, ten-year-old schoolchildren, female medical students, or business managers attending specific training courses can all form

such matched samples. It is not necessary to have *representative* samples from whole national populations such as public opinion polls, although these, too, can be used.

We usually ask the same set of at least 30 or 40 questions of all our subjects in various countries. In comparing the answers, we try to find the patterns of values and beliefs that distinguish countries from each other. We use one of several statistical methods that have been developed for this purpose; this procedure supplies us with suggested *dimensions of culture* on which we can locate our various countries. If our research has succeeded, such dimensions should be easy to interpret: They should represent fundamental problems of human societies for which there is no one solution but a range of solutions, of which each country's culture represents one particular choice.

A Case of Culture Measurement: The IBM Studies

A unique opportunity for culture measurement arose in the early 1970s when the IBM Corporation made its databank on international employee attitude surveys available for academic research. IBM had been holding worldwide comparative attitude surveys of its employees since 1967; by 1973, more than 116,000 questionnaires in 20 different languages from 72 countries had been collected. Employee attitude surveys have of course been held in many companies, but most of them are not internationally standardized and they contain only questions about satisfaction at work ("How do you like your boss, pay, working conditions," and so forth), which are not very suitable as cultural indices.

However, IBM's international questionnaire contained about 60 questions (out of a total of about 150) on the employee's basic values and beliefs that were eminently fit for measuring culture. They included such questions as "How important are each of the following to you in an ideal job?" followed by a list of 14 job characteristics such as earnings, job security, challenge, freedom, cooperation, and so forth. In addition, questions were included on the preferred style for one's ideal manager (from very directive to laissez-faire). Finally, judgments were asked about general issues at work, such as "Competition among employees usually does more harm than good." Employees were asked to rate their responses from "strongly agree" to "strongly disagree."

The IBM employees represented extremely well-matched subsets from each country's population: same company, job, and education, but different nationality. If anything, cultural differences among countries outside the corporation should be larger than they would be inside, so the national culture differences found inside IBM should be a conservative estimate of those existing for the countries at large.

Out of 72 countries covered, the national culture analysis at first used data from 40 of them, ignoring the smaller IBM subsidiaries. Later on, it became possible to use data from another 10 countries, while those of 14 more were grouped into three regions—East Africa, West Africa, and the Arab-speaking countries—that brought the total number of cultures targeted for comparison to 53.

The IBM studies revealed that these 53 cultures differed mainly along four dimensions:

1. *Power Distance—that is, the extent to which the less powerful members of organizations and institutions (like the family) accept and expect that power is distributed unequally.* This represents inequality that is defined from below, not from above; it suggests that a society's level of inequality is endorsed by its followers as much as by its leaders. Power and inequality are of course very fundamental aspects of any society, and any individual with some international experience is aware that all societies are basically unequal, but some are more unequal than others.

2. *Individualism on the one side versus its opposite (Collectivism) on the other.* This describes the degree to which individuals are integrated into groups. On the individualist side, we find societies in which the ties between individuals are loose: Everyone is expected to look after himself or herself and the immediate family. On the collectivist side, we find societies in which people from birth onward are integrated into strong, cohesive ingroups; often their extended families (with uncles, aunts, and grandparents) continue protecting them in exchange for unquestioning loyalty. The word "collectivism" in this sense has no political meaning: It refers to the group, not to the state. Again, the issue addressed by this dimension is an extremely fundamental one, involving all societies in the world.

3. *Masculinity versus its opposite, Femininity.* The distribution of roles between the sexes is another fundamental issue for any society that may involve a range of solutions. Analysis of the IBM data revealed that women's values differ less among societies than do men's values. Further, if we restrict ourselves to men's values (which vary more from one country to another), we find that they contain a dimension from very assertive, competitive, and maximally different from women's values on the one side, to modest and nurturing and similar to women's values on the other. We have called the assertive pole "masculine" and the nurturing pole "feminine." The women in the feminine countries have the same nurturing values as the men; in the masculine

countries they are somewhat more assertive and competitive, but not as much so as the men, so that these countries show a gap between men's values and women's values.

The three dimensions described so far all refer to three types of expected social behavior: behavior toward people higher or lower in rank (Power Distance), behavior toward the group (Individualism/Collectivism), and behavior according to one's sex (Masculinity/Femininity). The values corresponding to these cultural choices are obviously bred in the family: Power Distance by the degree to which children are encouraged to have a will of their own, Individualism/Collectivism by the cohesion of the family with respect to other people, and Masculinity/Femininity by the role models that the parents and older children present to the younger child.

If we compare the three dimensions with the Confucian teachings we described earlier, it will be no surprise that neo-Confucian countries generally score fairly high on Power Distance, low on Individualism, and mid-range on Masculinity/Femininity (except Japan, which scores quite high on Masculinity).

4. A fourth dimension found in the IBM studies refers not to social behavior but to man's search for Truth. We called it "Uncertainty Avoidance"; it indicates to what extent a culture programs its members to feel either uncomfortable or comfortable in unstructured situations. "Unstructured situations" are defined as novel, unknown, surprising, or different from usual. Uncertainty-avoiding cultures try to minimize the possibility of such situations by adhering to strict laws and rules, safety and security measures, and (on the philosophical and religious level) a belief in absolute Truth: "There can be only one Truth, and we have it." People in uncertainty-avoiding countries are also more emotional and are motivated by inner nervous energy. Uncertainty-accepting cultures are more tolerant of behavior and opinions that differ from their own; they try to have as few rules as possible, and on the philosophical and religious level they are relativist, allowing many currents to flow side by side. People within these cultures are more phlegmatic and contemplative; their environment does not expect them to express emotions.

Exhibit 4.2 lists scores for the 53 cultures in the IBM research, thereby permitting each country to be positioned on each of the four dimensions (plus a fifth that we will describe in the next section). These scores are *relative:* We have chosen our scales in such a way that the distance between the lowest- and the highest-scoring country is about 100 points.

At the company level, differences among cultures in these four dimensions have many consequences for management practices. For example, both Power Distance and Individualism affect the type of leadership most likely to be effective in a country. The ideal leader in a culture in which Power Distances

EXHIBIT 4.2. Scores on Five Dimensions for Fifty Countries and Three Regions in IBM's International Employee Attitude Survey

Country	Power Distance		Individualism		Masculinity		Uncertainty Avoidance		Confucian Dynamism	
	Index	Rank	Index	Rank	Index	Rank	Index	Rank	Index	Rank
Argentina	49	35-36	46	22-23	56	20-21	86	10-15		
Australia	36	41	90	2	61	16	51	37	31	11-12
Austria	11	53	55	18	79	2	70	24-25		
Belgium	65	20	75	-8	54	22	94	5-6		
Brazil	69	14	38	26-27	49	27	76	21-22	65	5
Canada	39	39	80	4-5	52	24	48	41-42	23	17
Chile	63	24-25	23	38	28	46	86	10-15		
Colombia	67	17	13	49	64	11-12	80	20		
Costa Rica	35	42-44	15	46	21	48-49	86	10-15		
Denmark	18	51	74	9	16	50	23	51		
Ecuador	78	8-9	8	52	63	13-14	67	28		
Finland	33	46	63	17	26	47	59	31-32		
France	68	15-16	71	10-11	43	35-36	86	10-15		
Germany (F.R.)	35	42-44	67	15	66	9-10	65	29	31	11-12
Great Britain	35	42-44	89	3	66	9-10	35	47-48	25	15-16
Greece	60	27-28	35	30	57	18-19	112	1		
Guatemala	95	2-3	6	53	37	43	101	3		

(Continued)

EXHIBIT 4.2. Continued

Country	Power Distance		Individualism		Masculinity		Uncertainty Avoidance		Confucian Dynamism	
	Index	Rank	Index	Rank	Index	Rank	Index	Rank	Index	Rank
Hong Kong	68	15-16	25	37	57	18-19	29	49-50	96	1
India	77	10-11	48	21	56	20-21	40	45	61	6
Indonesia	78	8-9	14	47-48	46	30-31	48	41-42		
Iran	58	19-20	41	24	43	35-36	59	31-32		
Ireland	28	49	70	12	68	7-8	35	47-48		
Israel	13	52	54	19	47	29	81	19		
Italy	50	34	76	7	70	4-5	75	23		
Jamaica	45	37	39	25	68	7-8	13	52		
Japan	54	33	46	22-23	95	1	92	7	80	3
Korea (S)	60	27-28	18	43	39	41	85	16-17	75	4
Malaysia	104	1	26	36	50	25-26	36	46		
Mexico	81	5-6	30	32	69	6	82	18		
Netherlands	38	40	80	4-5	14	51	53	35	44	9
New Zealand	22	50	79	6	58	17	49	39-40	30	13
Norway	31	47-48	69	13	8	52	50	38		
Pakistan	55	32	14	47-48	50	25-26	70	24-25	0	20
Panama	95	2-3	11	51	44	34	86	10-15		
Peru	64	21-23	16	45	42	37-38	87	9		

	1	2	3	4	5	6	7	8	9	10
Philippines	94	4	32	31	64	11-12	44	44	19	18
Portugal	63	24-25	27	33-35	31	45	104	2		
Salvador	66	18-19	19	42	40	40	94	5-6		
Singapore	74	13	20	39-41	48	28	8	53	48	8
South Africa	49	36-37	65	16	63	13-14	49	39-40		
Spain	57	31	51	20	42	37-38	86	10-15		
Sweden	31	47-48	71	10-11	5	52	29	49-50	33	10
Switzerland	34	45	68	14	70	4-5	58	33		
Taiwan	58	29-30	17	44	45	32-33	69	26	87	2
Thailand	64	21-23	20	39-41	34	44	64	30	53	7
Turkey	66	18-19	37	28	45	31-33	85	16-17		
Uruguay	61	26	36	29	38	42	100	4		
United States	40	38	91	1	62	15	46	43	29	14
Venezuela	81	5-6	12	50	73	3	76	21-22		
Yugoslavia	76	12	27	33-35	21	48-49	88	8		
Regions										
East Africa	64	21-23	27	33-35	41	39	52	36	25	15-16
West Africa	77	10-11	20	39-41	46	30-31	54	34	16	19
Arab Ctrs.	80	7	38	26-27	53	23	68	27		

Rank Numbers: 1 = Highest; 53 = Lowest (For Confucian Dynamism: 20 = Lowest) are small would be a resourceful democrat; on the other hand, the ideal leader in a culture in which Power Distances are large is a benevolent autocrat (or "good father"). In Collectivist cultures, leadership should respect and encourage employees' group loyalties; incentives should be given collectively, and their distribution should be left up to the group. In Individualist cultures, people can be moved around as individuals, and incentives should be given to individuals.

Masculinity and Uncertainty Avoidance affect people's motivations: Competition is more effective in a masculine culture, and personal risk is more acceptable if Uncertainty Avoidance is low. Power Distance and Uncertainty Avoidance together affect the image people form of what an organization should be; larger Power Distances are associated with greater centralization, while stronger Uncertainty Avoidance is associated with greater formalization.

At the national economic level, Individualism and national wealth (per capita gross national product in dollars) are quite strongly related. We have tested whether causality went from wealth to Individualism (people in wealthier countries becoming more individualist) or the other way round (individualist cultures becoming wealthier). We were able to test this because most of the IBM population was surveyed twice, with a four-year interval, so over this period we knew the changes in both wealth and Individualism. The data show convincingly that the arrow of causality goes from wealth to Individualism and not vice versa. If the resources in a country allow people to "do their own thing," they will start doing just that.

However, none of the four dimensions is related to national economic *growth*. Only for the wealthy countries (all of which tend to be individualist) is more Individualism associated with slower economic growth and vice versa. If everybody does his or her own thing, the economy grows less quickly than it would if at least some individuals worked for collective purposes. But this study revealed no relationship between culture and economic growth that holds true for all countries, including the poor ones that need such growth the most.

A Second Case of Culture Measurement: The Chinese Value Survey

The Rokeach Value Survey is a well-known questionnaire developed by psychologist Milton Rokeach for measuring values in American society. In 1979, a group of academic researchers from nine Asian and Pacific countries administered a modified version of this survey to 100 psychology students (50 males and 50 females) in each of ten different countries. The results of the survey were published about the same time as those of the IBM studies. When the two were compared, it appeared that all four dimensions identified in the IBM material, in addition to a fifth that we have not been able to interpret, were also present in the student data.

The overlap between the two research projects was demonstrated on the scores of six countries that were represented in both samples. This overlap is remarkable because the two projects used completely different questionnaires on different populations in different years in only partly overlapping sets of countries. The agreement between the two projects was strong support for the universality of the four IBM dimensions.

We were troubled, however, by another concern: the influence of the researchers' own culture on the results. Our data showed that people in different countries had different mental programming; this conclusion obviously also applies to the people who conceive the questionnaires and do the research. The IBM questionnaires evolved from work by U.S., British, Dutch, French, and Scandinavian researchers—all of them from Western countries. The Rokeach Value Survey was a purely U.S. instrument; thus respondents in non-Western settings were asked to answer questions that had been made up by Western researchers. Can we assume that the respondents' answers accurately reflect the essence of their own cultures? Some of the questions may have been irrelevant to them; others that were relevant may not have been included. These concerns led to the development of the Chinese Value Survey (CVS).

Michael Bond, based in Hong Kong, asked a number of Chinese social scientists to prepare a list of basic values for Chinese people. This led to the creation of a 40-item Chinese questionnaire that was subsequently translated into English. Through an international network of interested colleagues, this Chinese Value Survey was administered to 100 students (50 males and 50 females) in a variety of disciplines in each of 22 countries selected from all five continents. Wherever possible, translations into the local language were made directly from the Chinese. To a Western mind, some of the items seemed strange, such as "filial piety" (which was explained as "honoring of ancestors and obedience to, respect for, and financial support of parents"). Of course, to the Chinese mind, some of the items on the Rokeach Value Survey or IBM questionnaire may have seemed equally unusual.

A statistical analysis of the 22-country Chinese Value Survey results based on the *relative* importance attached in a country to each value as opposed to the other values again yielded four dimensions. Twenty out of 22 countries were covered earlier in the IBM studies; thus we could compare the scores of the countries on each CVS dimension with those for the IBM dimensions. Our findings were striking: One CVS dimension was very similar to Power Distance, another to Individualism/Collectivism, and a third to

Masculinity/Femininity—this again in spite of the completely different questions, different populations, different time periods, and different mix of countries.

The three dimensions common to the Chinese Value Survey and the IBM studies are the ones that refer to three types of expected social behavior: behavior toward seniors or juniors, toward the group, and as a function of one's sex. These represent cultural choices so fundamental to any human society that they are found regardless of whether the values surveyed were designed by a Western or an Eastern mind. They are truly universal human traits in the sense that all societies share the same problems, but different societies have "chosen" (historically rather than consciously) different solutions to these problems.

One dimension from the IBM studies, however, is missing in the CVS data: We did not find a CVS dimension related to Uncertainty Avoidance. We earlier associated this dimension with man's search for Truth; it seems that the Chinese do not believe this to be an essential issue. However, we did find another quite clearly marked dimension made up of the values indicated in Exhibit 4.3.

For countries scoring high on this dimension, the values on the left side of the exhibit are relatively more important; for countries scoring low, those on the right are more important. In fact, both the values on the right and those on the left are in line with the teachings of Confucius as we described them earlier. However, the values on the left select those teachings of Confucius that are more oriented toward the future (especially perseverance and thrift), whereas those on the right select Confucian values oriented toward the past and the present. We have called this dimension "Confucian Dynamism" to show that it deals with a choice from Confucius' ideas and that its positive pole reflects a dynamic, future-oriented mentality, whereas its negative pole reflects a more static, tradition-oriented mentality.

Scores for Confucian Dynamism for the countries surveyed with the CVS are listed in the last column of Exhibit 4.2. In discussing the IBM studies, we showed that none of the four IBM dimensions was associated with economic growth across all countries; however, we were stunned to discover that our new dimension, Confucian Dynamism, is strongly associated with economic growth over the period between 1965 and 1985 across all 22 countries, rich or poor, that were covered.

◼ Confucius and Economic Growth

A glance at Exhibit 4.2 shows that four of the Five Dragons—Hong Kong, Taiwan, Japan, and South Korea—hold the top positions on the "Confucian

EXHIBIT 4.3 Values Associated With Confucian Dynamism

The relative importance of:	*But the relative unimportance of:*
Persistence (perseverance)	Personal steadiness and stability
Ordering relationships by status and observing this order	Protecting your face
Thrift	Respect for tradition
Having a sense of shame	Reciprocation of greetings, favors, and gifts

Dynamism" scale. The next highest scores are found for Brazil, India, Thailand, and Singapore. The Netherlands, Sweden, and West Germany take a middle position. On the lower side we find the English-speaking countries Australia, New Zealand, the United States, Britain, and Canada; the African countries Zimbabwe and Nigeria; and the Philippines and Pakistan.

Let's do a quick recap of what happened: Chinese social scientists composed a values questionnaire and this was administered to male and female students in 22 countries. We learned from their answers that some values were preferred in some countries, while other values were preferred in others. We could form dimensions, clusters of values that appeared to be associated; one of these dimensions we called "Confucian Dynamism." Thus far, this was a completely psychological exercise; it was concerned, not with business or with economics, but with culture. It then appeared that the country scores on Confucian Dynamism derived from this exercise are strongly associated with those countries' economic growth. Thus we have found a cultural link to an economic phenomenon.

As in the case of the association between wealth and individualism, the causality could have gone either way. However, the values that compose the dimension of "Confucian Dynamism" do not seem to be recent developments caused by the fast economic development of certain countries (although they may have been reinforced by it). The Chinese and Japanese peoples were known to value thrift and perseverance before the present boom started; their belief in tradition and "face" (negative on the "Confucian Dynamism" scale) was heavily shaken by the events of the 1940s and 1950s; therefore, we assume the values to be at least part of the cause, and economic growth to be the effect.

The logical link between the two is East Asian entrepreneurship. We do not mean that the values we found are held only by entrepreneurs; rather, the way in which we found them (by surveying student samples) suggests that they are held broadly within entire societies, among entrepreneurs and future entrepreneurs, among their employees and their families, and among members of the society as a whole.

Let us look again at the values that compose our "Confucian Dynamism" dimension (see Exhibit 4.3). If this dimension is somewhat puzzling to the Western readers, they should not be surprised. The dimension is composed precisely of those elements that our Western instruments had not registered; a Westerner would not normally find them important. Thus we will try to explain them further.

At the outset, we must note that the label "Confucian" could be somewhat misleading. The values associated with the positive (left) side are also found in non-Confucian countries such as India or Brazil. In addition, a number of core Confucian values such as "filial piety" are not associated with this factor at all; and finally, the values on the negative (right) side, as we argued earlier, are as "Confucian" as those on the positive side.

Having issued this disclaimer, we should acknowledge that the shared value of "ordering relationship by status and observing this order" is quintessential Confucianism in action. As we showed earlier, hierarchical dualities and interrelatedness lie at the heart of the Chinese conception of being human (the "wu lun"). This sense of hierarchy and complementarity of relations undoubtedly makes the entrepreneurial role easier to play.

The value of having a "sense of shame" supports interrelatedness through sensitivity to social contacts. The value of "thrift" leads to savings, which means availability of capital for reinvestment, an obvious asset to economic growth; economists had been struck by the high savings quotas in the Five Dragon countries. Finally, "persistence" or "perseverance" suggests a general tenacity in the pursuit of whatever goals a person selects for himself or herself, including economic goals.

Low endorsement of the values on the right side of our "Confucian Dynamism" dimension facilitates economic growth. "Protecting one's face," if widely shared as a concern, would detract from getting on with the business. The "reciprocation of greetings, favors, and gifts" is a social activity more concerned with good manners than with performance. Too much "respect for tradition" impedes innovation; part of the secret of the Five Dragons' economic success is the ease with which they have accepted Western technological innovations. Finally, "personal steadiness and stability," if overstressed, would discourage the initiative, risk seeking, and changeability required of entrepreneurs trying to exploit the vicissitudes of world trade.

Culture in the form of certain dominant values is a necessary condition for economic growth; however, culture alone is not sufficient for such growth to occur. Two other necessary conditions are the existence of a market and a political context that allows development. The first condition explains why the growth of the Five Dragons started only after 1955, when for the first time in history the conditions for a truly global market were fulfilled. The supportive political context was fulfilled in all Five Dragons, although in quite different ways, with the role of government varying from active support to laissez-faire. Labor unions were weak and company-oriented in all five countries, and a relatively egalitarian income distribution meant that support for revolutionary social changes was weak. The Confucian sense of moderation affected political life as well, in spite of occasional outbreaks of unrest and violence.

The influence of the political context is evident in the country that was the cradle of Confucianism, the People's Republic of China. So far, data on the Chinese Value Survey for the People's Republic are missing. We can only infer that in spite of Maoism, many Confucian values remain strong in the People's Republic, and that those on the left side of our "Confucian Dynamism" dimension are currently boosted at the expense of those on the right side.

The economic growth of the People's Republic was obviously hampered by political factors. The Cultural Revolution of 1966-1976 was a period of economic shrinkage; nevertheless, the average annual rate of economic growth in the People's Republic over the 20-year period that included the Revolution was still 4.8% or higher than that of Japan. It also seems that under the leadership of Deng Xiaoping, the People's Republic has let economic expediency prevail over political purity. It is obviously more difficult to turn around a nation of 1,000 million people than it is to turn around a nation such as Singapore, which has a population of 2.5 million. So it is not unlikely that the People's Republic will follow the success of the Five Dragons—albeit at some distance—and eventually become the sixth—and most powerful—dragon of them all.

Western Minds and Eastern Minds

It is remarkable that the values dimension associated with the economic success of East Asiatic cultures over the past 20 years was not found with questionnaires developed by Western researchers. It took the Chinese Value Survey—an Eastern instrument—to identify this dimension. This is a powerful illustration of how fundamental a phenomenon culture really is. It not only affects our daily practices (the way we live, the way we are brought up, the way we manage, and the way we are managed); it also affects the theories we are able to develop to explain our practices. Culture's grip on us is complete.

What did our studies tell us about the difference between Western and Eastern minds? Besides the three previously mentioned dimensions common to both West and East (Power Distance, Individualism/Collectivism, and Masculinity/Femininity) we found one uniquely Western dimension: Uncertainty Avoidance. As we argued, this dimension deals with a society's search for Truth; uncertainty-avoiding cultures believe in an absolute Truth, and uncertainty-accepting cultures take a more relativist stance. We also found one uniquely Eastern dimension, Confucian Dynamism; we believe that this dimension deals with a society's search for Virtue. It is no accident that this dimension relates to the teachings of Confucius; as we described them earlier, he was a teacher of practical ethics without any religious content. He dealt with Virtue, but left the question of Truth open.

There is a philosophical dividing line in our world that separates Western from Eastern thinking. The West, in this case, includes the countries that are traditionally Judaean, Christian, or Muslim—three religions that are very much concerned with Truth. Throughout history, these religions have been split between fundamentalist, intolerant currents that believe they have the one Truth and all others are wrong, and liberal, tolerant currents that put a concern with humanity, also present in all three religions, above doctrine.

These two trends in thinking correspond to the two poles (strong or weak) of the Uncertainty-Avoidance dimension. The East, represented by Confucianism but also by Hinduism, Buddhism, Taoism, and Shintoism, does not assume that any one human being can have the Truth. Human truth is seen as partial, so that one truth does not exclude its opposite. This is why people in the East can easily adhere to more than one religion or philosophical school at the same time; Shintoism and Buddhism, for example, coexist in many Japanese households. Along this line of thinking, a practical, non-religious ethical system like Confucianism can become a cornerstone of society—more so than in the West, where we tend to derive ethics from religion.

During the Industrial Revolution that has shaken mankind for the past 200 years, the Western concern for Truth was at first an asset. It led to the discovery of the laws of nature, which could then be exploited for the sake of human progress. It is surprising that Chinese scholars, despite their high level of civilization, never discovered Newton's laws; they were simply not looking for them. The Chinese script also betrays this lack of interest in general laws: It needs 5,000 different characters, one for each syllable, while by splitting the syllables into separate letters Western languages need only about 30 signs. We could say that Western thinking is analytical, while Eastern thinking is synthetic.

By the middle of the 20th century, the Western concern for truth gradually ceased to be an asset and turned instead into a liability. Science may benefit from analytical thinking, but management and government are based on the art of synthesis. With the results of Western, analytically derived technologies freely available, Eastern cultures could start putting these technologies into practice according to their superior synthetic abilities. What is true or who is right is less important than what works, and how the efforts of individuals with different thinking patterns can be coordinated toward a common goal. Japanese management, especially with Japanese employees, is famous for this pragmatic synthesis. The strategic advantage, in this period of Eastern cultures that practice virtue without a concern for truth, is part of what our research has illustrated.

◼ The Quest For Global Management Synergy

The IBM values study, in which national cultural differences were measured across different subsidiaries within the same multinational corporation, shows that national culture does not stop at the gate of the foreign company. Whether they like it or not, the headquarters of multinationals are in the business of multicultural management.

Cultural differences among national subsidiaries easily lead to conflicts over corporate policies. Such conflicts arise not only between headquarters and local managers in the subsidiaries, but also between headquarters and expatriates from the home country nationality. In one U.S. corporation we know, the head of a headquarters staff department complained bitterly to the president about the noncompliance with certain rules by the East Asian regional manager, who was an expatriate American. "I fully agree," said the president. "His behavior is stupid and against company policy. I have only one question. From the time he worked in headquarters, I have known Mr. X to be an intelligent man. How can a man be so intelligent in Los Angeles and so stupid in Hong Kong?"

Policy conflicts are less likely to occur in technology and finance, which are relatively culture-independent, and more likely in marketing and personnel, where cultural diversity is largest. Multinational corporate cultures handle cultural diversity among subsidiaries according to the level of Uncertainty Avoidance in their headquarters. At one extreme is the position that "there is only one corporate truth, and we have it"; at the opposite extreme the subsidiaries are run at arm's length, without much attempt at integration. The president whom we quoted was a wise man who steered a middle way. He saw that cultural differences can easily go unrecognized by overzealous headquarters staff and can be interpreted as personality defects of the people in the subsidiaries, whether they are locals or expatriates.

National cultures can undoubtedly be complementary. Our experiences with the Chinese Value Survey are in themselves an example of cultural synergy, because the survey used a Western research approach with a Chinese questionnaire. We can also consider the economic success of the Five Dragons a case of cultural synergy, since it was based on the exploitation of technology originally developed in the West according to Eastern principles. Although there is no patent for developing cultural synergy, managers can be helped to recognize local cultural patterns. This opportunity may help them overcome the idea that the cultural choices of their own country are necessarily superior to those of other countries. Such an attitude is a luxury that the management of a multinational corporation can no longer afford.

◾ Selected Bibliography

Herman Kahn has formulated the neo-Confucian hypothesis in his book *World Economic Development: 1979 and Beyond* (Croom Helm, 1979). On the failure of economics to predict or explain the development of the Five Dragons, we recommend an article by George L. Hicks and S. Gordon Redding, "The Story of the East Asian 'Economic Miracle' " (*Euro-Asian Business Review*, Issues 3 and 4, 1983). Michael Harris Bond is the editor of a recent book entitled *The Psychology of the Chinese People* (Oxford University Press, 1986), which contains discussions of and references to the psychological aspects of Confucianism.

Geert Hofstede's description of the IBM studies can be found in his book *Culture's Consequences* (Sage Publications, 1984). Hofstede is also the author of a relevant article, "The Cultural Relativity of Organizational Practices and Theories" (*Journal of International Business Studies*, Fall 1983). The four dimensions associated with the IBM studies were first described in the same author's article "Motivation, Leadership, and Organization: Do American Theories Apply Abroad?" (*Organizational Dynamics*, Summer 1980).

Geert Hofstede and Michael Harris Bond compared the IBM studies with the modified Rokeach Value Study in their article "Hofstede's Culture Dimensions: An Independent Validation Using Rokeach's Value Survey" (*Journal of Cross-Cultural Psychology*, December 1984). Bond was also a member of "The Chinese Culture Connection," the group of authors of an article on the Chinese Value Survey entitled "Chinese Values and the Search for Culture-Free Dimensions of Culture" (*Journal of Cross-Cultural Psychology*, June 1987).

CHAPTER 5

The Work of Geert Hofstede

Commentary

The importance of Hofstede's work cannot be overestimated. His large-scale study of 53 nations provided evidence that there are at least five major dimensions along which national cultures tend to differ. Moreover, these dimensions are easily understandable and useful, not only to researchers but also to managers who want a cultural profile of a particular nation or nations. These dimensions have proved to be very helpful to researchers who have related them to measures of entrepreneurship, innovation, and even airline accidents per capita. For example, nations that tend to be collectivistic experience two and one-half times the accident rates of more individualistic nations (Phillips, 1991). Moreover, several other researchers have confirmed all or most of Hofstede's findings. For example, Hoppe (1983) gave foreign managers from 19 nations the 22-item Hofstede questionnaire and correlated their scores in 1983 with the original scores of respondents from these nations. The results were surprisingly consistent.

However, after pointing out the strengths of Hofstede's work, I typically ask students and managers about its weaknesses or limitations, and the normal response is silence. The reader might want to respond to this inquiry before proceeding.

One of the weaknesses of the Hofstede approach is that it is "etic," or culture-general. It provides an overall profile of a nation when compared to other nations, and in this sense, the resulting scores are similar to economic or institutional statistics that yield comparable profiles. However, Hofstede's approach does not provide an "emic," or culture-specific, level of understanding that gives the manager or investigator an in-depth feel for the nation. Also, this approach does not allow the manager to contrast regional differences within a nation, such as the marked difference between northern and southern Italy.

To complicate matters, there are many different types of individualism and collectivism, but the Hofstede perspective allows a nation to be categorized only as a point along this dimension. Furthermore, some of the dimensions are highly or at least moderately correlated; for example, as collectivism increases, both power distance and desire for certainty also rise. Fundamentally, the dimensional approach used by Hofstede and other cross-cultural psychologists is linear in nature and does not really consider the fact that many relationships between and even within dimensions are nonlinear and, at times, contradictory and paradoxical. The work of Alan Page Fiske helps us to address these problems, and in the next section, we describe it and its managerial implications in some detail.

Furthermore, as "the Confucius Connection" implies, there is a cultural metaphor underlying Hofstede's work, namely, that the characteristics of the Confucian value system or religion parallel the behavioral patterns found in Asian economies. The statistical work underlying Hofstede and Bond's analysis is good, but certainly not definitive, and various interpretations of their analysis have been offered (Fang, 1998). Similar to Samuel Huntington (1996), whose work is reviewed in this book, Hofstede and Bond have chosen one phenomenon (religion) to explain another (economic growth). But in so doing, they may have simplified reality too much. For example, they do not even mention the striking similarity between the Confucian Dynamic and the Protestant Ethic. As Max Weber (1930) so famously argued, there are several preconditions for capitalism, and one of the most important is an ideology justifying working hard and deferring short-term gratification for long-term rewards. According to Weber, this ideology was encouraged by Protestantism, and without this ideological underpinning, modern capitalism might not have developed. This thesis was challenged by several Catholic writers, who pointed out that Catholic nations such as Italy and France were quite adept at fostering capitalistic endeavors even before the rise of Protestantism.

Even given these caveats, what is extremely helpful about Hofstede's work is that it motivates and provokes us to look at culture in a new and different way. Although reviewers have tended to follow Hofstede's example by emphasizing his statistical results, his use of cultural metaphors deserves attention. As the first part of this book emphasizes, we live by metaphors, and they are not only nice but necessary. To the extent that nations develop the long-term time orientation that the metaphors of both the Confucian

Dynamic and the Protestant Ethic stress, it is probable that economic growth will rise rapidly.

References

Fang, T. (1998, August). Reflections on Hofstede's 5th dimension: A critique of "Confucian Dynamism." Paper presented at the annual meeting of the Academy of Management, San Diego, CA.

Hoppe, M. H. (1983). *A comparative study of country elites.* Unpublished doctoral dissertation, University of North Carolina at Chapel Hill.

Huntington, S. (1996). *The clash of civilizations.* New York: Simon and Schuster.

Phillips, D. (1991, August 21). Building a "cultural index" to world airline safety. *The Washington Post,* p. A8.

Weber, M. (1930). *The Protestant ethic and the spirit of capitalism* (T. Parsons, Trans.). New York: Scribner.

CHAPTER 6

Basic Types of Human Relations, Collectivism, and Individualism

Research Translation

As we have suggested, Hofstede provided the impetus for a large and growing body of important work, much of which emphasized different types of individualism and collectivism. The research completed by Harry Triandis and his associates (e.g., see Triandis & Gelfand, 1998) is particularly insightful and helpful in management, because he identified two basic types of individualism and two basic types of collectivism. He also argues that these four types provide a schema similar to the generic types of classification systems found in biology, and that more specific forms of both collectivism and individualism can be described after a particular culture has been categorized into one of the four general types. We begin our discussion with Triandis, after which we turn our attention to Fiske.

The first type of collectivism is horizontal; that is, members of the culture share the same values and even emotional responses, so much so that they are scarcely distinguishable from one another. Horizontal collectivism represents a high-context culture, and it is one in which there is little leeway given to members to deviate from norms and values. It is also a culture in which in-group members view out-groups in a distant and frequently even hostile fashion.

Under the second type, vertical collectivism, values are widely shared by in-group members, but there is an unequal distribution of power and authority. Typically, this form of collectivism emphasizes the "headman" style of leadership, both for organizational and political leaders. The headman, or national political leader, has much greater authority, power, and prestige than others, but he or she is also responsible for ensuring that the cultural values are upheld and that members of the group are provided for. Most Americans have never experienced this style of leadership because it involves a reciprocal psychological relationship, that is, followers defer to the headman, who in turn is responsible for looking out for their welfare.

Individualism also is classified as horizontal and vertical. When a culture emphasizes horizontal individualism, its members make decisions by themselves without worrying about group considerations. However, such a culture also believes that equality is the norm that should be stressed rather than rankings based on power and prestige. Under vertical individualism, individuals do make decisions by themselves with minimal regard to group considerations, but there are prestige and power rankings in terms of authority, income, and so forth.

Independently, Alan Page Fiske (1991) arrived at these four basic types. Fiske goes far beyond Triandis and argues that there are four elementary forms of human relations. His work relies heavily on ethnographic data and integrating the theories and research of other researchers. Most importantly, Fiske basically employs the theory of numerical data as a metaphor underlying these four elementary forms.

In statistics, it is common to distinguish between the following types of data: nominal, ordinal, interval, and ratio. Nominal data basically means that classifications or groups are established, but there is no attempt to say that one category is greater or less than others. For example, a student could be a student in University X or University Y, but not both. With ordinal data, it is possible to say that some members of a group are greater or more important than other members, but the distance between members is not uniform, so direct comparisons within the group are not possible. For example, John is more valued than Mary, and Mary is more valued than Peter, but it is not possible to say that Peter is twice as valued as John. With interval data, there is a uniform distance between each point of the scale, but there is no true zero point; hence, you must compare individuals within a group in terms of each criterion. For example, Peter may be one unit more sociable than Mary, and Mary may be one unit more sociable than John, so it is possible to say that Peter is twice as sociable as John. Finally, ratio data involve a true zero point, such as with money, so that it is possible to convert one scale into another scale without creating a new scale for each criterion such as sociability.

Fiske argues that the first elementary form of human relations, Collective Sharing (CS), is based on nominal groupings: One is either in the ingroup or the out-group, but not both. This corresponds to horizontal collectivism, and ethics is based on fulfilling the needs of all individuals within the group. Within the group, there is no such phenomenon as stealing because everything is shared, including food. However, out-group members are essentially treated as foreigners or barbarians, and sometimes even as non-humans. This form is found in small and economically underdeveloped villages throughout the world.

The second elementary form, Authority Ranking (AR), is based on ordinal data and corresponds to horizontal collectivism, or the headman perspective on leadership. As suggested previously, subordinate individuals are very obsequious to those in power. This is expressed frequently in the elaborate bows or gestures such as holding hands in a praying position, and then bowing much lower than the superior, who may merely nod in return. Such bowing is often seen in Asian nations such as Japan and Thailand, and it is in marked contrast to the Western handshake, which connotes only a greeting signifying equality on the part of those engaging in it. In an AR culture, ethics is based on status rather than need, and those at the higher rank receive proportionately more of the goods and rewards, even though they are expected to fulfill more responsibilities than those lower in status and power.

Horizontal individualism is characteristic of the third elementary form, Equality Matching. Individual decision making is respected and encouraged, even at the group's expense, or at least of some of its members. However, members of such a cultural group believe that some individuals will be superior to others on one measure but not another, because the measurement must be taken each time. In such national cultures, everyone is assumed to be equal, and ethical norms are based on this assumption. At the same time, it is assumed that everyone will make an equitable or equal contribution to the group, although the timing is not specified. The Scandinavian nations have constructed a social and cultural system in which Equality Matching is practiced, as they have very high but regressive tax rates and, at the same time, very high charitable contributions on a per capita basis.

Finally, there is Market Pricing (MP), which emphasizes a true zero point—money. Everything can be expressed in terms of money, and so it is now possible to rank individuals on several criteria and to compare their values directly across these criteria. Some criteria will be more important than others and will be so weighted, but it is now possible to come to a final, aggregated score for each individual. Market Pricing corresponds to vertical individualism, and it is the basis for performance evaluation in many nations, including the United States. In such a culture, a person's worth is assessed vis-à-vis that of others, and this worth can change dramatically over time.

Fiske provides some insightful examples of the manner in which these four elementary forms are played out in actual decisions. He asks the reader to consider the purchase of an expensive fire truck by a small town of 5,000 people. Given the information provided above, you and your fellow readers might want to discuss how the town should pay for this truck and whose homes should be protected. You might also consider various religions that practice one of these forms, and these include the Quakers; a messianic group whose leader—James Jones—was able to convince his 10,000 followers to engage in mass suicide; the Presbyterian Church; the Catholic Church; the Moslem religion; Buddhism; and so on.

As this discussion indicates, the use of a numerical measurement metaphor greatly enhances our understanding of actual organizational practices such as performance evaluation and executive compensation. For instance, how would you interpret the "pay for performance" approach in terms of these four forms, and what are the alternatives to it? When a nation such as Indonesia is ruled by one man for decades, what form is being followed? Also, how do you think cultures and organizations change when they follow each of these forms, but only one at a time?

References

Fiske, A. P. (1991). *Structures of social life: The four elementary forms of human relations*. New York: Free Press.

Triandis, H., & Gelfand, M. (1998). Converging measurement of horizontal and vertical individualism and collectivism. *Journal of Personality and Social Psychology, 74,* 118-128.

CHAPTER 7

French Wine

An Illustration of a
Cultural Metaphor

MARTIN J. GANNON
PETER BROWN
SHARON RIBAS

When it comes to doing things the European way or doing them the French way, then France generally prefers, yes, the French way.
—"The French Way" (1997, p. 17)

The French tend to evoke strong emotional reactions in many short-term and long-term visitors to their country. Frequently, visitors complain about the rudeness that greets them in France, and they regale listeners with horror stories about the stubborn French who refuse to speak any language other than French and who are emotionally cold. Some of this behavior is cultural in nature. For example, unlike most informally inclined Americans, the French tend to smile at someone only after they know a person for some time. However, the French themselves recognize

AUTHOR'S NOTE: This is a revised version of "French Wine," in Martin J. Gannon and Associates, *Understanding Global Cultures: Metaphorical Journeys Through 17 Countries* (Thousand Oaks, CA: Sage, 1994).

that their service to customers is well below the American standard, which has spurred the growth of the quality movement, even to the extent of teaching surly waiters and clerks to smile and speak in a friendly tone (Swardson, 1996).

However, many other visitors paint an opposite picture of the French, describing them as very concerned about their feelings and welfare and as going to extreme lengths to demonstrate hospitality and friendship. In fact, both portraits of the French have some validity, especially if one uses the metaphor of French wine.

One legacy of French society that has remained integral throughout the development of French history is that of French wine. In looking back over the years, it quickly becomes evident that wine and France are inextricably bound together. Indeed, wine has been part of France's history since the Romans first conquered and settled in southern France, bringing vine cuttings and the culture of wine with them.

Wine has played a vital role in determining economy, traditions, and attitudes. It has helped shape the country's disposition, weaving a common thread through all of the varying walks of French life. Just as there are more than 5,000 varieties of French wine, so, too, is there an abundance of French idiosyncrasies and personalities. Beneath these differences, however, lie an industry and a people that work together and grow together. Accordingly, wine appears to be an appropriate metaphor for describing and analyzing the French culture.

To focus this discussion within the metaphor of French wine, five principal elements of wine will serve as a guide: (a) pureness, (b) classification, (c) composition, (d) suitability, and (e) maturation.

Pureness

To more fully appreciate the metaphor, we must first understand what wine is, what its origins are, and how wine is made. A wine's characteristics are the summation of its past, as evidenced by the environment from which it develops. Viniculture is the precise and patient process that further shapes the destiny of the grape's transformation into wine. Fine wine is considered to be the distillation of 2,000 years of civilization. It is understandably viewed as an object of great pride; a survivor of nature's caprices and uncertainties; a product of patience and modesty; and, most importantly, a symbol of friendship, hospitality, and joie de vivre.

Vital to the quality of the wine are the soil, the climate, the vine type, and the viniculturalist who tends the wine-making process. The complex interplay of these factors determines whether pride or disappointment reigns once the wine flows from its bottled womb. Soil and climate nourish growth in mysterious ways that defy chemical analysis. Contrary to what might be expected, it is the type of soil on which little else grows that allows the vine to thrive. Climate and vine type must complement each other so as to produce healthy grapes, and the viniculturalist must ensure that the timing of harvest and maturation are meticulous and accurate.

Vines are also interbred, making it difficult to classify the wine produced because the offspring can resemble its parent or even display entirely new characteristics. Furthermore, what is recognized as the world's greatest wine is grown only in a few select vineyards in France. The art and science of viniculture also influences the wine's personality. Experience, diligent patience, and effort are required to propagate the wine through its various stages of cultivation. The *vendange,* or harvest time, brings a sudden preoccupation with time. A delay of even 12 hours between the harvest and preparation for fermenting can bring spoilage of both taste and aroma. After transfer from vats to bottles, the wine continues its aging process. Age, then, influences personality development, with great wines requiring more than 50 years to mature to perfection.

The French, much like Americans, have a romantic view of their country as being special and unique. Like a flawless bottle of vintage wine, it is as if God had decreed that there be perfection in the land and people of France. They have mentally massaged the image of their borders into a hexagon, perfectly situated midway between the Equator and the North Pole, balanced in soil and climate. Symmetry, balance, and harmony—it all coalesced in one great land because the French supposedly willed it. This perception of symmetry and unity in the physical dimensions of this geographically diverse land is more wishful thinking than reality.

The North and the South disagree even as to the origin of the French people; and in different parts of the country, people have different identities: the Northeast identifies with the Germans and Swiss, the Northwest with the English, the Southwest with the Catalans and Basques, and the Southeast with the Italians. Perhaps, then, the eternal struggle for unity has deep and stubborn roots in the past that dictate France's destiny as an aggregate of individuals struggling to forge themselves into a singular entity.

Thus, the French tend to give the impression that France is the center of the universe around which the rest of the world rotates. One can quickly learn to resent the French belief in their cultural superiority and lack of immediate friendliness. But they readily defend their position in part by noting that international business and diplomacy were conducted in the French language until World War I, and that French art, literature, and thought remain pervasive in modern education and society. They also band together by having shared a long and illustrious history of crusades, wars, and devastation.

The extent to which the French defend this supposed superiority is wide-ranging. A commission must decide which foreign words can be a part of the official language; there is a requirement to have proceedings of conferences published in French, even when English would suffice; and the seventh summit devoted to the French language was held in Vietnam in 1997, which France formerly ruled but in which only about 1% of the population speaks French.

The earliest traceable ancestry begins with the Celts, a Germanic people, who later became known as the Gauls. They planted an extensive empire that was subdued by the invasive Romans under Caesar in 52 BC. For the next 500 years, the Gauls were repeatedly subjected to invasions by other Germanic tribes, and, finally, by the Franks, who immigrated westward across the Rhine. From the Middle Ages and a feudalistic system, there emerged the Renaissance ("Rebirth"), a time of increasing wealth and power for France and continuing turmoil.

A golden age burst forth in the person of Louis XIV, the Sun King, who proclaimed, "L'Etat, c'est moi," or "I am the state." He orchestrated his rule from the extraordinarily lavish Palais de Versailles, and during his reign, France expanded and built an impressive navy. Its language was spoken and its culture was emulated all over Europe.

But the Sun King allowed a widening gap to develop between the wealthy and the poor, which, in an increasingly financially stressed economy, exploded in the French Revolution of 1789. The quest for "liberté, égalité, fraternité" first resulted in the brief rule of Napoléon. He allowed a more organized France to take shape by enforcing the Code Napoléon, which gathered, revised, and codified a vast, disorderly accumulation of laws, both old and new. Unfortunately, the oppressive restrictions that Napoléon placed upon laborers, peasants, and women are still felt today.

Moving closer to the modern era, France was also heavily affected by World Wars I and II. Although a victor in World War I, France lost nearly 2 million men. World War II still lives in the memories of many French people as a time of hopelessness and disgrace under German domination.

The history of French wine has also endured notable difficulties, one of which occurred from 1865 until 1895. During these years, a disease called *phylloxtera vastatrix* destroyed virtually every vineyard in France (Vedel, 1986). This was a tragedy of major proportions that adversely affected thousands of wine growers. But even in such dire circumstances, the French did not lose their resolve. After toiling for months by trial and error, they discovered that a viable solution was to graft French vine strains onto American stocks that were resistant to the disease. Forced into a corner, the French came together to save the industry. In subsequent years, the crops regained their health, and the wine industry flourished once again.

Even with this brief overview, it becomes apparent that the lives of the French people have been planted, uprooted, and replanted throughout history. It was the conquering Romans who left the French with an inherited sense of pageantry and grandeur, as well as with an affinity for control and bureaucratic organization. They introduced the concept of centralization and a complex bureaucracy, both of which have taken root in French hearts and minds. France's present concept of grandeur was first thrust upon the French people in the time of Louis XIV. From this epic era, there emerged the idea that the French were guardians of cherished universal values, and that their country was a beacon to the world. The French saw themselves as favored, as possessors of ideas and values coveted and treasured by the rest of mankind. As Peguy wrote, "God loves the French the best."

It is true that the purest, finest wines must be grown in very special soil. In this sense, the French consider France to be a very pure and proud country. Accordingly, those not born and raised in France need to guard against forming quick and negative first impressions without understanding past trials and tribulations as they relate to the formation of the French culture.

Classification

As noted earlier, France produces 5,000 varieties of wine precisely classified so that impostors cannot pass for superior wines. This incessant urge for nomenclature bestows upon wine a pedigree that is displayed on each label. Through fermentation and the aging process in the bottle, wine will develop its final personality, blend, and balance.

Although wine is classified in excruciating detail, one who is not a connoisseur would be so audacious as to divide it into four major classes:

1. *Appellation d'origine contrôlée* wines, which are the best and most famous

2. Respectable regional varieties, known as *vins délimités de qualité supérieur,* which are quite good for everyday use

3. *Vins de pays,* which are younger, fresher wines suitable for immediate consumption

4. *Vins de tables,* which are truly wine but lacking in taste and pedigree

Similarly, French society is also clearly stratified and divided into four principal and generally nonoverlapping classes: The *haute bourgeoisie,* which comprises the few remaining aristocrats along with top business and government professionals; the *petite bourgeoisie,* who are owners of small companies or top managers; *classes moyennes,* or the middle class—teachers, shopkeepers, and artisans; and *classes populaires,* or workers.

Each person may know his or her place in society, but it does not imply that one person feels inferior to another. The French are comfortable accepting and living within the confines of this classification system rather than resisting it. The worker in the classe populaire is just as accepted for his or her contribution to society as the elitist official in the haute bourgeoisie class. This norm extends to attitudes of the French to outsiders. Visitors to France sometimes have difficulty relating to the French, who can be just as ethnocentric as anyone else. The French tend to behave independently of others who mistakenly expect tacit cooperation from them in an undertaking. The reason for this outlook is quite simple. In the French mind, France and a person's own particular social class tend to come first. They interpret the phrase *tout le monde* (all the world) to mean all who are French or, even more specifically, all who are in their particular social class. Outsiders are countenanced but not openly welcomed.

Rules, regulations, and procedures give certainty, definition, and order to the French life, along with guaranteeing the preservation of a particular quality and tradition to the lifestyle. Still, *savoir-vivre* facilitates life, meaning that there is a certain way to do something, no matter what the situation or how trivial it may appear. It provides an avenue for security where a threat is presupposed, and certainty where fears and doubts exist. Consequently, it leaves nothing to chance. Even as Napoléon codified civil law, another Frenchman codified gastronomy in 12 volumes. Nothing has been omitted or forgotten; even slavery was codified, and it resulted in more humane treatment of France's slaves than of England's or Spain's.

On the other hand, savoir-vivre can lead to preoccupation of form over substance, transforming every aspect of life into a ceremony. Preoccupation with form is evident in the French sense of style and fashion—and a flair for elegance. Some first-class French hotels have decrepit furniture, yet the rooms have such utter charm that all is forgiven and overlooked. Image, and the stress on the sensual, is more important than the facts in business advertisements as well. French advertisements tend to be attention-getting. They concentrate on creating a mood or a response instead of informing (Hall & Hall, 1990). Their advertising campaigns must first produce pieces of art before trying to be efficient; this is why they believe that the American advertising products are not very good—they are too straightforward for French tastes (P. Pozzo Di Borgo, personal communication, November 21, 1990).

That the French love classifying things is apparent not only with regard to wine, but also with regard to titles and the French fastidiousness with regard to and insistence on politeness and attention to social forms. Like labels pasted on wine bottles, labels that are applied to people will stick.

There is little room in French society for impostors and little fluidity in crossing class barriers. They pay attention to status and titles and expect others to do likewise. Correct form must be followed. For example, when introductions are called for, the one who makes an introduction must be of the same status as the one being introduced. In a business meeting, it is essential that the person with the highest rank occupy the middle seat. The importance paid to social standing is so great that even salary takes second place. Likewise, when honor is an issue, keeping one's word has more value than profit (Hall & Hall, 1990). Given this situation, it is little wonder that many seeking social mobility have migrated to countries such as Canada and the United States in recent years, and that the rates of innovation and entrepreneurship are low.

In the following vignette depicting this typical but seemingly contradictory French behavior, Pierre B. showed his American guest the sights of Paris by car in a tour that culminated in a starlit evening in the hilly suburb of Montmartre. Making a swift right, Pierre gunned his car up a steep, narrow street. In choosing to ascend, he had deliberately ignored the one-way sign pointing downward, but no matter. He was about to reach the crest when spears of headlights turned downward and advanced upon his tiny car. Thus obstructed, Pierre halted—as did the handful of cars. Faced with a headbeam-to-headbeam standoff, Pierre argued vigorously out the car window. The other drivers did the same. As the discourse generated increasing heat and passion, the American occupants in Pierre's vehicle began to feel uneasy, but he motioned assurances to them that he was in control. Then, without warning, he leapt out of the car, as did the other drivers, and they all continued the escalating war of words in front of the interlocking headlights. Then, abruptly, it all ended. The drivers, in a unanimous movement, all piled back into their cars. Without a word, Pierre aggressively backed his car down the hill and lurched to a stop on the side street he had exited moments before. The handful of cars filed sedately past him and disappeared into the black night. Pierre paused a moment longer; then, with silent resolution, he revved the engine and gunned his car back up the same street. This time, he reached the top and, once there, perched on the crest. Without a sliver of compunction, he turned and looked smugly at his guests. He then sliced the air emphatically with his arm, and ejected a victorious, "Ah-*hah!*"

Like the viniculturist, the French generally have a need to control and refine life and to order the universe. A significant portion of this desire can be attributed to the thinking of Descartes, whose desire to make man the master of nature led him to ponder a rational meaning of the universe. Because he elected to discover this meaning without leaving his study, due to his belief that "I think, therefore I am," his findings were not always accurate. But that did not matter to him as long as he was convincing. He has been described as the "intellectual father of the French preoccupation with form" (De Gramont, 1969, p. 318). One example of Cartesian thought is the general who devises a perfect battle plan with incomplete knowledge of the enemy's strength and capacity and suffers defeat—but with style and elegance.

One can also witness the legacy of the Cartesian method in life's most commonplace occurrences. Preoccupation with shaping, organizing, and magically transforming raw material into a work of art is evident in food shop windows, where displays of colorful and elaborately prepared casseroles and desserts could vie with the Louvre in terms of master-crafted creations. In sum, Descartes, who is frequently described as the founder of modern philosophy, left nothing unexplained, and neither do the French today.

The French businessperson is no less concerned with form in his or her business life. Presentations are given from the heart, so the French display eloquence much more than Americans do. Their obsession with form shows in their belief that how one speaks makes as much of an impression as what one says. The French love to discuss abstract and complex ideas spontaneously, in detail, and at length, so that agendas, time factors, and conclusions appear to have less importance.

In addition, French business is highly centralized because of the long-lasting influence of the Romans. In a very autocratic and bureaucratic way, the person atop the hierarchy is most important and wields power in many, if not most, decisions. This norm encourages the French to bypass the many intervening layers and to appeal directly to the pinnacle of power. The person in authority demonstrates it physically, for he or she is the person whose desk is placed in the center of the office. Those with the least influence are relegated to the far corners of the room. It is little wonder that change in French organizations tends to come from the top downward, not from the bottom upward (Crozier, 1964).

Such a centralized social structure lends itself to the acceptance of autocratic behavior. Therefore, managers display almost total control over their subordinates. In fact, French managers are often accused of not delegating authority, instead sharing vital information only within their own elitist network. As a result, it can be very difficult for lower-level managers to move up the corporate ladder.

This tight inner circle of upper management can be likened to the tight inner circle of the highest quality wines that win awards year after year. Only those wines from the best regions, with the best color, brilliance, and taste, can gain the status of *appellation d'origine contrôlée*—the highest distinction available. In the same way, gaining a top management position frequently requires education at the finest of schools and upbringing in the most affluent regions.

This high level of centralization can also be regarded in a positive light, because it serves to maintain unity. The French remain a diverse people who tend to be proud of and loyal to their respective regions of origin. Throughout history, the French have strived for unity, but they tend to detest uniformity, for they are a people who generally love to differ. De Gaulle once asked, "How can you govern a country that makes 365 kinds of cheeses?" The answer may be in the modern autocracy of centralization, where people who exist in a hierarchy of niches can find their own niche, security, and sense of belonging among members of the same social class.

This knowledge of France's hierarchical business structure can be instructive to American business managers. Just as we save the best bottle of wine for presentation only to the most distinguished guests, so, too, should we save our most polished proposals for presentation to a top manager in a French corporation. Efforts to persuade lower- and middle-level managers may prove frustrating, because few final decisions can be made without approval from the top.

Another advisory note in business relations is to be aware of how the French handle the uncertainty of an unknown colleague at a typical business lunch. Uncertainty brings unease and implies a lack of control, for it entails a threat that must be thwarted. The lunch, then, gives the French colleague time and opportunity to reflect, study, and learn who the outsider is and how the person can be expected to behave in various situations. The French, who tend to be low risk-takers, find it imperative to become familiar with the person with whom they do business. Pleasure and business are intertwined, for there is no better way in the French mind to open up communication and understanding than with a leisurely repast of food and wine (Hall & Hall, 1990).

Interestingly, however, the average amount of time devoted to lunch during the busy day has decreased from 90 to 40 minutes, suggesting that the globalization of business has influenced even the diehard French (Swardson, 1998). Similarly, the number of French brasserie-cafés has decreased from more than 200,000 in 1960, when the population was 46 million, to 50,000 today, when the population is 58 million ("Mais où sont les cafés d'antan?" 1995).

Perhaps the best attempt to categorize and classify different types of French behavior was completed by the anthropologist Edward T. Hall (1966). According to Hall, France is at the middle of his context dimension, with Japan and the Arab countries representing high-context behavior and Germany and the United States representing low-context behavior. That is, the French are high context in the sense that they frequently do not need explicit and/or written communication to understand one another. However, the French tend to emphasize low-context behavior in the form of excessive bureaucratic rules and regulations. This seemingly contradictory behavior reflects the Roman emphasis on centralization and bureaucracy, and, at the same time, the innate desire of many French people to know one another deeply before transacting business.

Composition

Lichine states that "wine is an extraordinary, intricate, and inconstant complex of different ingredients," and so it can be said of the French. Who they are has been determined by their ancestry, the region of the country where they were raised, and the social and educational systems that influence the kind of people they become. Their society is changing, and so are they. Perhaps their adaptability is an outgrowth of their complexity and inconstancy. The French tend to do many things at once, and they do them with alacrity— especially in an urban setting such as Paris, where the pace is rapid. In this sense, the French are polychronic. This pace encourages quick decision making and contributes to their impetuousness, where, in a highly centralized structure, businesspeople skirt cumbersome intervening layers of hierarchy to accomplish their objectives.

To the consternation of Americans trying to do business in France, the French tend to tolerate disruptions for the sake of human interactions, because to them, it is all part of an interrelated process. This toleration makes planning difficult, even for the French. After all, given life's uncertainties, one never knows what obstacles may prevent promises from being kept.

Still, Hall points out that the French tend to be monochronic—doing one activity at a time—once they have defined a goal they wish to attain. This simultaneous emphasis on polychronism and monochronism is, once again, a reflection of the fact that France is at the midpoint of the high-context/low-context continuum. Given this intermediate position, it is easy to understand why foreigners have difficulty comprehending French behavior.

The French work hard and prefer to be their own bosses, although few have the opportunity. In fact, too much entrepreneurial spirit is considered disruptive to normal business activity (Taylor, 1990). Sporadic 70-hour work weeks are not uncommon for some small business owners. One prosperous flower shop owner drives his small van more than 350 miles from Nancy in northeastern France to the southern coast to pick up his weekly flower supply. However, his business is quite seasonal; therefore, one can compare these arduous trips to the vendange-like intensity of the vineyards. The French pride themselves on such devotion to work and tend to believe that people in other countries do not work with the intensity that they do.

By law, the French must devote 5 weeks, including all of August, to vacation—with approximately 40% of them migrating to vacation spots such as the Côte d'Azur. Holidays, like food and wine, are taken seriously, and the French tend to prepare carefully and meticulously for them.

Their weekends tend to be devoted to their families. Of the 85% who ascribe to Catholicism, only 15% attend Mass, usually on Saturday evenings or Sunday mornings. Saturday afternoons are often reserved for shopping. Some say that with regard to religion, there is an antichurch sentiment; others disagree, asserting instead that the French have no particular persuasion on religious matters—that they are more areligious than antireligious (P. Pozzo Di Borgo, personal communication, November 21, 1990).

Geert Hofstede's (1980) analysis of 40 nations in terms of four cultural dimensions tends to confirm the profile of the French and its apparent contradictions that emerge when the metaphor of wine is employed. Not surprisingly, the French tend to accept a high degree of power distance between individuals and groups in society, and to dislike uncertainty, preferring to be in familiar situations and working with long-term colleagues. But the French also tend to be individualistic and even iconoclastic, and they cluster with other nations who value a high degree of individualism.

Still, Hofstede shows that France is a "feminine society" in which aggressiveness, assertiveness, and the desire for material possessions are of much less importance than the quality and pace of life. The French have deep-seated needs for security and getting along with insiders, colleagues, and family members. In short, the French accept centralization and bureaucracy, but only insofar as it allows them to be individualistic and buffers them from life's uncertainty so that a high quality of life can be maintained.

An integral part of maintaining this high quality of life in France is through conversation. Like French business, however, conversation is not without classifications, rules, and hierarchical structure. Similarly, just as the process of making wine is complex, intricate, and meaningful, so, too, is the art of French conversation. There is an innate restlessness in the French to explore every conceivable issue or topic through lengthy and lively conversation. Whether it be politics, weather, history, or the latest film, contrasts and controversy challenge the French intellect and heighten morale.

Many consider the French to be argumentative—none more so than the French themselves. They can be quick to criticize, but this is often only to stimulate discussion. Few Frenchmen or Frenchwomen are satisfied by mere superficial discourse. If a conversation is worth beginning, like the production of a tasty Burgundy, it is worth cultivating into a meaningful discussion.

For example, late one evening, in the small town of Dijon, an American stepped into a cab to save himself about a 25-minute walk. No sooner had the American sat down when the cab driver quickly blurted out, "Ah, que vous êtes Américain?!" Not expecting such quick questioning, the American cautiously replied, "Oui, je suis Américain . . . pourquoi?" The cab driver responded excitedly that he had never been to America and wanted to learn more about it. Conversation continued briskly and was quite philosophical at times. The cab driver was mostly interested in comparing the respective styles and mannerisms of the Americans and the French. Meanwhile, time—and the money meter—were ticking away: 10 francs . . . 15 francs . . . 20 francs (about $4.00). The American knew pretty well the different ways to get home, and this was *not* one of them. Finally, after 20 minutes or so, the cab arrived at its destination. The American was a bit angry that the ride had taken so long and was worried that he did not have enough money. Just as he reached for his wallet, the driver said abruptly, "S'arrête! Je ne veux pas d'argent. Merci pour la conversation," and, after a pause, "Bonne nuit." What did this mean? "Stop yourself! I don't want any money. Thank you for the conversation. Good night." Other Americans have had similar experiences.

The finest wines result from following very carefully a detailed, meticulous set of rules (Johnson, 1985). If one of these rules is forgotten or ignored, the quality of the wine will be greatly diminished. The same is true of speaking and conversation in France. Even small mispronunciations have the unnerving effect of fingernails scraping on a blackboard. It is a highly developed art and follows very specific rules.

Not surprisingly, the French language is governed by a seemingly endless (and annoying, in many eyes) set of rules. For example, all French nouns are either masculine or feminine, and article and adjectives must agree. Verbs have so many different endings and participles that they are almost impossible to keep track of. And, sometimes difficult for English speakers to understand, proper sentence structure often places the verb at the end of the sentence as opposed to its beginning or middle.

In conversational circles, there are two very different forms of addressing a person in French. The second person singular, *tu* or *toi*, is reserved for only the closest of friends and family members of the same age or younger. *Vous,* which is the second person plural as well as singular, is used on a more formal level. Care needs to be taken in using *tu* and *vous,* as the wrong usage can spoil a conversation or jeopardize a relationship at an early stage. Until you know a person well, the *vous* form should be used. As you become better acquainted, an occasional usage of *tu* is not considered offensive. But only much later, when friendships have thoroughly developed, should you use the *tu* or *toi* form regularly—but not with your elders or superiors.

A helpful guide to building a meaningful friendship in France is to recognize the parallels of this process to cultivating wine: Do not rush the process, and allow quality to improve over time. That is, approach the relationship in a high-context manner. For Americans venturing into France for the first time, it is important to acknowledge that the American conversational style is quite different from the French conversational style. Whereas Americans tend to have many small conversations with a number of people, the French prefer fewer conversations on much deeper levels.

Another inherent conversational rule is that to smile at someone you do not know and say "hello" is frequently considered provocative, not friendly. On the other hand, to pass a friend on the street or bump into family acquaintances without offering conversation would be considered rude (Taylor, 1990). These differing interaction styles for different levels of friends in France are not so common in the United States, where a friendly hello and small talk are the norm.

Like a glass of vintage Bordeaux, the family tends to be important to the French because it is a source of acceptance, nourishing them in the midst of life's vicissitudes. The French often look to their families for emotional and economic support. Similarly, as when the horrible disease struck the wine industry in the late 1800s, wine growers look to each other in times of trouble. Relationships among family members are very close. Family bonds are strengthened by eating weekend meals and taking extended holidays together. These are times for catching up on family matters, planning, and simply enjoying each other's company.

Interestingly, however, although French people can be very romantic about love, the concept of marriage and children tends to be approached in a businesslike, practical manner. Children are considered the parents' obligation, and children's behaviors directly reflect proper (or improper) upbringing. French parents are not as concerned about playing with the child as they are about civilizing him or her (Carroll, 1987). This parental guidance continues through adolescence, and often through university. In fact, it is not uncommon for parents to help out their children considerably with housing or other expenses, even after marriage. One foreigner who had lived in France most of his life described this orientation in the following way: "The French support their children until they are stepping on their beards."

The French are very private with regard to their homes, so an invitation to dinner implies a high level of intimacy. The home is mostly reserved for family or very close friends. Restaurants are used for acquaintances and first-time get-togethers. One should never ask to visit a French home if not invited, and if you want to stop by for some reason, telephone first.

Furthermore, similar to a fine vintage selection patiently awaiting its proper time for opening and enjoying, the women's movement in France has been in no great rush for full equality in societal roles. The Frenchwoman sees herself, and is regarded, as the equal of man—equal but different. Presented with opportunities to play the same roles as men, she has shied away from doing so. Accordingly, many milestones in women's rights came about much later in France than in other countries. Only in 1980 did the Académie Française admit its first woman member. Until 1964, a wife still had to obtain her husband's permission to open a bank account, run a shop, or get a passport; and only in 1975 and 1979 did further laws remove inequalities in matters of divorce, property, and the right to employment. Even the American reaction to Bill Clinton's relationship with Monica Lewinsky is puzzling to the French, and one prominent French politician formed a group to support Clinton. The French easily countenance the fact that politicians such as former President François Mitterand had a second, unofficial family.

Politically, women were given the vote in 1945, but they have not been overly eager to enter active politics. Even so, progress is being made, and in business, most expectations about the ideal woman staying at home have diminished greatly. About 45% of the workforce is now female, the 28th highest percentage among nations (*The Economist*, 1998).

So, given the Frenchwoman's tendency to prefer femininity over feminism, it is not surprising that the growth of the women's liberation movement has been relatively slow in France. This movement will most likely be just as successful, or even more so, in France than in America, but like the superior wines of France, its growth will be patient and organized.

◼ Suitability

The most meaningful occasions in the French person's life often center around food and drink. Certain wines "marry" certain foods; furthermore, the type of wine served dictates the shape of the glass. The wine must be drunk properly with one's hand on the stem so as not to warm the liquid. A fine wine must be gently swirled, checked with a discerning eye for clarity, sniffed to detect bouquet, and tasted critically before it can be accepted for guests. Meals can linger for hours, consisting of several courses served in proper sequence and with appropriate wines to match each course.

This challenging and often controversial business of putting wine together with the proper food requires much mating and matching, contrasting and complementing (Johnson, 1985). In the same way, the French people constantly struggle to find a political system that matches best with the desires of the nation. During the Third Republic alone, from 1872 until 1940, France had 102 governments, whereas the United States had only 14 over the same period. In the 12 years of the Fourth Republic, from 1946 until 1958, there were 22 governments.

From 1986 until 1988, France was governed by what the French themselves called *cohabitation*: a president, François Mitterand, from the leftist Socialist Party, and a prime minister, Jacques Chirac, from the rightist

"Rassemblement Pour la République" party. The two were directly at odds with each other on many issues, particularly in that Mitterand advocated the nationalization of private industry, whereas Chirac was a proponent of privatizing a number of state-run organizations.

Part of the reason for such political instability is that the president, with the consent of the prime minister, has the power to dissolve the National Assembly at any time other than a crisis. This would be the equivalent of a U.S. president telling the 535 members of the Senate and House of Representatives that their jobs have been terminated. Dissolving can also work from the other side; that is, the president or prime minister can resign of his own free will, causing a new round of National Assembly elections to take place. Such upheaval and constant change make matching the government (wine) with the people (food) extremely difficult.

Internationally, France has been very careful to guard its individual sovereignty. For example, in 1966, President de Gaulle informed the North Atlantic Treaty Organization (NATO) that France was going to withdraw its land and air forces from NATO "to regain her whole territory and the full exercise of sovereignty." In 1982, when U.S. President Ronald Reagan was planning an air strike on Libya, French President Mitterand refused to allow U.S. aircraft to fly over French air space. France's allies tend to react negatively to such controversial stances.

Ironically, governmental instability and the penchant for controversy are welcomed by the French people. They tend to be proud of their wide range of active political parties—six in all. Abundant political choice is consistent with the concept of French devotion to individual freedom. Furthermore, the political process is helped along by a free press and a love of political discussion. It is little wonder that France averages about 10,000 public protests of all types per year (Fleming & Lavin, 1997).

It seems that the French are determined to maintain their governmental system even though this may often result in controversy. Many observers point out that no matter where you set foot on French soil, you will find yourself engaged in political discussions. So, although the wine and food of French politics are not always suitable to each other, it is their very *un*suitability that stimulates conflict, controversy, and a spirited involvement of the citizens in the political arena.

The Maturation Process

The viniculturist strives for disciplined growth, tirelessly pruning and training the vines to conform to his or her will (Carroll, 1987). This disciplined growth is also reflected in the French educational system, which is strictly controlled by the state and where children begin their education at the age of 6, with many enrolling in preschool by age 2. Unlike other countries, such as Japan, where promotion from one grade to another is generally automatic, students do not advance until they attain certain skills. The result is that children of widely varying ages are in the same class. French education is known to be rigorous, with 30 days of the school year tagged for examinations. But unlike the vendage and its intense preoccupation with accomplishing its mission in 12 hours, young students must focus their developing minds on 35 intense hours of instruction each week. Mercifully, it is also the shortest school year in the world.

For the child who continues in the French school system, controlled educational growth signifies growth that is directed toward a certain diploma. The teachers who tend their crops of young students make the decisions that guide their paths and, ultimately, careers. There is a tendency to stress mathematics because proficiency in that area is seen as a key to success and guarantees treatment as a member of the elite. Today, the most able children are being trained as scientists to operate in an international culture. Some observers are critical that this preoccupation with math reaches into inappropriate realms of study, such as music classes, which also require math proficiency.

The destiny of less able or privileged children is to glean careers from the leftovers. Parents of these children lack the education and influence to help mold a bright future for their offspring. In a real sense, though, social status, more than anything else, determines a child's educational opportunity or fate. The elite who understand the importance of education begin to prepare their children early in life for entrance to the *grandes écoles* (elite universities similar to American Ivy League universities) and universities or *facultés* (specialty colleges and universities; e.g., journalism), and this practice tends to reinforce the sharp social class differences. Still, although there is discrimination at an intellectual level (ability), there is none at a financial level, as occurs in the United States, for tuition at the Sorbonne is the same as everywhere else in France.

Educational choices are limited in other ways. It is very difficult for those who do not belong to the upper social groups to have any freedom of choice in their vocations. Rather, the system categorizes them early on and shapes and defines their destinies. One young Frenchman, the son of a successful flower shop owner who had built his business from selling flowers on the street, did not want to carry on the family business. Because of the intense competition in his country, he was convinced that he had no chance of going to the *lycées* (elite secondary schools) or universities, grandes écoles, and facultés that most privileged students attend. As a result, he pursued educational opportunities in the United States that were better than his choices in

France. A somewhat similar situation exists for women who might wish to return to school after raising families or who might harbor thoughts of changing careers. Such opportunities are generally not realistic possibilities for them.

In recent years, this elite approach to education has been widely criticized, because it tends to lead to a narrow perspective on problems, both in business and in government. For example, the 5,000 graduates of the elite École Nationale d'Administration (ENA) tend to dominate government bureaucracies and then, later in life, frequently become chief executives in firms they once regulated. Jacques Chirac and other prominent politicians have openly criticized the graduates of this école as being too conservative and shortsighted, even though Chirac is one of their most prominent graduates (Drozdiak, 1995).

The French tend to take many things seriously, even life's joys. One of life's greatest pleasures are friends; therefore, friendship is taken seriously, as might be expected of a society emphasizing high-context behavior. Friendship must be carefully cultivated and tended over the years. The growth of friendship is a slow and deliberate thing. The French are critical of the quick and seemingly casual manner in which Americans make and discard friendships. Such behavior is uncouth—not unlike chugging down a glass of wine when a sip is properly called for. A friendship, then, is not to be taken lightly; rather, like a carefully selected wine, it is to be savored and enjoyed to the fullest. A good wine and a good friend—they are the joie de vivre. For example, an American businessman had been in France for more than 3 weeks, working on a 1-year project, when he came into contact with a French colleague critical to the success of the project. The two businessmen naturally had to spend a great deal of time together. The American appreciated this opportunity to brush up on his French-speaking skills, because his colleague was a purebred Frenchman who supposedly did not speak English. The American did his best to communicate effectively, but often felt frustrated that he could not express himself clearly and feared that he might convey the wrong message unintentionally. Then, suddenly, after 4 or 5 weeks of such effort, the two were preparing for a business meeting when the Frenchman said, "You can speak in English if you would feel more comfortable." The American was astonished. The Frenchman then explained that the French are very cautious in dealing with foreign business colleagues and are careful not to overexpose themselves before a more serious, respectful relationship is established.

Another area where maturation—as well as adaptation—appears in France is in the country's gradual response to the modern health and fitness craze sweeping from the United States into European countries. Traditionally, the French have shown a disdain for such trends, choosing continued adherence to national pastimes such as fine wine and cuisine. But times are changing. Today, joggers are everywhere—in the Parc de la Tête in Lyon, or on the coastal roads of Brittany, or at the foot of the Eiffel tower. Ten years ago, chances were that the person running along the Seine worked for the American Embassy. Now he or she is a trader at the Banque Nationale de Paris (Thomas, 1992).

Smoking, which has traditionally been popular in France, has become decidedly unfashionable. According to the Health Ministry, tobacco consumption has dropped sharply. The government has taken advantage of this social change by passing a law that makes smoking more difficult in public places.

By most accounts, the health craze began about 1990. In 1979, the Gymnase Club opened its first gym. Today, there are 18 Gymnase Clubs in Paris alone, all filled with people eager to trim down or get into and stay in shape. As if this were not enough, today's French are actually concerned about what they eat. They are subscribing to nutritionist services in record numbers, and the book *Eat Yourself Slim* was a bestseller for more than a year.

Not surprisingly, the consumption of wine among the French has declined significantly, from 137 liters per person in 1957 to 70 liters or less ("Losing Its Bottle: French Wine," 1992, p. 56). But in true French fashion, this decline has been accompanied by an increase in the consumption of high-quality wines, from 7 liters in 1957 to 20 liters. Although this increase may reflect the greater spending power of the French, it is also consistent with the desire to make life more pleasurable and enjoyable.

The Changing Portrait

As our discussion implies, the French have a predilection to think in terms of greatness. This is understandable given the glories of their past. It also applies to the reputation the French have developed and maintained in the wine industry. French wines are the best—a fact that the whole world acknowledges, and for the French, the assumption tends to extend to their other accomplishments and themselves as well. Assumption of greatness tends to be inbred in the French, down to the most humble villager.

Undoubtedly, the French imagine greatness to be part of their future. In an era of technological upheavals, they are excelling in high-tech areas. De Gaulle exhorted his people to shape their own destinies independent of the United States, to find their own place in the sun and space, and to become a nuclear power in their own right. This they have done with lightning speed, making rapid advances in numerous areas of importance. They enjoy an impressive network of highways, and 75% of the nation's energy is provided by nuclear power.

Sometimes, however, the French penchant for going it alone hurts the economy. For example, the French developed Minitel, which was the world's largest database just a few years ago, and it connects every conceivable service in Paris, and some other cities as well, by computer. However, the French were very slow to use the Web as an alternative.

With the building of the Concorde, the French married high-tech grace and excellence; it is, indeed, a work of art on winds. Ironically, the Concorde was a joint project with the British, but people commonly attribute the accomplishment to France rather than Great Britain. Could it be because prestige and grandeur seem to be typically French concepts?

The famous train *de grand vitesse* (TGV) is the bullet-shaped orange train that streaks past vineyards and villages at more than 170 miles per hour. Riding the TGV at night with blackened windows is to experience complete absence of motion. To incorporate both transport and motionlessness in this train is a typical sort of French creation—a mastering of nature, a striving for perfection, a blending of unlikely and diverse elements.

In spite of its various wrinkles, the societal system in France functions quite well, giving its citizens a safety net that cuddles them like a blanket at birth and softens the unpleasant jolts that life can bring in old age. It provides 98% of its approximately 58 million citizens with a level of medical care and benefits unknown to Americans. Income is guaranteed to those over 65 even if they have never worked, and the wealthy collect, too, for it is their right under the law.

This is a system that the French would revolt for if it were to be taken away from them, and it is costly. At a yearly price tag of $250 billion, it is more than triple their defense budget. And, although its benefits are being pared cautiously to reduce a large accumulated federal deficit, it still gives pension benefits almost equal to an average wage and lavishes free care on mothers and babies alike in order to boost the sagging birthrate and elevate standards of living.

Even as wine has a maturation or aging process that alters its personality, so do the French. Also, just as the flavor of wine changes with different blends of ingredients, France's cultural composition is evolving. They have experienced many changes in their history, and more will follow. One out of 12 people in France is a foreigner; one out of 20 is a Muslim. France is one of the few European countries that actually encourages assimilation by granting citizenship to all who are born on French soil. More recently, many have emigrated from France's former colonies, with more than 1.5 million coming from northern Africa alone. Well over 100,000 political refugees have been allowed into the country. There is resentment, prejudice, and discrimination against these newcomers, and some politicians, such as Le Pen, openly appeal to this xenophobic bias. Still, it is a fact that France is one of the few nations that has welcomed so many outsiders and refugees.

However, although the face of France is slowly changing in numerous and complex ways, short-term and long-term visitors to this country will most likely continue to react to the French in strong emotional terms. The French most likely will continue to spend a great amount of time nurturing relationships, being wary of outsiders, being sensitive to social class differences, accommodating themselves to the centralized bureaucracy, and being individualistic and iconoclastic. Although such activities on the surface may appear to be contradictory, they reflect an approach to life that welcomes, and even thrives on, many different and contrasting ideals. The secret to being able to accommodate such difference is moderation—and wine offers good training in the exercise of moderation. Healthy in itself, it must be taken in proportion, because it is the excess of it that can cause serious problems.

In more than 2,000 years of wine cultivation, French winemakers have accumulated a wealth of experience from which they have established successful techniques and procedures. Throughout the history of vinification and cultural development in France, the quest for quality has mobilized their collective energy. Although nature ensures that each vintage will be different, it is the human element at each step along the way that determines the ultimate outcome. The best wines are objects of great pride and, at the same time, a lesson in patience and modesty. In this respect, the French obsession with rules, procedures, classifications, and form certainly help to develop a product—and culture—that is world renowned. Thus, whatever paths the people of France choose to follow, the metaphor of composing a fine wine will continue to give insights into their fundamental motivations and system of values.

References

Carroll, R. (1987). *Cultural misunderstandings: The French American experience.* Chicago: University of Chicago Press.

Crozier, M. (1964). *The bureaucratic phenomenon.* Chicago: University of Chicago Press.

De Gramont, S. (1969). *The French.* New York: Putnam.

Drozdiak, W. (1995, October 14). Alumnus Chirac leads charge against elite Paris school. *Washington Post,* p. A17.

The Economist: Pocket world in figures. (1998). New York: Wiley.

Fleming, C., & Lavin, D. (1997, November 5). How many protests can the French take? About 10,000 a year. *The Wall Street Journal Europe*, p. 1.

The French way. (1997, November 8). *The Economist*, pp. 17-18.

Hall, E. (1966). *The hidden dimension*. Garden City, NY: Doubleday.

Hall, E., & Hall, M. (1990). *Understanding cultural differences*. Yarmouth, ME: Intercultural Press.

Hofstede, G. (1980). *Culture's consequences*. Beverly Hills, CA: Sage.

Johnson, H. (1985). *How to enjoy wine*. New York: Simon & Schuster.

Losing its bottle: French wine. (1992, September 5). *The Economist*, p. 56.

Mais où sont les cafés d'antan? (1995, June 10). *The Economist*, p. 50.

Swardson, A. (1996, November 30). Surly Parisians taught to grin and bare their friendly side. *Washington Post*, p. A12.

Swardson, A. (1998, January 12). A Paris tradition gets sacked. With changing life-styles, takeout food takes off in France. *Washington Post*, pp. A1, A14.

Taylor, S. (1990). *Culture shock! France*. Portland, OR: Graphic Arts Center.

Thomas, D. (1992, November 9). The French accent on fitness rigeur. *Washington Post*, pp. D1, D2.

Vedel, A. (Ed.). (1986). *The Hachette guide to French wines*. New York: Knopf.

PART III

Winners
and Losers

This part of the book examines the use of game theory as a metaphor for describing cultural, social, political, and economic systems. Game theory is highly influential and has been used to describe and explain many phenomena such as small group dynamics, risk-taking behavior, business negotiations, and the origins of wars.

However, there are many different types of games. One useful general categorization is between zero-sum and non-zero-sum games. A zero-sum game is one in which one party wins at the expense of the other, and the possible gains and losses are considered fixed. There is no way to play the zero-sum game so that everyone wins while, simultaneously, the total number of gains expands rather than remains fixed or static. Non-zero-sum games occur when both parties have the potential of gaining simultaneously, and the total number of gains has the potential of expansion.

Much of the metaphorical writing on culture by political scientists and journalists employs the metaphor of zero-sum games. In this part of the book, we focus on the influential work of Samuel Huntington, a prominent political scientist who has argued that the clashes and wars between nations will be replaced by the clashes and wars between civilizations. Huntington's use of zero-sum gaming as a metaphor for civilizational cultural clashes is instructive on some levels but ultimately fails. This work is a classic example of using metaphorical thinking inappropriately, at least in part because it is so simplistic.

Similarly, but to a lesser extent, writers emphasizing the power shift from nations to other entities, such as large trading blocs like the European Union, tend to view the possible gains and losses as fixed, when, in fact, the power of nations and other entities can increase as nations coordinate their efforts. Thus, this section cautions that metaphors and cultural metaphors should definitely be used, but appropriately.

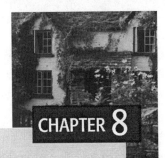

CHAPTER 8

Samuel P. Huntington's
The Clash of Civilizations

Research Translation and Commentary

The journal *Foreign Affairs* published an article in 1993 on the clash of civilizations that generated a great amount of discussion and controversy, and seemingly more than any article published in this journal since the 1940s. Its author, the well-known political scientist Samuel P. Huntington, then expanded this article into a full-length book published by Simon and Schuster in 1996. In summarizing this book, I am using the Touchstone paperback edition published in 1997.

Huntington's basic thesis is provocative: In the post-Cold War era in which the distinction between the West and the communist or Eastern bloc has faded, the most important classification system is civilizational. He believes that people and groups are searching for identities, as they always have, and that this search is now being acted out at the civilizational level. Some of his subthemes are that the world is, in a sense, separated into two camps, but they are a Western one and a non-Western many; that nation-states will still be important, but they will be influenced heavily by cultural and civilizational identities; and that the conflicts that are the most dangerous involve those from either states or groups within states from different civilizations. He presents various types of data to prove his thesis and subtheses; for example, in early 1993, slightly less than half of the 48 ethnic conflicts in the world were between groups from different civilizations, and the barbarous war in the former Yugoslavia was civilizational (Muslim Bosnians,

Roman Catholic Croats closely identified with Germany, and Serbs closely linked with Russia).

For Huntington, religion is the most important defining element of civilization, followed by language. Huntington feels that a civilization "is defined by the common objective elements, such as language, history, religions, customs, institutions, and by a subjective self-identification of people" (p. 43). He then identifies eight modern civilizations: Sinic or Chinese-based, Japanese, Hindu, Islamic, Orthodox in which Russia is the core state, Western, Latin American, and African. Ideally, a civilization should have one core state surrounded by concentric circles of other states with decreasing levels of power in its orbit. However, some civilizations, such as the Islamic and African civilizations, do not have core states, whereas Japan is both a civilization and a core state. Other core states include China in the Sinic civilization, India in the Hindu civilization, and the United States in the Western civilization. Latin America currently has no core state, but there are some potential core states.

There is an impressive amount of evidence that Huntington presents on a variety of issues to support his thesis and subtheses. For example, in 1490, Western societies controlled about 1.5 million square miles out of 52.5; in 1923, 25.5; and by 1993, only 12.7. Islamic societies rose from 1.8 square miles in 1920 to over 11 million in 1993. In 1920, the West ruled 48% of the world's population, but by 1993, the corresponding figure was only about 13%, and it is scheduled to decline even further. A similar pattern can be found in terms of the relative percent share of the world's gross production output. He also debunks the belief that Western culture is dominant and spreading universally because of consumption patterns and global communications. Throughout history, one nation or civilization, such as Japan, has borrowed heavily from another, such as China, but remained intact as a civilization or culture. Also, in opposition to many popular articles that emphasize the spreading use of English, he cites data indicating that the use of English as the primary language has actually declined from 9.8% of the world's population in 1958 to 7.6% in 1992, and that it will soon be surpassed by Hindi and Spanish, whereas Mandarin is clearly in the lead at 15.2%. At this point, he compares the use of English for business and political purposes to the use of French in the 18th century and allows the reader to use his or her imagination.

His view of culture is that it follows or is critically influenced by the distribution of power. As he clearly states, "The distribution of cultures in the world reflects the distribution of power. Trade may or may not follow the flag, but culture almost always follows power" (p. 91). Similarly, he shows that trade expansion follows economic union. EC trade within its nations increased from 50.6% in 1980 to 58.9% in 1989. Similar patterns can be found in the North American Free Trade Agreement involving the United States, Canada, and Mexico. He points out that there are four levels of economic integration: free trade area, customs union, common market, and economic union. Nations are typically reluctant to grant full economic union or even a common market to a friendly nation from a different civilization that has supported them several times in the past, as is the case with the European Union's rejection of Muslim Turkey in its formal application for membership.

In this book, Huntington introduces a valuable distinction between a torn nation and a cleft nation. A torn nation is one that is in one civilization, but its leaders want it to be in another, as was the case of Slavic Russia under Peter the Great, who wanted it to be European, or in the case of modern Mexico, which is seeking to become economically integrated with the United States. A cleft nation is one in which large groups belong to different civilizations, as is the case with Malaysia, which is about 60% Muslim, 30% Chinese, and 10% Indian. Such a nation faces the potential of a fault line or civilizational war within its borders, and periodically, nations such as Indonesia and Malaysia have had situations in which their native populations destroy the shops of Chinese and kill them, sometimes in the hundreds of thousands. These situations are related to the great gap in wealth between the poorer natives, who are typically Muslim, and the Chinese.

Also, this book contains an intriguing discussion of the Muslim world. Huntington states that President Bill Clinton is arguing against 1,400 years of history when he takes the position that the West does not have problems with Islam, only with violent Islamic extremists. Muslim nations are disproportionately involved in terrorist activity, fault line wars between civilizational groups within one nation, and civilizational wars across two or more nations. Although Muslims make up only one fifth of the world's populations, they were participants in 26 of the 50 ethnic conflicts in early 1993. Huntington does not give a definitive answer as to why, but he points out that the major explanatory factor may well be that this civilization does not have a core state to ensure that the other states within its orbit behave in a controlled and responsible manner.

In the final chapter of the book, Huntington attacks the Western belief in the universality of Western culture on the basis that it is false, immoral, and dangerous. The data presented above offer some support for the charge of falsity. Also, Huntington feels that it is immoral in that culture follows power, which would suggest that Western imperialism would need to be stressed, something that is clearly seen as immoral not only elsewhere but also in the United States. And it is dangerous simply because civilizations are likely to react negatively and to engage in wars. Thus, he argues that there are three rules for world peace: The abstention rule, or do not try to impose your culture on another civilization; the joint mediation rule, especially involving the core states; and the searching for commonalties rule, both within and across nations, and across civilizations. These rules are encapsulated in the book's final sentence: "In the emerging era, clashes of civilizations are the greatest threat to world peace, and an international order based on civilization is the surest safeguard against world war" (p. 321).

Commentary

This is a cogently argued but flawed book. The metaphor underlying it is game theory, and almost exclusively game theory as formulated in zero-sum terms, that is, when one group or civilization wins, the other loses. Only in the final few pages does Huntington venture into viewing the world and its groupings in non-zero-sum terms, that is, everyone can win, and the size of the pie is not fixed but can be expanded as resources throughout the world accumulate.

Also, although Huntington poses the issues in terms of power and its loss or gain, there are at least two other metaphors or frameworks for analyzing a conflictual international situation: interest groupings based on a variety of factors, and sometimes, religion may not even be sufficiently important to be among them; and cognitive frameworks that allow the leaders to understand how interests can be shared so that the game can become non-zero-sum rather than zero-sum (see Hasenclever, Mayer, & Rittberger, 1997).

Most importantly, the black-and-white manner in which Huntington frames his theoretical perspective sometimes forces him to attribute great power to culture, and at other times, much less power. He believes that cultural assertion follows material success, that is, hard power generates soft power (p. 109). Similarly, he states, "The distribution of cultures in the world reflects the distribution of power. Trade may or may not follow the flag, but culture almost always follows power" (p. 91). But if culture follows power or is the dependent variable being acted upon by the power or the independent variable, then it may not be culture itself that is creating actions, but the dynamics of the situation forcing or allowing some leaders to use pseudo-cultural arguments as a subterfuge for undertaking war and warlike activities. My basic perspective is that there are three overlapping and interacting systems that are dynamically but not linearly related to one another: culture, the social system (e.g., type of government and educational system), and the economic system. From a systems perspective, it is the dynamic interactions that are critical rather than the influence of one independent variable (power as manifested in different ways; e.g., trade) on the dependent variable (culture).

Still, Huntington is correct in his assertion that leaders whose nations are experiencing economic prosperity frequently feel free to criticize other nations with different cultures. This certainly was the case of the criticisms leveled against the West by Malaysian and Singaporean leaders in the 1980s and even early 1990s, and perhaps in the case of American criticism of Japan. However, such criticism is not inevitable, especially if the leaders can cognitively see the advantages accruing to all interest groups.

Additionally, Huntington himself points out that about half of the ethnic conflict in early 1993 did not involve civilizational wars. By emphasizing civilizational differences so much, he may well be creating rigid and inaccurate stereotypes of "us versus them" that explain, at best, only about 50% of the conflicts that he cites. Whether such conflicts will increase in the future is a matter of debate. Most importantly, he ascribes overriding importance to religion as the critical basis of civilizations, and he describes civilizational wars primarily in terms of religion (e.g., Muslim vs. Christian nations). But although he is correctly describing some parts of the past and the present, the future may be quite different. At one time, Catholics and Protestants waged barbarous wars, such as the Thirty Years War, but over time, they learned to live with one another in peace, in spite of the fact that Huntington's second most important criterion for civilization, language, varies widely in Western civilization. If Huntington's thesis were correct, differences in religious beliefs and language should have been more than sufficient to lead to disastrous civilizational war rather than to the integration of Western civilization.

As this commentary suggests, the basic theoretical model is quite simplistic, and it leaves out of consideration many key factors, such as the rising levels of education in many nations, overall world prosperity that was increasing at more than twice the yearly rate of 2% between 1990 and 1997, increasing contact between nations, and the uniform manner in which business leaders are being trained throughout the world in the very popular MBA programs that stress internationalization and globalization.

Still, in spite of these criticisms, Huntington's book deserves a wide reading, because he has posed many difficult questions and offered an exploratory framework that differs greatly from those emphasized in most universities' departments, including business schools. Such opposing frameworks usually highlight the differences across nations, but they simultaneously attempt to offer proposals and programs that will enhance cross-cultural understanding in a non-zero-sum manner. As one who has devoted many years to developing such frameworks, I was alternately appalled at the black-versus-white framework that Huntington poses and respectful of the cogency of his arguments, which are frequently not raised in polite company. Let us read Huntington and seriously consider his arguments, and fervently hope that he is wrong.

Finally, Huntington's hypothesis about the importance of religion as it relates to culture has been tested by Inglehart (2000) using data from the World Values Survey. As Inglehart convincingly shows, there is support for the following civilizational cultures or clustering of nations based on his analysis of values in 65 nations: Orthodox, Islamic, hierarchically Catholic, historically Protestant, and Confucian. Some values were influenced by the domination of Communist forms of government, but the historical religious trends are clearly apparent. These findings confirm that religion is a major influence on the values of nations and individuals, even in the modern world where religion is sometimes not emphasized in and outside of schools.

References

Hasenclever, A., Mayer, P., & Rittberger, V. (1997). *Theories of international regimes.* Cambridge, UK: Cambridge University Press.

Huntington, S. (1997). *The clash of civilizations: Remaking of world order.* New York: Simon & Schuster.

Inglehart, R. (2000). Culture and democracy. In Harrison, L., & S. Huntington (Eds.), *Culture matters,* pp. 80-97. New York: Basic Books.

CHAPTER 9

Powershift and the Assumed Decline of Nations

Research Translation and Commentary

The unit of analysis for cultural metaphors is the group, which can be a small group, an ethnic group, a nation, and so on. Gannon's work on cultural metaphors focuses on the nation as the unit of analysis, for example, using the characteristics of French wine to describe the characteristics of French culture. In recent years, a large number of articles (e.g., Frank, 1998; "The Myth of the Powerless State," 1995; "The Nation-State Is Dead," 1996; Pennar, 1995) have appeared proclaiming the decline of national power. Jessica Matthews (1997) has coined the imaginative term "powershift" to highlight this decline of power.

According to Matthews and others, because of such factors as the increasing amount of trade between nations and modern communication systems, members of the various trading blocs, such as the European Union and the United States-Canada-Mexico entity (North American Free Trade Agreement), have taken away national sovereignty. There is some truth in this assertion. For example, the European monetary system sets one interest rate for all nations in this system; hence, one nation cannot adjust its monetary policy unilaterally. This loss of power over the monetary system is clearly a powershift.

Similarly, multinational corporations have vast economic resources and can use them to persuade and even coerce nations. If a multinational corporation does not like the business laws and practices of a nation, it can shut down operations and move elsewhere very rapidly. Factories today are modularized, at least in part so that they can be quickly disassembled and moved to another nation, sometimes within 1 or 2 days. Even nongovernmental organizations (NGOs) can organize their activities on a worldwide basis—for example, environmental groups—and pressure national governments to change their policies and practices.

Although powershift is a reality, one issue is whether the underlying metaphor is a zero-sum game or a non-zero-sum game. Frequently, writers study the problem only from the perspective of a zero-sum game, that is, nations lose and other entities, such as larger trading blocs and multinational corporations and even NGOs, gain. However, viewing powershift from the perspective of a non-zero-sum game suggests that all can gain power in the process. For example, world trade before 1990 increased at the rate of about 2% per year and, between 1990 and 1997, by about 4% per year. This augmented national power in that nations were able to sponsor many more activities than previously, even though they did have to abide by the rules of the larger trading blocs.

There is no final answer to the complex issues that the metaphor of powershift suggests. But the reader is cautioned to expand the range of metaphors so that reality can be approached from wider and more realistic perspectives in which the outcomes do not need to be fixed but can be expansive.

References

Frank, R. (1998, October 10). Culture clash: Europeans search for a shared identity amid dark memories. *Wall Street Journal,* pp. A1, A12.

Matthews, J. (1997). Powershift. *Foreign Affairs, 76*(1), 51-66.

The myth of the powerless state. (1995, October 7). *The Economist,* pp. 15-16.

The nation-state is dead: Long live the nation-state. (1995, December 23-1996, January 5). *The Economist,* pp. 15-18.

Pennar, K. (1995, July 17). Is the nation-state obsolete in a global economy? *Business Week,* pp. 80-81.

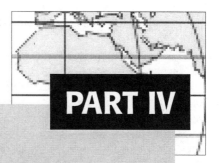

PART IV

Symbolism of
Cultural Metaphors

A cultural metaphor by definition includes a significant amount of symbolism. One phenomenon, activity, or institution, such as French wine, is used to describe the values, attitudes, and behaviors of a group, such as France. In this part of the book, we present some powerful readings on the symbolism of cultural metaphors.

We begin with a classic article on football and rock concerts. These cultural metaphors are used to explain the success model (football) and the creative model (rock concerts) in American life. Although this article was written in 1976, its keen insights are just as applicable today as then, and perhaps even more so.

Next, we highlight Robert Putnam's insightful examination of modern American life through his use of the cultural metaphor of bowling. As he shows, bowling is as popular as ever, but it is now done individually much more often than in groups. He presents an array of data to suggest that modern American life is becoming more fractionated and alienated, as suggested by his metaphor.

We then complete a research translation of Clifford Geertz's classic article on the Balinese cockfight and its metaphorical meaning in Bali. This is considered one of the most important studies of cultural metaphors and represents a shift from treating metaphors as literary devices to treating them as reflective of underlying values and attitudes.

The final article in this section focuses on cross-cultural negotiations. One of the most heated debates in today's world is whether people from different ethnic groups and nations are fundamentally different from one another. However, the debate is typically framed as an either-or proposition, that is, there is no difference or there is a fundamental difference. Weiss employs the classic metaphor of Romans and barbarians, showing that there are different classes of barbarians or groups differing from one's own. The issue becomes one's level of knowledge of the barbarian's culture, and their corresponding level of understanding of your "Roman" culture. Thus, Weiss accepts the symbolism of barbarism or foreignness, but only to the extent to which you and the other party should be willing to adapt to one another's culture.

CHAPTER 10

Football Games and Rock Concerts

The Ritual Enactment of American Success Models

SUSAN P. MONTAGUE
ROBERT MORAIS

This paper stems from a particularly insightful comment made by anthropologist Clifford Geertz about ritual. He writes that rituals are "not only models *of* what . . . [men] . . . believe, but also models for the believing of it. In these plastic dramas men attain their faith as they portray it" (1966: 29). Anthropologists have long recognized that myth and ritual function as vehicles to remind people of the basic ideology that underlies society's organization. Geertz touches on the still remaining question of faith: How is it that people become convinced that the ideology presented to them is actually truthful and correct? This question has remained unexplored, largely due to the anthropological conception of "primitives" as people who live in an ideologically monolithic universe. It is assumed that in the absence of alternative ideologies the question of faith does not arise. But this conceptualization

AUTHORS' NOTE: Originally published in W. Arens (Ed.), *The American Dimension: Cultural Myths and Realities* (pp. 32-52). Port Washington, NY: Alfred Publishing. Copyright © 1975 by Susan P. Montague and Robert Morais. Reprinted by permission.

is too naive, and certainly cannot handle questions of how faith in the existing social system is generated in societies (such as our own) that offer a variety of alternative ideologies.

Geertz does not elaborate on his idea, but his comment provides a starting point for exploring the question of why Americans find such disparate performances as football games and rock concerts so emotionally compelling. Unfortunately, informants cannot provide an adequate explanation to account for their attraction to these phenomena. This has left scholars with the task of coming up with indirect explanations, which most often are psychological, and focus on the American predilection toward violence. Various writers differ on just why Americans find violence so stimulating and desirable, but they agree that this factor does attract Americans. However, these explanations are inadequate because they fail to account for why certain standardized expressions of violence are so much more popular than others.

More importantly, the explanations miss the point. Football games and rock concerts are standardized cultural performances. Viewers find them compelling insofar as they embody significant messages. From this perspective, it is striking that the symbolic content of both these entertainment forms is heavily oriented toward the definition of success in our society. In this paper, we argue that it is impossible to directly verify in everyday life that the tenets of American success models are correct. Actors cannot readily prove to themselves that application of the models will in fact result in success. Consequently, faith in these models must be generated in some other way. This is done through symbolic validation, which is embodied in, among other things, ritual performances including football games and rock concerts. We will examine how these performance modes provide validation of American success models.

To begin it is necessary to examine the concept of success. Success is an articulating concept bridging the gap between, on the one hand, the American cosmological model of the social universe and, on the other, actor-grounded behavioral models. The cosmological model, based on traditional Christian theology, portrays a perfect universe created by God, functioning according to His laws. Man, however, violated these laws out of greed; therefore, he must wage a never-ceasing battle against his human failing. Due to his flawed character, he can never achieve God's perfection, but the price of relaxed vigilance is personal and social disaster. This model underwent gradual modification, which culminated in the late nineteenth century in the scientific-physicalist revolution wherein the laws of nature competed with and partially replaced the laws of God. However, the scientific-physicalist model of the cosmos compounded man's difficult situation, since the laws of God manifest two useful properties missing in the laws of nature. First, they are directly revealed and written down in wholly legitimized sacred books. Second, they are moral laws, which provide direct guidelines for man's behavior. The laws of nature are neither directly revealed nor moral, but instead must be discovered through an indirect process of experimentation. Further, since they are physical and not moral laws, men must also find a means for deriving behavioral guidelines from them.

The more pertinent problem for the individual is to translate universal behavioral guidelines, however formulated, into specific actions. In contemporary American culture, the concept of success constitutes one bridge between these two levels, facilitating the conversion of the general into the specific and vice versa. It does this in two ways, first by stating criteria by which the two levels are to be articulated, and second by defining a social feedback system that provides the actor with a means for monitoring the adequacy or inadequacy of his behavior. The feedback system demands our attention first.

Until the late Middle Ages, this mediation between the individual and the universal was the monopoly of Catholicism's monolithic institutional structure, and was expressed through the concepts of grace and salvation. The mediating ability was embodied in anointed individuals who participated in rituals of direct spiritual communion with God. This relationship also legitimized their role as moral arbiters of people's behavior. However, with the rise of Protestantism, the mediating role of the priest was greatly diminished, and in theory each individual was left to confront God directly and alone. This in fact meant that behavioral monitoring gradually moved outside any one given institution and was taken over by society at large. However, the result, which is still with us, is a nebulous feedback system that is both impersonal and indirect. If there is no oracle to consult, there can be no one person the actor can turn to for authoritative interpretation. Instead, feedback is provided by an intricate system of social rewards, anonymously conferred. The actor himself must attempt to monitor his behavior by examining how well he is doing in the process. This means that there must be a reward currency, and indeed there is—the so-called status symbol.

Because the reward system is indirect and impersonal, it is difficult for any given actor to verify that it actually works. According to the ideology, the system functions automatically. But how can the individual be assured that he is actually receiving his just and due reward? Further, while the rewards are conceived of as coming from society at large, they are actually conferred by a number of independent institutions. This raises the problem of standardization, since again it is difficult for the actor to determine whether or not he would receive the same reward if he worked for a different institution. Thus, in order for the system to be accepted by society's members as suitable and just, two directly unverifiable points must somehow be verified: first, that it works, and second, that it works uniformly across the board.

The other feature of the success concept is that it functions to bridge the ideological gap between universal law and the individual's behavioral guidelines in such a way as to facilitate the construction of behavioral rules that are consonant with cosmological law. This is accomplished by avoiding the question of the actual content of the universal law, and focusing instead on the motivation that underlies that content. The motivation is love. Just as the universe was created out of God's love, so the individual who acts with love can assume that he is behaving properly. Ironically, this device, which is appropriate to the Christian model of the universe, is even more important for the formulation of behavioral guidelines under the scientific-physicalist model, which does not actually contain any motivational component. Since scientific-physicalist laws are not social laws, it is difficult to derive behavioral interpretations directly from them. This difficulty enhances the value of a cultural mechanism that avoids the direct confrontation of universal law and individual behavior. Thus our culture fosters and reinforces the nature-love equation, even though that equation is not necessarily valid.

The concept of success shifts the problem of formulating behavioral guidelines from correct interpretation of universal law to correct application of universal motivation. This means that the actor and society must define which behaviors are loving. This type of definition constitutes the subject matter of success models.[1] Let us look at how the two success models embodied in football and rock define loving behavior.

Within the traditional American success model, love is defined as altruistic self-sacrifice. The properly oriented actor dedicates his life to working to improve the lives of others. In its more general form, this means that men hold jobs in the world of commerce, and women run the home and raise children. Success is defined in terms of men's work accomplishments. Women do not participate directly in the success system, but measure their status in terms of that of their husbands' accomplishments. The success system rewards moral character, which is manifested for men through work, and for women by domestic performance. A proper marriage is one that matches the moral character of the partners. Given such a union, the reward to the man can validly extend to cover the woman.

This model not only defines proper behavior, but also improper. A popular "success" author informs us that: "In time I came to recognize four basic causes for failure among salesmen; they apply equally, of course, to the pursuit of success in any line of endeavor. They are: illicit sex, alcohol, deception, and stealing" (Stone, 1962: 133). Other writers on contemporary morality and success go further, and condemn smoking and gambling. Such acts are seen as indulgences that deter the individual from the path of altruistic self-sacrifice, and thus lead to failure.

The second success model, which we call the creative model, is the converse of the first. It argues that love is manifested through self-expression, other than altruistic self-denial. Each individual possesses unique talents, and by allowing these to flower, he makes his contribution to the world. In this system, creativity replaces altruism as the valued personal commodity. This model is directly in line with scientific-physicalism, and its earliest manifestations in American pulp literature convert the ideal worker from the dedicated drudge (Alger's bank clerks and busboys) to the explorer, inventor, and scientist (Stratemeyer's Tom Swift and Don Sturdy): actors bent on discovery of the laws of the physical world. The traditional model is a straightforward application of the Protestant Ethic, and the creative model is a response to the adoption of scientific-physicalism.

The creative model raises the same sort of difficulties that plague scientific-physicalism itself. If natural laws are difficult to discover and verify, it is also difficult to specify how to socialize individuals capable of discovering and verifying them. The valued, but routine, tasks under the traditional model can be accomplished by virtually anyone who works at them hard enough. However, creativity is more than a matter of hard work. It involves personal inventiveness, based on a recombination of elements drawn from the actor's past experiences that gives him insight into a hitherto unsolved problem. It is impossible to predict precisely which elements the creative actor will draw together to obtain his fruitful insight, which means that any and all personal experiences are appropriate, whether or not society has previously defined them as moral or immoral. Further, creativity is not amenable to a rigid timetable, and it is difficult to argue that the actor should do any specific thing at any given time. Both these facts are socially unpalatable. As a result, although the creative model appeared in America in the early twentieth century, it was not until the late 1960s that its logic was pushed to completion with the argument that the truly moral member of society is the one who orients his behavior toward "doing his own thing."

With this background, let us look at how the success models are presented and validated in football games and rock concerts. In another essay in this collection, Arens has examined football as ritual, and we shall draw on some of the points he makes. He notes that football is a uniquely American game, but more than that, a cultural feature that distinguishes us from other peoples with whom we share a good many cultural traits, including language. In the United States, football is an extraordinarily popular phenomenon. Arens suggests that this is because football reflects characteristics that have a high priority in American culture: technological complexity, coordination, and specialization. He points out that the tendency to violence, which native informants stress as a captivating feature of football, is not unique to the sport. What is unique is that the violence is "expressed within the framework of teamwork, specialization, mechanization, and variation." In short, to push Arens' observations a bit further, the football team looks very much like a small-scale model of the American corporation: compartmentalized, highly sophisticated in the coordinated application of a differentiated, specialized technology, turning out a winning product in a competitive market. Football ideology bears out this analogy. Successful football coaches frequently function during the off-season as business-management consultants. Some, such as Phil Krueger, a coach at U.S.C., preach that the value of football lies not in the game itself, but in its effectiveness as a vehicle that prepares men for successful business careers (Fiske, 1975: 66). Indeed, the late Vince Lombardi, coach of the perennial champion Green Bay Packers, spent a good portion of his off-season delivering inspirational lectures to middle-management on how to be a winner and rise to the top.

If there is good reason to conclude that Americans watching football are watching a model of their own work world, the question that confronts us is why Americans should actually choose to spend leisure time in this pursuit. The function of leisure as we ordinarily think of it is to get away from work. We argue that at least two factors account for this seemingly peculiar phenomenon. First, football, as a small-scale enactment of the commercial structure and process, renders visible and directly comprehensible a system that is far too large and complex to be directly comprehended by any individual. Even economists, specialists who devote themselves to attempting to obtain an overview of the structure and processes of the American economy, find the task impossible. The ordinary individual is of course at a loss as to how to begin. It is likely that he finds it difficult even to comprehend the internal structure of the company that employs him. This difficulty is a concomitant of the size and complexity of corporations in contemporary America. Football, through a reduction of scale and visual presentation, solves these dilemmas through concrete expression. The viewer, following the progress of teams within a league, can comprehend the functioning of the entire system. In addition he can watch a single team, his team, and observe its organization and performance as an internally coherent entity. Insofar as football is directly equated with the business world, the invisible and incomprehensible is rendered visible and comprehensible. It is inferred by the viewers that the processes that are seen to work in one system also operate in the other.

The second reason Americans spend leisure time watching their symbolic work world is an extension of the first. If the structure and processes that govern the world of football are equated with those of the world of commerce, then the principles that govern the actor's success on the football field must also apply in the world of work. As indicated above, Krueger feels that football is invaluable precisely because it trains men for success in business. But, as Fiske notes, the players are objects of respect and admiration, and "the values which they represent are emulated by their male peers" (1975: 65). The audience, too, learns by watching the players. "Peers" in this instance include a widely heterogeneous population of American men. As Arens comments, "Personally, I can think of precious little else that I have in common with our former or current president, with a rural Texan, or an urban black other than a mutual passion for this game. Football represents not only 'Middle America,' . . . but the whole of America." The values that are held up to this widely diversified audience are strikingly similar to the values of the traditional success model. The greatest football coaches are not seen to work with talent significantly superior to that on other teams. Rather, fine coaches inspire their men on to greater heights of dedication, hard work, and self-sacrifice. The televised game commentary (often provided by former idols) and the press reports focus largely on the teams' training. As Arens points out, it is here that football becomes extremely ritualistic, in the sense that the elements selected for positive comment actually have little to do directly with improving the athletic skills of the players. Instead, they are elements symbolic of dedication, hard work, and most of all, self-sacrifice for the good of the team. Let us see how this works.

Football players are required to report to summer training camps each year to prepare for the fall playing season. The purpose of the camp is to improve player skills, develop team coordination, and get the players into condition to undergo the rigors of game combat. While team coordination is probably the most significant rational activity, both the camp schedule and the publicity place equal, if not greater, emphasis on the development of physical toughness. "Hitting," or physical collision with an adversary, is an emphasized activity. At the same time, while it is clear that hitting is an important component of the game, players express fears of suffering injuries that might sideline them during the playing season or end their careers. However, they remain, despite the validity of their fears, under heavy pressure to hit during training. Refusal to do so is taken as a sign of cowardice, lack of dedication, refusal to be self-sacrificing for the team. Actual signs of physical incapacity are interpreted in the same manner. Players shun their injured comrades, and one insider reports that his college coach accused him of cowardice for refusing to compete after sustaining a broken neck. The epitome of the truly great player, held up for others to emulate, is Joe Namath, who supposedly quarterbacked the underdog Jets to a Super Bowl victory when he was sleeping in the living room of his parents' house because his knees were so bad he could not climb the stairs to his second-floor bedroom. His personal pain did not deter him from accomplishing the almost impossible on behalf of his team.

In addition, great emphasis is placed on forms of self-denial. During the training period players are prohibited from indulging not only in illicit sex, but also in licit sex, by being segregated from their wives. Also, the players must not smoke or drink. A movie version of training camp shows team members sneaking out after bed check for a few beers at a local tavern like naughty boys on an adventurous escapade. Gambling is also taboo at all times. The football commissioner went so far as to threaten to ban Joe Namath from competition until he sold his interest in a New York bar and restaurant, which numbered among its clientele several suspected syndicate gamblers.

All of these self-sacrificing, self-denying behaviors are utilized as indices of player and team worthiness. The audience is told repeatedly that winning teams deserve to win, and do win, because their players are dedicated, hard-working, and self-sacrificing. These attributes are stressed even though the true problem of the game lies in the effective application of a complex division of labor. While this is recognized in football commentary, it is not stressed to the extent that the attributes of the success model are. Players often complain that the public, which eats up their self-sacrifices, is not as interested in the content of the various different highly skilled roles required to play the game. This makes sense because the viewer can directly comprehend specialization: he too works at a specialized job. What he cannot comprehend as easily, but what is of greater personal interest, is how the traditional success model actually works. The discrepancy here is between the problem of the game, coordination, and the problem of the viewer's life, behavioral guidelines. Football's popularity rests to a large part on the demonstration of the components of the success model at work, rather than on the concrete realities of the game itself.

Football validates the success model by staging a real event in which the principles of success are shown to work as promised by society. The contest actually happens before the viewer's eyes. The reality of the event is then transferred to the ideology of the success model, which is presented as accounting for the winning team's superior performance. Of course, there is a sleight of hand going on here, because "the best team always wins." The team that wins is not necessarily best; it is best because it wins. In order to set the stage for the legitimacy of the assertion that the best team does indeed win, the teams must rigidly and publicly adhere to behaviors symbolic of the success model during their training. It can then be argued that a team's superior performance is consonant with the expectations of the success model. The burden of proof switches to the losers: If the team that abided by the rules wins, then the team that loses must have failed to dedicate itself seriously enough.

Football not only provides the viewer with a working demonstration of the traditional success model, but also of the accompanying monitor-reward system. Again, the actor who cannot directly comprehend the structure of the business world, or even that of his own company, where he must compete for success, cannot directly verify that this system works. This explains why a good deal of football commentary is devoted to a careful statistical monitoring of each player's performance. Players' accomplishments are compared and contrasted with those of fellow team members and competitors. Rewards in the form of salary and recognition are then extended as a result of this evaluation. Again, insofar as the equation is drawn between football and business, the viewer is reassured that the system really works, for he sees actors being dispassionately and accurately monitored and rewarded according to the merits of their performance. He can also appreciate that the monitor-reward system is standardized and thus equitable.

Rock as a performance mode shares many of the basic characteristics of football. Although rock is not a uniquely American phenomenon (it has been enthusiastically received in other countries), it began here. The book *Rock Dreams* portrays the five kings of rock on its cover. Two are Americans: Elvis Presley and Bob Dylan. The other three are English: John Lennon, Mick Jagger, and David Bowie. Contemporary rock may be dominated by the English, but it grew from roots in American blues, and has, even in the hands of foreigners, retained its preoccupation with American culture. Rock, like football, thus is essentially an American phenomenon.

The recording industry is one of America's largest businesses, and its profits are anchored solidly in rock music. The avid buyers and listeners are just as inarticulate about their fascination with rock as are football fans about their sport. The release of power is also a common feature, although in rock it is accomplished through complex coordinated sounds rather than by physical violence. Armed with instruments, voices, and microphones, the Rolling Stones become the power equivalent of the Pittsburgh Steelers.

Although it is more difficult to sharply differentiate rock from other types of music than football from other sports, this is consonant with the creative success model. Rock bands face the problem of putting out a product that is qualitatively, not quantitatively, unique. There is only so much room for originality within the framework of straight rock. Performers solve this problem by amalgamating elements from other musical modes into their presentations. However, the wholly impregnable kings are the purists: Elvis, Lennon, and Jagger. Significantly, artistic success within the rock world can be measured by getting one's picture on the cover of *The Rolling Stone,* the rock newspaper, named after the purest of the pure.

Just as football preaches the traditional success model, rock preaches its opposite, the creative success model. An analysis of the ideology of rock as presented by the five superstars illustrates this point. The idols epitomize creativity derived from self-indulgence. The rock press focuses on how the stars satiate themselves, in contrast to the football press, which focuses on how players deny themselves. *Shooting Stars,* a book of rock star portraits, shows no one practicing or rehearsing. The entire book contains only ten or eleven pictures of stars performing or recording. The rest of the pictures are devoted to leisure activities: sleeping, lounging, drinking, traveling, partying, and picnicking. Performer interviews also generally fail to consider the work that goes into actually producing rock music. The image of the rock band is that of a collection of individually talented players who simply get it together musically. The frequent dissolution of rock groups is presented as an inevitable concomitant of the difficulties inherent in the continued association of individually creative people, each bent on "doing his own thing."

Self-indulgence is expressed through overt participation in activities that are taboo under the traditional success model. Performers both drink and smoke, often onstage, and make no secret of drug use. The most significant departure from the self-denial tenets of the traditional success model is in the area of sex. Football players are restricted from sexual activity during training and before a game. The converse is true for rock stars. The asexual rock star is a contradiction in terms because sexuality is the idiom of power in rock music. The star is expected to behave in an overtly sexual manner, suggestive onstage and promiscuous offstage. While the congratulatory crowd may go so far as to carry their favorite football players off the field after a dramatic victory, rock stars are physically attacked by hordes of would-be lovers, each bent on securing some token of intimate physical contact—a kiss if possible, a piece of hair or clothing, if not. The freshly scrubbed, girl next door cheerleader, whose formal role is to rally the team on to victory during the game, is replaced in the rock world by the whore-like groupie, whose formal role is to sleep with the star after the performance. Groupies have no place in the performance itself, because the star onstage is expected to direct his sexuality toward the audience. Elvis led the way in the 1950s with his pelvic contortions, but his gyrations were mild compared to Jagger and Bowie, the current kings. There is a telling scene in the movie *Gimme Shelter,* of Jagger watching the warm-up band, Ike and Tina Turner, on the backstage video monitor. He becomes annoyed when Tina begins to powerfully pantomime oral sex with her microphone. To the star, a warm-up band should build up the audience, not bring it to a climax.

Though rock lyrics also treat other topics, they are often blatantly sexual. To a fan any Stones song is great, but "Satisfaction," "Let's Spend the Night Together," "Brown Sugar," and "Honky Tonk Woman" are the real classics. Similarly, Dylan's most frequently played "oldie" on A.M. radio is "Lay Lady Lay." "Suffragette City," a song about a man being interrupted by a friend during intercourse, is one of Bowie's most popular audience numbers.

Obviously, the validation problem facing rock is different from that facing football. The traditional success model is fully consonant with the tenets of the success concept. However, the monitor-reward system is not really geared to handling creativity. Creativity is not amenable to precise statistical measurement, since it is a qualitative phenomenon. It can be measured only on some scale of social importance, but even this presents problems, because any given creation may or may not have much relevance at the time of its inception. The actor's contribution may thus go unheralded for years, perhaps forever. Further, the monitor-reward system is wholly ungeared to monitoring and rewarding the self-indulgence held to be a prerequisite of the creative act. These difficulties cast a doubt on the merits of the creative success model, for it would seem less consonant with the concept of success than the traditional model. However, the dual-component feature of the success concept supplies a way out. Remember that the concept contains both the monitor-reward system and the behavior motivation component. Rock argues that the traditional success model may be consonant with the monitor-reward system, but that it is not, and by definition cannot be, consonant with the behavior motivation component, love. This is because the traditional success model is competitive.[2] For every football team that wins, another goes down to defeat. Rock makes explicit this fact that in the real world the few win, the many lose—hence the prevalence of wars, famine, poverty, and social injustice. In the rock world, competition, a virtue under the traditional success model, is transformed into the scourge of mankind, the essence of evil. This means that those who achieve "success" by adhering to the tenets of the traditional model are not really successful. Theirs is a hollow accomplishment. Further, traditionally successful individuals who tout their own virtues are either hypocrites or naive fools. Jagger presents the devil as a far more sympathetic character than the powerful people who would shun him while piously espousing traditional goodness; unlike them, the devil is straightforward about the damage he does. The unhypocritical idealist is, according to Bowie, the person who would "Kill for the Good of the Fight for the Right to be Right." He would not only slaughter his enemies who, fools themselves, are only fighting for the same thing, but also make unnecessary grief for those who love him: "she kneels before the grave. A brave son—who gave his life to save the slogan."

Rock lyrics not only point up the negative consequences of competition for mankind, but also for the competing individual himself. The most the traditionally successful actor can hope for is retaliation. As Jagger puts it, "Under my thumb, the girl who once had me down." If he commands admiration, he also inspires jealousy. Bowie writes of band members eyeing their guitarist-lead singer, Ziggy Stardust: "And so we bitched about his fans, and should we crush his sweet hands." More commonly, the person who achieves success is portrayed as living a hollow, lonely life, isolated from love because he has devoted himself to excelling over his fellows, rather than helping them. Probably the most powerful indictment is contained in Dylan's "Ballad of a Thin Man," in which a conscientious, hard-working, successful man winds up totally lost and disoriented in the hostile environment of his own making, and is sneeringly taunted with the fact that he knows something is happening but he doesn't know what it is. Hell has rarely been more powerfully portrayed in any medium.

Rock begins validating the creative success model by discrediting the traditional model as not really loving. However, this is only the stage setting for the more important validation, a dramatic demonstration that the creative model does itself meet the love criterion. This demonstration is of a different sort from that found in football, where the audience watches the model being acted out by the two teams in competition. In contrast, with a rock concert the audience itself participates in the drama. Performers address the audience, and with its responses it becomes part of the performance. The rock star attempts to wed himself and the audience into an experience of love. Instead of merely seeing others and generalizing from them to himself, the audience member is encouraged to join with others and experience with them.

Loneliness, caused by isolation from others, is defined in the world of rock as the essence of nonlove, and it is by breaking down the barrier of isolation that the performer creates the emotional experience of love. The audience expects this breakdown and takes steps to initiate it even before the performer comes onstage. People talk with those sitting near them, and often smoke the same "joint," which is passed among total strangers. The first task of the performer, then, is to establish some sort of personal bond with the audience. A typical example is Jagger coming onstage after several warmup bands. He apologizes for the long delay, and explains that he has been chafing to get onstage, just as the audience has been yearning for him to appear. Rock performers not only allude to feelings that they and the audience share, they also talk in language heavy with the symbolism of interpersonal bonds. Audience members are not strangers, they are brothers and sisters, friends, fellow dope smokers.

The order of material in the concert is aimed at gradually heightening the performer-audience bond. Bowie, noted for his masterful stage performances, begins with songs of alienation and gradually intersperses sexual songs, building toward the salvation climax, "Rock and Roll Suicide." This song in turn encapsulates all that has gone before, beginning with a portrayal of the anguishing loneliness of everyday existence, and winding up with the ringing affirmation: "You're *not* alone, gimme your hand! And you're *wonderful,* gimme your hand!" On a typical night, throngs surge forward, their hands outstretched, and as he takes them, one after another, each audience member can share in belonging, being valued, being loved. The audience leaves the warm, intimate satisfaction of the theater to confront the cold, competitive, lonely world outside, yet is reassured that love can be realized, for it has just happened.

The rock audience, like the football crowd, is asked to generalize from one set of experiences to another, from the professional performance to his own life. However, the two generalizations differ radically. The football fan is encouraged first to equate two separate systems, and then how individuals function within them. The key relationship is between the individual and the system. Rock, though, does not ask the audience to equate systems since it is ideologically antisystem. Instead, the rock fan is encouraged to equate one actor, the star, with another, himself. The key relationship is individual to individual. On the contrary, the football fan can watch the contest without ever identifying with any given player. However, there is no rock without the star, no fan without his personal favorite performer or performers. Indeed, as opposed to a football contest, the rock concert lacks a broader organizational context because it stands apart from the system. The concert is simply an event without meaning beyond the "happening," whereas a football game has meaning for the future actions of a whole host of teams in the larger context of league competition. The lack of context that characterizes rock concerts is itself an important part of the message encouraging individuals to relate to one another. Rock implies that context should always be subordinated to people. The rock performer takes a collection of individuals who have no particular reason beyond their common humanity for wanting to relate to one another, and tries to turn them into a community of love. It matters little that the community is highly transitory. The argument is that all people are the same but unable to perceive this fact, because so much of their time is spent participating in various competing systems. The star, freed from systemic context, demonstrates both that love can be realized, and how to go about experiencing it. The members of the audience need only keep their sights set firmly on this goal and emulate the rock star, and they too will be able to create and enjoy love as he does, which is the essence of true success.

In this paper we have outlined the content of two mutually contradictory success models. While we have not traced the historical development of each in detail, we have noted that the creative model has gradually developed as an increasingly complete inversion of the traditional model. However, the complete development of the creative model has not caused the traditional model to become outmoded or to fall into disuse. The question then is, why does our society possess and utilize two contradictory success models? We argue that this is the case because neither strikes a workable mean between the individual's and society's needs, and that they err in opposite directions.

The traditional model (which ironically is associated with a personalized, Christian model of the universe) sacrifices the individual and his emotional satisfaction to society. The creative model (associated with an impersonalized, scientific-physicalist model of the universe) sacrifices society for the sake of the individual. These points are illustrated with reference to rock and football, which expect the performers to adhere rigidly to only one of the two models.

The problem with the traditional model is the degree to which the individual is expected to deny himself pleasure and emotional fulfillment and still lead a personally rewarding life. Football exposés point out that far from building character, the game produces sadomasochistic brutes. Players are transformed into so many hunks of moving meat to be exploited and then discarded when their self-sacrifice has rendered them physically useless. No consideration is given to their needs as people (i.e., to their feelings). They become human machines that are expected to tolerate and mete out punishment. Participants turned writers argue that football players face a choice: to reject the ideology of the game, or to reject their own humanity. The most common solution is a compromise. When players appear in public they adhere to the game's ideology, and in private consciously violate it by indulging in the taboo behaviors often characteristic of the creative success model.

In contrast, the weakness of the creative model is the extent to which it encourages each individual to "do his own thing," rather than perform routine, but socially necessary, tasks. Any society can contain only so much freedom and anarchy. Rock performers find themselves in a double bind. Ironically, while they publicly epitomize the creative success model, their work demands that they succumb to the tenets of the traditional success model. They must practice regularly, make frequent public appearances, show up for concerts and play the same songs over and over again. In general, they have to subordinate their individual or even collective desires to those of their manager, recording company, and ever-demanding audience. Their work is largely routinized, so that what they preach and what they actually do are two separate things.

In addition, they too confront the question of meaning. If, for football players, meaning is impersonalized and lies outside the system, for the rock star, it is personalized and lies within the individual. However, the result is the same—a sense of personal loss. For as *every* conceivable personal experience becomes meaningful, *no* individual experience remains very meaningful. As a result, the lives of rock stars are often characterized by a constant search for meaning derived from novel or more intense experiences. Rock performers are noted for dying from overdoses of drugs, which are taken either to produce heightened states of consciousness, or at least to provide a temporary escape from the intolerability of what becomes a meaningless everyday existence.

The difficulties that beset both football players and rock stars as they try to act out only one of the two models are largely related to lack of flexibility. There are times when social needs are paramount, and times when the individual must act on his own needs. Further, meaning is located neither wholly within an external system nor wholly within the individual, but in the interplay between the two. Taken together, the two models provide the actor with flexible guidelines. Further, because the two models share legitimacy under the same success umbrella, the individual need never feel he is acting inconsistently as he switches back and forth between them. And because the concept of success is articulated with universal law, both the individual and society recognize that his actions are at all times consonant (unless he applies the wrong success model to the situation) with the higher goal, the management of human affairs according to the rules of the universe. That indeed is success.

In this paper, we have attempted to describe how two success models, the traditional and the creative, are enacted and grounded as truth in two performance modes, football games and rock concerts. We have also examined the question of why American culture contains two radically different success models. However, we have barely scratched the surface, and have left untouched a host of questions, among the most important of which is: What are the criteria individuals use in deciding which success model to apply to which life situation? At this point, we simply do not know.

Notes

We wish to thank the many American informants who patiently discussed football, rock, and success with us. We are also grateful to W. Arens, Richard Feinberg, Julia Hecht, and Michael Moffatt for their thoughtful comments on an earlier draft of the paper.

1. Success models thus propose behavioral guidelines that are only indirectly linked to the universal laws. However, the symbolism of love maintains the illusion of a direct linkage.

2. Huber notes that competition has been a continual problem for traditional success-model writers. They play down interpersonal competition, preferring the view that the actor competes with himself (i.e., with his baser desires) to achieve. He also notes that Social Darwinism has only rarely been advocated by traditional success-model writers precisely because its dog-eat-dog tenets conflict with the Christian love ethic (1971).

▗ References

Cohn, Nik, 1974, *Rock Dreams*. New York: Popular Library.

Fiske, Shirley, 1975, "Pigskin Review: An American Initiation." In Michael A. Rynkiewich and James R. Spradley, eds. *The Nacirema: Readings on American Culture*. Boston: Little, Brown.

Geertz, Clifford, 1966, "Religion as a Cultural System." In M. Banton, ed. *Anthropological Approaches to the Study of Religion*. London: Tavistock.

Huber, Richard M., 1971, *The American Idea of Success*. New York: McGraw Hill.

Leibovitz, Annie, ed., 1973, *Shooting Stars: The Rolling Stone Book of Portraits*. San Francisco: Straight Arrow Books.

Shaw, Bernard, 1961, *The Millionairess*. London: Penguin.

Shaw, Gary, 1972, *Meat on the Hoof*. New York: Dell.

Stone, W. Clement, 1962, *The Success System That Never Fails*. Englewood Cliffs, N.J.: Prentice Hall.

CHAPTER 11

Bowling Alone

America's Declining
Social Capital

ROBERT D. PUTNAM

M any students of the new democracies that have emerged over the past decade and a half have emphasized the importance of a strong and active civil society to the consolidation of democracy. Especially with regard to the postcommunist countries, scholars and democratic activists alike have lamented the absence or obliteration of traditions of independent civic engagement and a widespread tendency toward passive reliance on the state. To those concerned with the weakness of civil societies in the developing or postcommunist world, the advanced Western democracies and above all the United States have typically been taken as models to be emulated. There is striking evidence, however, that the vibrancy of American civil society has notably declined over the past several decades.

Ever since the publication of Alexis de Tocqueville's *Democracy in America,* the United States has played a central role in systematic studies of the links between democracy and civil society. Although this is in part because trends in American life are often regarded as harbingers of social modernization, it is also because America has traditionally been considered

AUTHOR'S NOTE: Originally published in *Journal of Democracy,* 6(1), 65-78. Copyright © 1995 by the *Journal of Democracy.* Reprinted by permission.

unusually "civic" (a reputation that, as we shall later see, has not been entirely unjustified).

When Tocqueville visited the United States in the 1830s, it was the Americans' propensity for civic association that most impressed him as the key to their unprecedented ability to make democracy work. "Americans of all ages, all stations in life, and all types of disposition," he observed, "are forever forming associations. There are not only commercial and industrial associations in which all take part, but others of a thousand different types—religious, moral, serious, futile, very general and very limited, immensely large and very minute. . . . Nothing, in my view, deserves more attention than the intellectual and moral associations in America."[1]

Recently, American social scientists of a neo-Tocquevillean bent have unearthed a wide range of empirical evidence that the quality of public life and the performance of social institutions (and not only in America) are indeed powerfully influenced by norms and networks of civic engagement. Researchers in such fields as education, urban poverty, unemployment, the control of crime and drug abuse, and even health have discovered that successful outcomes are more likely in civically engaged communities. Similarly, research on the varying economic attainments of different ethnic groups in the United States has demonstrated the importance of social bonds within each group. These results are consistent with research in a wide range of settings that demonstrates the vital importance of social networks for job placement and many other economic outcomes.

Meanwhile, a seemingly unrelated body of research on the sociology of economic development has also focused attention on the role of social networks. Some of this work is situated in the developing countries, and some of it elucidates the peculiarly successful "network capitalism" of East Asia.[2] Even in less exotic Western economies, however, researchers have discovered highly efficient, highly flexible "industrial districts" based on networks of collaboration among workers and small entrepreneurs. Far from being paleo-industrial anachronisms, these dense interpersonal and interorganizational networks undergird ultramodern industries, from the high tech of Silicon Valley to the high fashion of Benetton.

The norms and networks of civic engagement also powerfully affect the performance of representative government. That, at least, was the central conclusion of my own 20-year, quasi-experimental study of subnational governments in different regions of Italy.[3] Although all these regional governments seemed identical on paper, their levels of effectiveness varied dramatically. Systematic inquiry showed that the quality of governance was determined by long-standing traditions of civic engagement (or its absence). Voter turnout, newspaper readership, membership in choral societies and football clubs—these were the hallmarks of a successful region. In fact, historical analysis suggested that these networks of organized reciprocity and civic solidarity, far from being an epiphenomenon of socioeconomic modernization, were a precondition for it.

No doubt the mechanisms through which civic engagement and social connectedness produce such results—better schools, faster economic development, lower crime, and more effective government—are multiple and complex. While these briefly recounted findings require further confirmation and perhaps qualification, the parallels across hundreds of empirical studies in a dozen disparate disciplines and subfields are striking. Social scientists in several fields have recently suggested a common framework for understanding these phenomena, a framework that rests on the concept of *social capital*.[4] By analogy with notions of physical capital and human capital—tools and training that enhance individual productivity—"social capital" refers to features of social organization such as networks, norms, and social trust that facilitate coordination and cooperation for mutual benefit.

For a variety of reasons, life is easier in a community blessed with a substantial stock of social capital. In the first place, networks of civic engagement foster sturdy norms of generalized reciprocity and encourage the emergence of social trust. Such networks facilitate coordination and communication, amplify reputations, and thus allow dilemmas of collective action to be resolved. When economic and political negotiation is embedded in dense networks of social interaction, incentives for opportunism are reduced. At the same time, networks of civic engagement embody past success at collaboration, which can serve as a cultural template for future collaboration. Finally, dense networks of interaction probably broaden the participants' sense of self, developing the "I" into the "we," or (in the language of rational-choice theorists) enhancing the participants' "taste" for collective benefits.

I do not intend here to survey (much less contribute to) the development of the theory of social capital. Instead, I use the central premise of that rapidly growing body of work—that social connections and civic engagement pervasively influence our public life, as well as our private prospects—as the starting point for an empirical survey of trends in social capital in contemporary America. I concentrate here entirely on the American case, although the developments I portray may in some measure characterize many contemporary societies.

▚ Whatever Happened to Civic Engagement?

We begin with familiar evidence on changing patterns of political participation, not least because it is immediately relevant to issues of democracy in the narrow sense. Consider the well-known decline in turnout in national elections over the last three decades. From a relative high point in the early 1960s, voter turnout had by 1990 declined by nearly a quarter; tens of millions of Americans had forsaken their parents' habitual readiness to engage in the simplest act of citizenship. Broadly similar trends also characterize participation in state and local elections.

It is not just the voting booth that has been increasingly deserted by Americans. A series of identical questions posed by the Roper Organization to national samples ten times each year over the last two decades reveals that since 1973 the number of Americans who report that "in the past year" they have "attended a public meeting on town or school affairs" has fallen by more than a third (from 22 percent in 1973 to 13 percent in 1993). Similar (or even greater) relative declines are evident in responses to questions about attending a political rally or speech, serving on a committee of some local organization, and working for a political party. By almost every measure, Americans' direct engagement in politics and government has fallen steadily and sharply over the last generation, despite the fact that average levels of education—the best individual-level predictor of political participation—have risen sharply throughout this period. Every year over the last decade or two, millions more have withdrawn from the affairs of their communities.

Not coincidentally, Americans have also disengaged psychologically from politics and government over this era. The proportion of Americans who reply that they "trust the government in Washington" only "some of the time" or "almost never" has risen steadily from 30 percent in 1966 to 75 percent in 1992.

These trends are well known, of course, and taken by themselves would seem amenable to a strictly political explanation. Perhaps the long litany of political tragedies and scandals since the 1960s (assassinations, Vietnam, Watergate, Irangate, and so on) has triggered an understandable disgust for politics and government among Americans, and that in turn has motivated their withdrawal. I do not doubt that this common interpretation has some merit, but its limitations become plain when we examine trends in civic engagement of a wider sort.

Our survey of organizational membership among Americans can usefully begin with a glance at the aggregate results of the General Social Survey, a scientifically conducted, national-sample survey that has been repeated 14 times over the last two decades. Church-related groups constitute the most common type of organization joined by Americans; they are especially popular with women. Other types of organizations frequently joined by women include school-service groups (mostly parent-teacher associations), sports groups, professional societies, and literary societies. Among men, sports clubs, labor unions, professional societies, fraternal groups, veterans' groups, and service clubs are all relatively popular.

Religious affiliation is by far the most common associational membership among Americans. Indeed, by many measures America continues to be
(even more than in Tocqueville's time) an astonishingly "churched" society.
For example, the United States has more houses of worship per capita than
any other nation on Earth. Yet religious sentiment in America seems to be
becoming somewhat less tied to institutions and more self-defined.

How have these complex crosscurrents played out over the last three or
four decades in terms of Americans' engagement with organized religion?
The general pattern is clear: The 1960s witnessed a significant drop in reported weekly churchgoing—from roughly 48 percent in the late 1950s to
roughly 41 percent in the early 1970s. Since then, it has stagnated or
(according to some surveys) declined still further. Meanwhile, data from the
General Social Survey show a modest decline in membership in all "church-
related groups" over the last 20 years. It would seem, then, that net participation by Americans, both in religious services and in church-related groups,
has declined modestly (by perhaps a sixth) since the 1960s.

For many years, labor unions provided one of the most common organizational affiliations among American workers. Yet union membership has
been falling for nearly four decades, with the steepest decline occurring between 1975 and 1985. Since the mid-1950s, when union membership
peaked, the unionized portion of the nonagricultural work force in America
has dropped by more than half, falling from 32.5 percent in 1953 to
15.8 percent in 1992. By now, virtually all of the explosive growth in union
membership that was associated with the New Deal has been erased. The solidarity of union halls is now mostly a fading memory of aging men.[5]

The parent-teacher association (PTA) has been an especially important
form of civic engagement in twentieth-century America because parental
involvement in the educational process represents a particularly productive
form of social capital. It is, therefore, dismaying to discover that participation
in parent-teacher organizations has dropped drastically over the last generation, from more than 12 million in 1964 to barely 5 million in 1982 before
recovering to approximately 7 million now.

Next, we turn to evidence on membership in (and volunteering for)
civic and fraternal organizations. These data show some striking patterns.
First, membership in traditional women's groups has declined more or less
steadily since the mid-1960s. For example, membership in the national Federation of Women's Clubs is down by more than half (59 percent) since
1964, while membership in the League of Women Voters (LWV) is off
42 percent since 1969.[6]

Similar reductions are apparent in the numbers of volunteers for main-
line civic organizations, such as the Boy Scouts (off by 26 percent since 1970)
and the Red Cross (off by 61 percent since 1970). But what about the possi-

bility that volunteers have simply switched their loyalties to other organizations? Evidence on "regular" (as opposed to occasional or "drop-by") volunteering is available from the Labor Department's Current Population Surveys of 1974 and 1989. These estimates suggest that serious volunteering declined by roughly one-sixth over these 15 years, from 24 percent of adults in 1974 to 20 percent in 1989. The multitudes of Red Cross aides and Boy Scout troop leaders missing in action have apparently not been offset by equal numbers of new recruits elsewhere.

Fraternal organizations have also witnessed a substantial drop in membership during the 1980s and 1990s. Membership is down significantly in such groups as the Lions (off 12 percent since 1983), the Elks (off 18 percent since 1979), the Shriners (off 27 percent since 1979), the Jaycees (off 44 percent since 1979), and the Masons (down 39 percent since 1959). In sum, after expanding steadily throughout most of this century, many major civic organizations have experienced a sudden, substantial, and nearly simultaneous decline in membership over the last decade or two.

The most whimsical yet discomfiting bit of evidence of social disengagement in contemporary America that I have discovered is this: more Americans are bowling today than ever before, but bowling in organized leagues has plummeted in the last decade or so. Between 1980 and 1993 the total number of bowlers in America increased by 10 percent, while league bowling decreased by 40 percent. (Lest this be thought a wholly trivial example, I should note that nearly 80 million Americans went bowling at least once during 1993, *nearly a third more than voted in the 1994 congressional elections* and roughly the same number as claim to attend church regularly. Even after the 1980s' plunge in league bowling, nearly 3 percent of American adults regularly bowl in leagues.) The rise of solo bowling threatens the livelihood of bowling-lane proprietors because those who bowl as members of leagues consume three times as much beer and pizza as solo bowlers, and the money in bowling is in the beer and pizza, not the balls and shoes. The broader social significance, however, lies in the social interaction and even occasionally civic conversations over beer and pizza that solo bowlers forgo. Whether or not bowling beats balloting in the eyes of most Americans, bowling teams illustrate yet another vanishing form of social capital.

Countertrends

At this point, however, we must confront a serious counterargument. Perhaps the traditional forms of civic organization whose decay we have been tracing have been replaced by vibrant new organizations. For example, national environmental organizations (like the Sierra Club) and feminist groups (like the National Organization for Women) grew rapidly during the 1970s and 1980s and now count hundreds of thousands of dues-paying members. An even more dramatic example is the American Association of Retired Persons (AARP), which grew exponentially from 400,000 card-carrying members in 1960 to 33 million in 1993, becoming (after the Catholic Church) the largest private organization in the world. The national administrators of these organizations are among the most feared lobbyists in Washington, in large part because of their massive mailing lists of presumably loyal members.

These new mass-membership organizations are plainly of great political importance. From the point of view of social connectedness, however, they are sufficiently different from classic "secondary associations" that we need to invent a new label—perhaps "tertiary associations." For the vast majority of their members, the only act of membership consists in writing a check for dues or perhaps occasionally reading a newsletter. Few ever attend any meetings of such organizations, and most are unlikely ever (knowingly) to encounter any other member. The bond between any two members of the Sierra Club is less like the bond between any two members of a gardening club and more like the bond between any two Red Sox fans (or perhaps any two devoted Honda owners): they root for the same team and they share some of the same interests, but they are unaware of each other's existence. Their ties, in short, are to common symbols, common leaders, and perhaps common ideals, but not to one another. The theory of social capital argues that associational membership should, for example, increase social trust, but this prediction is much less straightforward with regard to membership in tertiary associations. From the point of view of social connectedness, the Environmental Defense Fund and a bowling league are just not in the same category.

If the growth of tertiary organizations represents one potential (but probably not real) counterexample to my thesis, a second countertrend is represented by the growing prominence of nonprofit organizations, especially nonprofit service agencies. This so-called third sector includes everything from Oxfam and the Metropolitan Museum of Art to the Ford Foundation and the Mayo Clinic. In other words, although most secondary associations are nonprofit, most nonprofit agencies are not secondary associations. To identify trends in the size of the nonprofit sector with trends in social connectedness would be another fundamental conceptual mistake.[7]

A third potential countertrend is much more relevant to an assessment of social capital and civic engagement. Some able researchers have argued that the last few decades have witnessed a rapid expansion in "support groups" of various sorts. Robert Wuthnow reports that fully 40 percent of all

Americans claim to be "currently involved in [a] small group that meets regularly and provides support or caring for those who participate in it."[8] Many of these groups are religiously affiliated, but many others are not. For example, nearly 5 percent of Wuthnow's national sample claim to participate regularly in a "self-help" group, such as Alcoholics Anonymous, and nearly as many say they belong to book-discussion groups and hobby clubs.

The groups described by Wuthnow's respondents unquestionably represent an important form of social capital, and they need to be accounted for in any serious reckoning of trends in social connectedness. On the other hand, they do not typically play the same role as traditional civic associations. As Wuthnow emphasizes,

> Small groups may not be fostering community as effectively as many of their proponents would like. Some small groups merely provide occasions for individuals to focus on themselves in the presence of others. The social contract binding members together asserts only the weakest of obligations. Come if you have time. Talk if you feel like it. Respect everyone's opinion. Never criticize. Leave quietly if you become dissatisfied. . . . We can imagine that [these small groups] really substitute for families, neighborhoods, and broader community attachments that may demand lifelong commitments, when, in fact, they do not.[9]

All three of these potential countertrends—tertiary organizations, nonprofit organizations, and support groups—need somehow to be weighed against the erosion of conventional civic organizations. One way of doing so is to consult the General Social Survey.

Within all educational categories, total associational membership declined significantly between 1967 and 1993. Among the college-educated, the average number of group memberships per person fell from 2.8 to 2.0 (a 26-percent decline); among high-school graduates, the number fell from 1.8 to 1.2 (32 percent); and among those with fewer than 12 years of education, the number fell from 1.4 to 1.1 (25 percent). In other words, at *all* educational (and hence social) levels of American society, and counting *all* sorts of group memberships, *the average number of associational memberships has fallen by about a fourth over the last quarter-century.* Without controls for educational levels, the trend is not nearly so clear, but the central point is this: *more Americans than ever before are in social circumstances that foster associational involvement (higher education, middle age, and so on), but nevertheless aggregate associational membership appears to be stagnant or declining.*

Broken down by type of group, the downward trend is most marked for church-related groups, for labor unions, for fraternal and veterans' organizations, and for school-service groups. Conversely, membership in professional associations has risen over these years, although less than might have been predicted, given sharply rising educational and occupational levels. Essentially the same trends are evident for both men and women in the sample. In short, the available survey evidence confirms our earlier conclusion: American social capital in the form of civic associations has significantly eroded over the last generation.

Good Neighborliness and Social Trust

I noted earlier that most readily available quantitative evidence on trends in social connectedness involves formal settings, such as the voting booth, the union hall, or the PTA. One glaring exception is so widely discussed as to require little comment here: the most fundamental form of social capital is the family, and the massive evidence of the loosening of bonds within the family (both extended and nuclear) is well known. This trend, of course, is quite consistent with—and may help to explain—our theme of social decapitalization.

A second aspect of informal social capital on which we happen to have reasonably reliable time-series data involves neighborliness. In each General Social Survey since 1974 respondents have been asked, "How often do you spend a social evening with a neighbor?" The proportion of Americans who socialize with their neighbors more than once a year has slowly but steadily declined over the last two decades, from 72 percent in 1974 to 61 percent in 1993. (On the other hand, socializing with "friends who do not live in your neighborhood" appears to be on the increase, a trend that may reflect the growth of workplace-based social connections.)

Americans are also less trusting. The proportion of Americans saying that most people can be trusted fell by more than a third between 1960, when 58 percent chose that alternative, and 1993, when only 37 percent did. The same trend is apparent in all educational groups; indeed because social trust is also correlated with education and because educational levels have risen sharply, the overall decrease in social trust is even more apparent if we control for education.

Our discussion of trends in social connectedness and civic engagement has tacitly assumed that all the forms of social capital that we have discussed are themselves coherently correlated across individuals. This is in fact true. Members of associations are much more likely than nonmembers to participate in politics, to spend time with neighbors, to express social trust, and so on.

The close correlation between social trust and associational membership is true not only across time and across individuals, but also across countries. Evidence from the 1991 World Values Survey demonstrates the following:[10]

1. Across the 35 countries in this survey, social trust and civic engagement are strongly correlated; the greater the density of associational membership in a society, the more trusting its citizens. Trust and engagement are two facets of the same underlying factor—social capital.

2. America still ranks relatively high by cross-national standards on both these dimensions of social capital. Even in the 1990s, after several decades' erosion, Americans are more trusting and more engaged than people in most other countries of the world.

3. The trends of the past quarter-century, however, have apparently moved the United States significantly lower in the international rankings of social capital. The recent deterioration in American social capital has been sufficiently great that (if no other country changed its position in the meantime) another quarter-century of change at the same rate would bring the United States, roughly speaking, to the midpoint among all these countries, roughly equivalent to South Korea, Belgium, or Estonia today. Two generations' decline at the same rate would leave the United States at the level of today's Chile, Portugal, and Slovenia.

▰ Why Is U.S. Social Capital Eroding?

As we have seen, something has happened in America in the last two or three decades to diminish civic engagement and social connectedness. What could that "something" be? Here are several possible explanations, along with some initial evidence on each.

The movement of women into the labor force. Over these same two or three decades, many millions of American women have moved out of the home into paid employment. This is the primary, though not the sole, reason why the weekly working hours of the average American have increased significantly during these years. It seems highly plausible that this social revolution should have reduced the time and energy available for building social capital. For certain organizations, such as the PTA, the League of Women Voters, the Federation of Women's Clubs, and the Red Cross, this is almost certainly an important part of the story. The sharpest decline in women's civic participation seems to have come in the 1970s; membership in such "women's" organizations as these has been virtually halved since the late 1960s. By contrast, most of the decline in participation in men's organizations occurred about ten years later; the total decline to date has been approximately 25 percent for the typical organization. On the other hand, the survey data imply that the aggregate declines for men are virtually as great as those for women. It is logically possible, of course, that the male declines might represent the knock-on effect of women's liberation, as dishwashing crowded out the lodge, but time-budget studies suggest that most husbands of working wives have assumed only a minor part of the housework. In short, something besides the women's revolution seems to lie behind the erosion of social capital.

Mobility: The "re-potting" hypothesis. Numerous studies of organizational involvement have shown that residential stability and such related phenomena as homeownership are clearly associated with greater civic engagement. Mobility, like frequent re-potting of plants, tends to disrupt root systems, and it takes time for an uprooted individual to put down new roots. It seems plausible that the automobile, suburbanization, and the movement to the Sun Belt have reduced the social rootedness of the average American, but one fundamental difficulty with this hypothesis is apparent: the best evidence shows that residential stability and homeownership in America have risen modestly since 1965, and are surely higher now than during the 1950s, when civic engagement and social connectedness by our measures were definitely higher.

Other demographic transformations. A range of additional changes have transformed the American family since the 1960s: fewer marriages, more divorces, fewer children, lower real wages, and so on. Each of these changes might account for some of the slackening of civic engagement, since married, middle-class parents are generally more socially involved than other people. Moreover, the changes in scale that have swept over the American economy in these years—illustrated by the replacement of the corner grocery by the supermarket and now perhaps of the supermarket by electronic shopping at home, or the replacement of community-based enterprises by outposts of distant multinational firms—may perhaps have undermined the material and even physical basis for civic engagement.

The technological transformation of leisure. There is reason to believe that deep-seated technological trends are radically "privatizing" or "individualizing" our use of leisure time and thus disrupting many opportunities for social-capital formation. The most obvious and probably the most powerful instrument of this revolution is television. Time-budget studies in the 1960s showed that the growth in time spent watching television dwarfed all other changes in the way Americans passed their days and nights. Television has made our communities (or, rather, what we experience as our communities) wider and shallower. In the language of economics, electronic technology enables individual tastes to be satisfied more fully, but at the cost of the positive social externalities associated with more primitive forms of entertainment. The same logic applies to the replacement of vaudeville by the movies and now of movies by the VCR. The new "virtual reality" helmets that we will soon don to be entertained in total isolation are merely the latest extension of this trend. Is technology thus driving a wedge between our individual interests and our collective interests? It is a question that seems worth exploring more systematically.

◾ What Is to Be Done?

The last refuge of a social-scientific scoundrel is to call for more research. Nevertheless, I cannot forbear from suggesting some further lines of inquiry.

- We must sort out the dimensions of social capital, which clearly is not a unidimensional concept, despite language (even in this essay) that implies the contrary. What types of organizations and networks most effectively embody—or generate—social capital, in the sense of mutual reciprocity, the resolution of dilemmas of collective action, and the broadening of social identities? In this essay I have emphasized the density of associational life. In earlier work I stressed the structure of networks, arguing that "horizontal" ties represented more productive social capital than vertical ties.[11]

- Another set of important issues involves macrosociological crosscurrents that might intersect with the trends described here. What will be the impact, for example, of electronic networks on social capital? My hunch is that meeting in an electronic forum is not the equivalent of meeting in a bowling alley—or even in a saloon—but hard empirical research is needed. What about the development of social capital in the workplace? Is it growing in counterpoint to the decline of civic engagement, reflecting some social analogue of the first law of thermodynamics—social capital is neither created nor destroyed, merely redistributed? Or do the trends described in this essay represent a deadweight loss?

- A rounded assessment of changes in American social capital over the last quarter-century needs to count the costs as well as the benefits of community engagement. We must not romanticize small-town, middle-class civic life in the America of the 1950s. In addition to the deleterious trends emphasized in this essay, recent decades have witnessed a substantial decline in intolerance and probably also in overt discrimination, and those beneficent trends may be related in complex ways to the erosion of traditional social capital. Moreover, a balanced accounting of the social-capital books would need to reconcile the insights of this approach with the undoubted insights offered by Mancur Olson and others who stress that closely knit social, economic, and political organizations are prone to inefficient cartelization and to what political economists term "rent seeking" and ordinary men and women call corruption.[12]

■ Finally, and perhaps most urgently, we need to explore creatively how public policy impinges on (or might impinge on) social-capital formation. In some well-known instances, public policy has destroyed highly effective social networks and norms. American slum-clearance policy of the 1950s and 1960s, for example, renovated physical capital, but at a very high cost to existing social capital. The consolidation of country post offices and small school districts has promised administrative and financial efficiencies, but full-cost accounting for the effects of these policies on social capital might produce a more negative verdict. On the other hand, such past initiatives as the county agricultural-agent system, community colleges, and tax deductions for charitable contributions illustrate that government can encourage social-capital formation. Even a recent proposal in San Luis Obispo, California, to require that all new houses have front porches illustrates the power of government to influence where and how networks are formed.

The concept of "civil society" has played a central role in the recent global debate about the preconditions for democracy and democratization. In the newer democracies this phrase has properly focused attention on the need to foster a vibrant civic life in soils traditionally inhospitable to self-government. In the established democracies, ironically, growing numbers of citizens are questioning the effectiveness of their public institutions at the very moment when liberal democracy has swept the battlefield, both ideologically and geopolitically. In America, at least, there is reason to suspect that this democratic disarray may be linked to a broad and continuing erosion of civic engagement that began a quarter-century ago. High on our scholarly agenda should be the question of whether a comparable erosion of social capital may be under way in other advanced democracies, perhaps in different institutional and behavioral guises. High on America's agenda should be the question of how to reverse these adverse trends in social connectedness, thus restoring civic engagement and civic trust.

▀ Notes

1. Alexis de Tocqueville, *Democracy in America,* ed. J.P. Maier, trans. George Lawrence (Garden City, N.Y.: Anchor Books, 1969), 513-17.

2. On social networks and economic growth in the developing world, see Milton J. Esman and Norman Uphoff, *Local Organizations: Intermediaries in Rural Development* (Ithaca: Cornell University Press, 1984), esp. 15-42 and 99-180; and Albert O. Hirschman, *Getting Ahead Collectively: Grassroots Experiences in Latin America* (Elmsford, N.Y., Pergamon Press, 1984), esp. 42-77. On East Asia, see Gustav Papanek, "The New Asian Capitalism: An Economic Portrait," in Peter L. Berger and Hsin-Huang Michael Hsiao eds., *In Search of an East Asian Development Model* (New Brunswick, NJ.: Transaction 1987), 27-80; Peter B. Evans, "The State as Problem and Solution: Predation, Embedded Autonomy and Structural Change," in Stephan Haggard and Robert R. Kaufman, eds., *The Politics of Economic Adjustment* (Princeton: Princeton University Press, 1992), 139-81, and Gary G. Hamilton, William Zeile, and Wan-Jin Kim, "Network Structure of East Asian Economies," in Stewart R. Clegg and S. Gordon Redding, eds., *Capitalism in Contrasting Cultures* (Hawthorne, N.Y.: De Gruyter, 1990), 105-29. See also Gary G. Hamilton and Nicole Woolsey Biggart, "Market, Culture, and Authority: A Comparative Analysis of Management and Organization in the Far East," *American Journal of Sociology* (Supplement) 94 (1988): S52-S94; and Susan Greenhalgh, "Families and Networks in Taiwan's Economic Development," in Edwin Winckler and Susan Greenhalgh, eds. *Contending Approaches to the Political Economy of Taiwan* (Armonk, N.Y.: M.E. Sharpe 1987), 224-45.

3. Robert D. Putnam, *Making Democracy Work: Civic Traditions in Modern Italy* (Princeton: Princeton University Press, 1993).

4. James S. Coleman deserves primary credit for developing the "social capital" theoretical framework. See his "Social Capital in the Creation of Human Capital," *American Journal of Sociology* (Supplement) 94 (1988): S95-S120, as well as his *The Foundations of Social Theory* (Cambridge: Harvard University Press, 1990), 300-21. See also Mark Granovetter, "Economic Action and Social Structure: The Problem of Embeddedness," *American Journal of Sociology* 91 (1985): 481-510; Glenn C. Loury, "Why Should We Care About Group Inequality?" *Social Philosophy and Policy* 5 (1987): 249-71, and Robert D. Putnam, "The Prosperous Community: Social Capital and Public Life," *American Prospect* 13 (1993): 35-42. To my knowledge, the first scholar to use the term "social capital" in its current sense was Jane Jacobs, in *The Death and Life of Great American Cities* (New York: Random House, 1961), 138.

5. Any simplistically political interpretation of the collapse of American unionism would need to confront the fact that the steepest decline began more than six years before the Reagan administration's attack on PATCO. Data from the General Social Survey show a roughly 40-percent decline in reported union membership between 1975 and 1991.

6. Data for the LWV are available over a longer time span and show an interesting pattern: a sharp slump during the Depression, a strong and sustained rise after World War II that more than tripled membership between 1945 and 1969, and then the post-1969 decline, which has already erased virtually all the postwar gains and continues still. This same historical pattern applies to those men's fraternal organizations for which comparable data are available—steady increases for the first seven

decades of the century, interrupted only by the Great Depression, followed by a collapse in the 1970s and 1980s that has already wiped out most of the postwar expansion and continues apace.

7. Cf. Lester M. Salamon, "The Rise of the Nonprofit Sector," *Foreign Affairs* 73 (July-August 1994): 109-22. See also Salamon, "Partners in Public Service: The Scope and Theory of Government-Nonprofit Relations," in Walter W. Powell, ed., *The Nonprofit Sector: A Research Handbook* (New Haven: Yale University Press, 1987), 99-117. Salamon's empirical evidence doss not sustain his broad claims about a global "associational revolution" comparable in significance to the rise of the nation-state several centuries ego.

8. Robert Wuthnow, *Sharing the Journey: Support Groups and America's New Quest for Community* (New York: The Free Press, 1994), 45.

9. Ibid., 3-6.

10. I am grateful to Ronald Inglehart, who directs this unique cross-national project, for sharing these highly useful data with me. See his "The Impact of Culture on Economic Development: Theory, Hypotheses, and Some Empirical Tests" (unpublished manuscript, University of Michigan, 1994).

11. See my *Making Democracy Work,* esp. ch. 6.

12. See Mancur Olson, *The Rise and Decline of Nations: Economic Growth, Stagflation and Social Rigidities* (New Haven: Yale University Press, 1982), 2.

CHAPTER 12

The Persistence of Cultural Stability: Applying the Fiske Framework to North and South Italy

Research Translation

It is often stated that cultures are constantly changing, and that, in many cases, the change is dramatic and rapid. A few years ago, *Fortune* magazine published a widely cited article concerning the bedrooms of teenagers around the world that contained this message, at least implicitly. Teenagers tend to have posters of the same pop musicians, such as Michael Jackson, and of athletes such as Michael Jordan, as well as posters of basketballs, footballs, soccer balls, and Nike sport shoes. However, as Samuel Huntington (1997) has argued so persuasively and cogently, using American products does not indicate that people from other nations have accepted American cultural values. Huntington offers statistic after statistic to demonstrate that cultural differences, particularly at the civilizational level, tend to persist over many centuries.

In this section, we employ Fiske's (1991) framework of the four types of human relations to analyze the persistence of cultural stability once major institutions that reinforce particular values are put into place. Again, these four types are Community Sharing (CS), Authority Ranking (AR), Equality Matching (EM), and Market Pricing (MP). We apply this framework to

Robert Putnam's (1993) classic study *Making Democracy Work*. Putnam has studied the rise of democratic citizenship behavior in some parts of Italy (primarily the North) and its absence in other parts (primarily the South). His analysis is based on the study of historical documents, extensive and in-depth interviews with prominent Italian leaders, and large-scale questionnaire surveys completed at different points in time so that comparisons could be made.

Putnam demonstrates that the problems facing southern Italy are due, in large part, to the integration of its many small political units under the iron rule of King Frederico in the 11th century. Frederico was extremely successful in this attempt, but he brooked no opposition and demanded total fealty from all subjects. His was the classic Authority Ranking framework taken to its logical extreme: All major issues and decisions had to be handled through him and no one else. There was no sharing of power with anyone else.

However, over time, this system became inefficient, particularly after Frederico's death. Many of his successors proved to be incompetent and/or corrupt. They practiced a distorted form of AR in which all rewards flowed to them, but they had scant regard for the citizens. Thus, a key aspect of AR was violated, namely, that the psychological dependency relationship involving mutual obligations flowing from subject to ruler and vice versa was broken. Putman shows that, under such a corrupt form of AR in which power flows only downward, there is an automatic need for countervailing power or a middleman between the king and the citizens. These middlemen became the Mafia, whose power seems to have actually increased in recent years (Richard, 1995). In many southern towns, Mafia representatives are more powerful than the local police, and there are some Mafia-controlled areas in which the police do not enter, or else enter at their own risk. Richard points out that newer and more violent strains of the Mafia have arisen, and that they are now linked through the Internet with other such groups throughout the world.

Some of the results of this situation are inevitable. There is a great amount of corruption and inefficient law enforcement officers, and prosecutors have been killed in an open and brazen manner; also, fealty must be given to the Mafia chieftains before any favors are handed out. Such is the legacy that King Frederico has left in southern Italy, and it has persisted and has been strengthened since the 11th century.

No such iron rule enveloped northern Italy. Rather, there were autonomous towns and political groupings in which citizens actively participated in the life of the community. Guilds flourished, and through them, an emphasis on education. Citizens voted in local elections, and there was a high voting rate among them. Under these conditions, northern Italy became the bustling business and economic center that it is today. To cite one bit of evidence, the GNP per capita in northern Italy is higher than that of Germany, which has been the leading economic power in Europe for decades. From Fiske's perspective, northern Italy primarily emphasizes Market Pricing, although vestiges of some earlier emphases on AR still exist in some northern Italian businesses. Promotions are based to some degree on length of service, but competence is a strong and competing criterion that can sometimes override service. Most importantly, the aspect of AR that has been retained in northern Italy is the psychological relationship between ruler and ruled and the acceptance of mutual obligations on both sides of the equation.

Hence, periodic wars and other disasters have not changed the basic profiles of northern and southern Italy since the 11th century, thus confirming the persistence of cultural stability once the institutional framework reinforcing particular values has been put into place. However, it may well be that the birthrate will lead to new cultural changes. Italy has the lowest birthrate in Europe at 1.2, and thus its population is not replacing itself and is becoming much older. This is a particular problem in the North, where there is a group of citizens known as the Northern League that has been arguing for years that northern Italy should become a separate nation. However, most northern businesspeople and politicians are opposed to this movement, because the North needs the workers that the South is able to supply, and migration has tended to move from south to north where opportunities exist.

Still, it is clear that there is an Italian culture integrating the North and South. As Huntington points out, an international traveler clearly recognizes the difference between a German and an Italian village, whether it is located in the South or North. Elsewhere (Gannon, 1994), we describe Italian culture in depth in terms of the cultural metaphor of the opera. There is pageantry and splendor in Italy; voice or the close correspondence between talking and singing due to the musical and lyrical nature of the language; the interaction between soloists and chorus or the relationships between the various parts of the country; and externalization, which refers to the belief that thoughts and emotions must be expressed, first in the family and then in the piazza. Although Italy as a nation emerged only in 1860, this metaphor effectively captures the essence of the Italian culture rather than only one of its parts.

Finally, although we have emphasized the persistence of cultural stability, we do not deny that some cultures can be changed dramatically and rapidly. It was only a little more than 50 years ago that Japanese citizens could not look at or touch their emperor, who was considered godlike. Although the position of emperor still exists in terms of ceremonies and special treatment, today, the emperor is a citizen rather than a godlike person. However, Japanese culture is still highly collectivistic and has retained most, if not all, of its major cultural characteristics, as our cultural metaphor of the Japanese Garden suggests (Gannon, 1994). Although we do not deny that cultures change, it is our contention that the change at the deepest levels is much slower than the story in *Fortune* magazine and other sources of data would suggest. Sharing technology, clothes, and other aspects of modernity have an influence on culture, but much less so than the changes in basic institutions reinforcing values that sustain a group and its members.

References

Fiske, A. (1991). *Structures of social life*. New York: Free Press.

Gannon, M., & Associates. (1994). *Understanding global cultures*. Thousand Oaks, CA: Sage.

Huntington, S. (1997). *The clash of civilizations: Remaking of world order*. New York: Simon & Schuster.

Putnam, R. (1993). *Making democracy work: Civic traditions in modern Italy*. Princeton, NJ: Princeton University Press.

Richard, C. (1995). *The new Italians*. New York: Penguin.

CHAPTER 13

The Balinese Cockfight

Research Translation

Although cockfighting is illegal in many nations, it is still quite popular, and there are many illegal cockfights held throughout the world. Essentially, cockfighting is a contest in which two gamecocks or fighting roosters battle each other in a fight to the death. Most probably, cockfighting originated in Asia several thousand years ago. Enthusiasts spend a great amount of time and money breeding cocks to achieve a high level of power, quick speed, courage, and the killer instinct.

Although the cocks have natural spurs on their legs, their owners trim them and attach deadly spurs of steel or brass that the birds use to attack their opponents. Cockfights take place in an enclosed pit. At the beginning of each fight, and there are frequently several during an event, handlers hold the birds and allow them to peck each other. After becoming enraged, the birds are released by the trainers to attack one another. Some fans are so enthusiastic that they lean too far over the pit, losing an eye or receiving another serious injury.

Clifford Geertz (1973), a Princeton anthropologist, studied 500 cockfights in Bali, an Indonesian island with approximately 2 million inhabitants. Although 95% of the Indonesians are Muslim, the Balinese practice a unique form of Hinduism that combines this religion and traditional Balinese beliefs, which include animism and ancestor worship.

Geertz points out that the Balinese have a conception of time that is similar to that of the Thai, that is, work punctuated with periods of *sanuk,* or fun. According to Geertz, the Balinese see time as pulsating in an on-and-off manner, and during the off periods, nothing of significance happens. During

129

the on periods, religious festivals and cockfights take place, and they are enthusiastically enjoyed by the entire population of a village or region. However, Geertz was initially perplexed by the extent of the emotions that cocks and cockfighting arouse in the Balinese. Everyone talks about them, many Balinese spend incredible amounts of time raising cocks, and some Balinese become so enmeshed in the contest that they risk their entire fortunes betting for a particular cock with whom they identify intensely. Bankruptcies and suicides have been known to occur because of this passionate attachment to cockfights.

However, Geertz's analysis of the 500 cockfights began to suggest that it is a metaphor for the entire society, particularly its male members. To understand this metaphor, it is necessary to understand how betting takes place. There are two types of bets, or *toh,* the most important of which involves two groups—families, friends, and even entire villages and regions— that pool their money in support of their cocks and that place their bet in the center of the pit. Although a great amount of ritual accompanies this toh, the odds are usually even. However, it is the amount of money that is bet in the center of the pit that is critical. If it is low, then it is assumed that one cock is superior to the other, and that one group does not want to suffer embarrassment or the loss of too much face in public if its cock loses. If the amount is high, it is assumed that the cocks are approximately equal to one another, and that each group is willing to accept the risk of losing face.

The second type of toh occurs on the outside of the pit, and it is a direct reflection of what happened in the center. The smaller the amount of money bet in the center, the higher the odds that will be accepted for the cock that is supposedly inferior. However, the larger the amount of money bet in the center, the lower the odds that will be accepted for either cock. This period of betting is quite colorful, as bettors signal their choices with a show of fingers and shouts. According to Geertz, the betting outside of the pit tends to be somewhat mindless, and it is here that addiction among the bettors tends to occur. The true aficionado is the one who bets at the center of the pit. In both instances, however, there is a built-in protection against an excessive amount of betting, because all bets have to be paid in cash immediately after the fight, and lending is not allowed.

What do all of these things mean symbolically to the Balinese? Although cockfighting is frequently described as a sport, it is similar to the Spanish bullfight, which is a ritual rather than a sport (see "The Spanish Bullfight" in Gannon and Associates, 1994). According to Geertz, the Balinese are very courteous to one another in daily interactions, as we might expect. However, the cockfight allows groups, families, villages, and even entire regions to give an indirect and delicious insult to their counterparts that would not be countenanced in the normal course of affairs. Geertz (1973) explains the symbolism in the following way:

> To anyone who has been in Bali any length of time, the deep psychological identification of Balinese men with their cocks is unmistakable. The double entendre here is deliberate. It works in exactly the same way in Balinese as it does in English, even to producing the same tired jokes, strained puns, and uninventive obscenities. . . .
>
> In the cockfight, man and beast, good and evil, ego and id, the creative power of aroused masculinity and the destructive power of loosened animality fuse in a bloody drama of hatred, cruelty, violence, and death. It is little wonder that when, as is the invariable rule, the owner of the winning cock takes the carcass of the loser—often torn limb from limb by its enraged owner—home to eat, he does so with a mixture of social embarrassment, moral satisfaction, aesthetic disgust, and cannibal joy. Or that a man who has lost an important fight is sometimes driven to wreck his family shrines and curse the gods, an act of metaphysical (and social) suicide. Or that in seeking earthly analogues for heaven and hell the Balinese compare the former to the mood of a man whose cock has just won, the latter to that of a man whose cock has just lost. (pp. 417, 421)

The Balinese cockfight encompasses only a part of Balinese society. Indeed, it is most probably not possible to construct a metaphor that includes all aspects of a society. Such a metaphor, however, provides a rich understanding of a culture that goes far beyond a profile based on cross-cultural dimensions such as power distance and individualism/collectivism.

■ References

Gannon, M., & Associates. (1994). *Understanding global cultures*. Thousand Oaks, CA: Sage.

Geertz, C. (1973). *The interpretation of culture*. New York: Basic Books.

CHAPTER 14

Negotiating
With "Romans"*

STEPHEN E. WEISS

Managers are increasingly called on to negotiate with people from other cultures. Cross-cultural negotiation need not be as frustrating nor as costly as it is often made out to be; it can be a productive and satisfying experience. Which of these outcomes a manager achieves depends in part on the negotiation strategies taken in response to—or better, in anticipation of—the counterpart's plans and behavior. There are eight culturally responsive strategies for a manager to consider (see Figure 14.1).[1] Clearly, the quality of a negotiation outcome and a manager's satisfaction with it also depend on how well he or she chooses and implements one of these approaches.

This article presents five steps for selecting a culturally responsive strategy and then offers various tips for implementation, such as making the first move, monitoring feedback, and modifying the approach. These guidelines

AUTHOR'S NOTE: Reprinted from "Negotiating With 'Romans'—Part 2" by Stephen E. Weiss, *Sloan Management Review,* Spring 1994, pp. 85-99, by permission of the publisher. Copyright 1994 by Sloan Management Review Association. All rights reserved.

FIGURE 14.1. Culturally Responsive Strategies and Their Feasibility

High	Induce Counterpart to Follow One's Own Script	Improvise an Approach [Effect Symphony]
	Adapt to the Counterpart's Script [Coordinate Adjustment of Both Parties]	
Low	Employ Agent or Adviser [Involve Mediator]	Embrace the Counterpart's Script
	Low	**High**

Counterpart's Familiarity with Negotiator's Culture

Negotiator's Familiarity with Counterpart's Culture

Brackets indicate a joint strategy, which requires deliberate consultation with counterpart. At each level of familiarity, a negotiator can consider feasible the strategies designated at that level and any lower level.

reflect four basic, ongoing considerations for a strategy: its *feasibility* for the manager, its fit with the counterpart's likely approach and therefore its capacity to lead to *coherent interaction*, its *appropriateness* to the relationship and circumstances at hand, and its *acceptability* in light of the manager's values. There are challenges involved in all of these efforts, and they are pointed out below rather than ignored or belittled, as happens in much cross-cultural negotiation literature. Thus, from this article, managers stand to gain both an operational plan and the heightened awareness necessary to use a culturally responsive negotiation strategy effectively.

■ Selecting a Strategy

Every negotiator is advised to "know yourself, the counterpart, and the situation."[2] This advice is useful but incomplete, for it omits the relationship—the connection—between the negotiator and the counterpart.[3] (For clarity, the negotiator from the "other" culture will be called the "counterpart" in this article.) Different types of relationships with counterparts and even different phases of a relationship with a particular counterpart call for different strategies.

For the cross-cultural negotiator, the very presence of more than one culture complicates the process of understanding the relationship and "knowing" the counterpart. In contrast to the "within-culture" negotiator, the cross-cultural negotiator cannot take common knowledge and practices for granted and thereby simply concentrate on the individual. It becomes important to actively consider the counterpart in two respects: as a member of a group and as an individual.

The right balance in these considerations is not easily struck. An exclusive emphasis on the group's culture will probably lead the negotiator off the mark because individuals often differ from the group average. Members of the same group may even differ very widely on certain dimensions. At the same time, the degree of variation tolerated between group members is itself an aspect of culture. For example, Americans have traditionally upheld the expression, "He's his own man," while Japanese believed that "the protruding nail is hammered down." The cross-cultural negotiator should thus consider both the counterpart's cultural background and individual attributes, perhaps weighting them differently according to the culture involved, but mindful always that every negotiation involves developing a relationship with a particular individual or team.[4]

> For years, Japanese managers have come to one of my classes each term to negotiate with graduate students so the students can experience nego-

tiating first-hand and test the often stereotypical descriptions they have read about Japanese negotiating behavior. I deliberately invite many Japanese, not just one or two. The students invariably express surprise when the Japanese teams "deviate" from the Japanese negotiating script, as the students understand it, and when differences appear in the behavior of various Japanese teams.

The five steps for selecting a culturally responsive negotiation strategy take into account these complexities:

1. Reflect on your culture's negotiation script.

2. Learn the negotiation script of the counterpart's culture.

3. Consider the relationship and circumstances.

4. Predict or influence the counterpart's approach.

5. Choose your strategy.

These steps take minutes or months, depending on the parties and circumstances involved. Each step will probably not require the same amount of time or effort. Furthermore, the sequencing of the steps is intended to have an intuitive, pragmatic appeal for an American negotiator, but it should not be treated rigidly. Some steps will be more effective if they are coupled or treated iteratively. Nor should these efforts start at the negotiation table when time, energy, resources, and introspection tend to be severely limited. Every one of these steps merits some attention by every cross-cultural negotiator before the first round of negotiation.

It is important to remember that the procedure represented by these five steps is itself culturally embedded, influenced by the author's cultural background and by that of the intended audience (American negotiators).[5] Not all counterparts will find the pragmatic logic herein equally compelling. As two Chinese professionals have observed, "In the West, you are used to speaking out your problems. . . . But that is not our tradition," and "In our country, there are so many taboos. We're not used to analytic thinking in your Western way. We don't dissect ourselves and our relationships."[6] Even with this procedure, culture continues to influence what we do and how we do it.

One way to deal with this inescapable cultural bias is to acknowledge it and remain aware of the continual challenges of effectively choosing and implementing a strategy. Often these challenges do not stand out—books on international negotiation have not addressed them—yet they can hamper, even ruin, a negotiator's best efforts. Each step below thus includes a list of cautions for cross-cultural negotiating.

1. Reflect on Your Culture's Negotiation Script

Among members of our "home" group, we behave almost automatically.[7] We usually have no impetus to consider the culture of the group because we repeatedly engage in activities with each other without incident or question. It is easy to use these "natural," taken-for-granted ways in a cross-cultural situation—too easy.

> A book on international negotiation published by the U.S. State Department displays the flags of six nations on its front cover. On initial copies of the book, the French flag appeared in three bands of red, white, and blue. The actual French flag is blue, white, and red.[8]

A cross-cultural negotiator should construct a thoughtful, systematic profile of his or her culture's negotiation practices, using personal knowledge and other resources. Let's say you want to develop an "American negotiator profile." There is a vast amount of research and popular literature on negotiation in the United States.[9] For insights about American culture more broadly, consider both Americans' self-examinations and outsiders' observations.[10] Then organize this information into the profile represented in Figure 14.2.[11] The profile consists of four topic areas: the general model of the negotiation process, the individual's role, aspects of interaction, and the form of a satisfactory agreement. The left side of the ranges in Figure 14.2 generally fit the American negotiator profile (e.g., the basic concept is distributive bargaining, the most significant issues are substantive ones, negotiators are chosen for their knowledge, individual aspirations predominate over community needs, and so forth).

This profile should also uncover the values that support these tendencies. For instance, distributive bargaining implies certain attitudes toward conflict and its handling (direct), toward business relationships (competitive), and toward the purpose of negotiation (to maximize individual gains). Since some of your group's tendencies and values may not align with your own, develop a personal profile as well. Doing so does not require probing deeply into your unconscious. Simply ask yourself, "What do I usually do at times like this? Why? What do I gain from doing it this way?" These kinds of questions resemble those used in basic negotiation training to distinguish an underlying interest from a bargaining position, namely, "What does this bargaining position do for me? Why?"

> In the mid-1980s, a white American banker planned to include an African-American analyst on his team for a forthcoming visit to white clients in South Africa. When they learned about this, the clients intimated their

FIGURE 14.2. Negotiator Profile

General Model

1. Basic Concept of Process
   Distributive bargaining/Joint problem-solving/Debate/Contingency bargaining/Nondirective discussion
2. Most Significant Type of Issue
   Substantive/Relationship-based/Procedural/Personal-internal

Role of the Individual

3. Selection of Negotiators
   Knowledge/Negotiating experience/Personal attributes/Status
4. Individuals' Aspirations
   Individual ◄─────────────────────► Community
5. Decision Making in Groups
   Authoritative ◄─────────────────► Consensual

Interaction: Dispositions

6. Orientation Toward Time
   Monochronic ◄─────────────────► Polychronic
7. Risk-Taking Propensity
   High ◄─────────────────────────► Low
8. Bases of Trust
   External sanctions/Other's reputation/Intuition/Shared experiences

Interaction: Process

9. Concern with Protocol
   Informal ◄─────────────────────► Formal
10. Communication Complexity
    Low ◄──────────────────────────► High
11. Nature of Persuasion
    Direct experience/Logic/Tradition/Dogma/Emotion/Intuition

Outcome

12. Form of Agreement
    Contractual ◄─────────────────► Implicit

Source: Adapted from S. E. Weiss with W. Stripp, *Negotiating With Foreign Business Persons* (New York: New York University Graduate School of Business Administration, Working Paper #85-6, 1985), p. 10.

TABLE 14.1 Cautions: Understanding Your Own Culture's Script

- Beware of psychological and group biases, such as denial and "group think."
- Probe for assumptions and values; they are seldom identified explicitly in day-to-day life.
- Don't become rigidly wedded to your own ways.
- Take time during negotiations to step out of the action and reflect on your behavior.

---

preference that she not attend. While the banker wanted to serve his clients, he also had strong feelings about including the analyst and about basing qualifications on merit. She was the best analyst on his staff. The banker's values swayed his decision: he told his clients that he would not make the trip without this analyst on his team.[12]

Developing cultural and personal profiles is an ongoing task. Instead of writing them up once and moving on, return to them and refine them as you gain experience and understanding. The value of such a process is considerable. It increases your self-awareness; it helps you explain your expectations and behavior to a counterpart; it prepares you to make decisions under pressure; it allows you to compare your culture to another on a holistic rather than fragmented basis; it helps you determine a counterpart's level of familiarity with your culture; its products—profiles—can be used in future negotiations with other cultural groups; it motivates interest in other cultures; and it enables you to act consistently and conscientiously.

This process demands a good deal of effort, especially at the outset (note the cautions in Table 14.1). But as a negotiator, you will find such reflection to be a good basis for developing a cross-cultural negotiation strategy.

2. Learn the Negotiation Script of the Counterpart's Culture

This step applies to both the negotiator highly familiar with a counterpart's culture and the one who knows next to nothing about it.[13] The highly familiar negotiator should review what he or she knows and gather additional information to stay current. The uninitiated negotiator should begin to construct a negotiator profile from the ground up. Ideally, this process involves learning in the active sense: developing the ability to use the counterpart's cultural and personal negotiation scripts, as well as "knowing" the scripts and related values.

Learning these scripts enhances the negotiator's ability to anticipate and interpret the counterpart's behavior. Even a negotiator with low familiarity who is likely to employ an agent needs some information in order to interact effectively with the agent and to assess the agent's performance. Although few negotiators learn everything about a counterpart before negotiation, advance work allows for assimilation and practice, provides a general degree of confidence that helps the negotiator to cope with the unexpected, and frees up time and attention during the negotiation to learn finer points.

Again, the negotiator profile framework is a good place to start. Try especially to glean and appreciate the basic concept of negotiation because it anchors and connects the other dimensions. Without it, a negotiator, as an outsider, cannot comprehend a counterpart's actions; they appear bizarre or whimsical. Moreover, if you focus merely on tactics or simple "do and don't"-type tips and reach a point in a transaction for which you have no tip, you have no base—no sense of the "spirit of the interaction"—to guide you through this juncture. For instance, the "spirit" of French management has been described like this:

> French managers see their work as an intellectual challenge requiring the remorseless application of individual brainpower. They do not share the Anglo-Saxon view of management as an interpersonally demanding exercise, where plans have to be constantly "sold" upward and downward using personal skills. The bias is for intellect rather than for action.[14]

Continuing with this example, let's say you are preparing to negotiate with a French counterpart. You may find information about French negotiation concepts and practices in studies by French and American researchers and in natives' and outsiders' popular writings.[15] In addition to general nonfiction works on French culture, novels and films can convey an extraordinary sense of interactions among individuals and groups.[16] Other sources include intensive culture briefings by experts and interviews with French acquaintances, colleagues, and compatriots familiar with French culture, and, in some cases, even the counterpart.

Here, as in reflections on your own culture, make sure to consider core beliefs and values of the culture. Keep an eye on the degree of adherence to them as well as their substantive content.

A Frenchman involved in the mid-1980s negotiations between AT&T and CGE over a cross-marketing deal revealed his own culture's concern for consistency in thought and behavior as he discussed AT&T's conduct. He described the AT&T representatives' style as "very strange" because they made assurances about "fair" implementation while pushing a very "tough" contract.

Moving from information gathering to assimilation and greater familiarity with a culture usually requires intensive training on site or in seminars.[17] Some Japanese managers, for example, have been sent overseas by their companies for three to five years to absorb a country's culture before initiating any business ventures. When the time comes, familiarity may be assessed through tests of language fluency, responses to "critical incidents" in "cultural assimilator" exercises, and performance in social interactions in the field.[18]

Whether or not you have prior experience working with a particular counterpart or other inside information, try to explore the counterpart's own negotiation concepts, practices, and values. They can be mapped in a negotiator profile just as you mapped your own values.

This entire undertaking poses challenges for every negotiator, regardless of the strategy ultimately chosen. One of the highest hurdles may be the overall nature of the learning itself. Learning about another culture's concepts, ways, and values seems to hinge on the similarity between that culture and one's own. Learning is inhibited when one is isolated from members of that culture (even if one is living in their country) and "may fail to occur when attitudes to be learned contradict deep-seated personality orientations (e.g., authoritarianism), when defensive stereotypes exist, or at points where home and host cultures differ widely in values or in conceptual frame of reference."[19] Other significant challenges can be seen in Table 14.2. Remember that, ultimately, you have access to different strategies for whatever amount of learning and level of familiarity you attain.

3. Consider the Relationship and Circumstances

Negotiators and counterparts tend to behave differently in different relationships and contexts.[20] One does not, for instance, act the same way as a seller as one does as a buyer. So a negotiator should not count on the same strategy to work equally well with every counterpart from a given cultural group (even if the counterparts have the same level of familiarity with the negotiator's culture) or, for that matter, with the same counterpart all the time. The peaks and valleys that most relationships traverse require different strategies and approaches. In the same vein, circumstances suggest varying constraints and opportunities.

TABLE 14.2 Cautions: Learning About the Counterpart's Culture

---

■ Don't be too quick to identify the counterpart's home culture. Common cues (name, physical appearance, language, accent, and location) may be unreliable. The counterpart probably belongs to more than one culture.

■ Beware of the Western bias toward "doing." In Arab, Asian, and Latin groups, ways of being (e.g., comportment, smell), feeling, thinking, and talking can more powerfully shape relationships than doing.

■ Try to counteract the tendency to formulate simple, consistent, stable images. Not many cultures are simple, consistent, or stable.

■ Don't assume that all aspects of the culture are equally significant. In Japan, consulting all relevant parties to a decision (*nemawashi*) is more important than presenting a gift (*omiyage*).

■ Recognize that norms for interactions involving outsiders may differ from those for interactions between compatriots.

■ Don't overestimate your familiarity with your counterpart's culture. An American studying Japanese wrote New Year's wishes to Japanese contacts in basic Japanese characters but omitted one character. As a result, the message became "Dead man, congratulations."

To continue your preparations for a negotiation, consider particular facets of your relationship with the counterpart and the circumstances. The most important facets on which to base strategic choices have not yet been identified in research and may actually depend on the cultures involved. Furthermore, laying out a complete list of possibilities goes beyond the scope of this article.[21] But the following considerations (four for relationships, four for circumstances) seem significant.

Life of the relationship. The existence and nature of a prior relationship with the counterpart will influence the negotiation and should figure into a negotiator's deliberations. With no prior contact, one faces a not-yet personal situation; general information and expectations based on cultural scripts will have to do until talks are under way. Parties who have had previous contact, however, have experienced some form of interaction. Their expectations concerning the future of the relationship will also tend to influence negotiation behavior.[22] In sum, the negotiator should acknowledge any already established form of interaction, assess its attributes (e.g., coherence) and the parties' expectations of the future, and decide whether to continue, modify, or break from the established form. These decisions will indicate different culturally responsive strategies.

> **TABLE 14.3** Cautions: Considering the Relationship and Circumstances
>
> - Pay attention to the similarities and differences, in kind and in magnitude, between your negotiator profiles and those of the counterpart.
> - Be careful about judging certain relationship aspects as major (big picture issues) and minor (fine details). This dichotomy, let alone the particular contents of the two categories, is not used in all cultures.
> - Consider the relationship from the counterpart's perspective.
> - Identify the relationship factors and circumstances most significant to you and the counterpart.
> - Beware of the use and abuse of power.
> - Discover the "wild cards" either party may have.
> - Remember that the relationship will not remain static during negotiation.

Fit of respective scripts. Having completed steps 1 and 2, you can easily compare your negotiator profiles, both cultural and individual, with those of the counterpart. Some culture comparisons based on the negotiator profile in Figure 14.2 have already been published.[23] Noting similarities as well as differences will enable you to identify those aspects of your usual behavior that do not need to change (similarities) and those aspects that do (major differences) if you choose a strategy that involves elements of both your negotiation script and the counterpart's (e.g., the adapt strategy). The number and kinds of differences will also suggest how difficult it would be to increase your level of familiarity with the counterpart's culture or to use certain combinations of strategies.

Do not allow such a comparison to mislead you. Some people overemphasize differences. Others, focusing on superficial features, overestimate similarities and their understanding of another culture (e.g., when Americans compare American and Canadian cultures). The cautions in Table 14.3 can help you stay on track.

Of course, a negotiator highly familiar with the counterpart's culture who plans to adopt an embrace strategy, operating wholly within that culture, has less need for these comparisons.

Balance of power. It may seem that power would have a lot to do with the choice of strategy. A more powerful party could induce the other to follow his or her cultural script. A less powerful party would have to embrace the other's script. A balance of power might suggest an adapt or improvise strategy.

But the issue is not so simple. The tilt of the "balance" is not easily or dearly determined; parties often measure power using different scales.[24] Indeed, forms of power, their significance, and appropriate responses are all culturally embedded phenomena.[25] Furthermore, it makes little sense to rely on power and disregard a counterpart's familiarity with one's culture when one's goal is coherent interaction. This is not to say that one could not benefit from an imbalance of power *after* choosing a culturally responsive strategy or in other areas of negotiation. Still, since power is culturally based and Americans have a general reputation for using it insensitively, American negotiators should be extremely careful about basing the strategy decision on power.

Gender. Consider the possible gender combinations in one-on-one cross-cultural relationships: female negotiator with female counterpart, male negotiator with male counterpart, male negotiator with female counterpart, and female negotiator with male counterpart. Within most cultures, same-gender and mixed relationships entail different negotiating scripts. There are few books on negotiation designated for American women, but communication research has shown that men tend to use talk to negotiate status, women tend to use it to maintain intimacy, and they are often at cross-purposes when they talk to each other.[26] The debates over how American women should act in male-dominated workplaces further substantiate the existence of different scripts. In a sense, gender groups have their own cultures, and mixed interaction within a national culture is already cross-cultural.

Mixed interaction across national and other cultures holds even greater challenges. One of the primary determinations for a woman should be whether a male counterpart sees her first as a foreigner and second as a woman, or vice versa. According to some survey research, Asian counterparts see North American businesswomen as foreigners first.[27] The opposite may be true in parts of France. Edith Cresson, former French prime minister, once said, "Anglo-Saxons are not interested in women as women. For a [French] woman arriving in an Anglo-Saxon country, it is astonishing. She says to herself, 'What is the matter?' "[28] Thus, although current information about negotiating scripts for other countries tends to be based on male-male interactions, complete culturally-based negotiator profiles should include gender-based scripts.

Whether your negotiation involves mixed or same-gender interaction, try to anticipate the counterpart's perception of the gender issue and review your core beliefs. Gender-based roles in France, for instance, may appear so antithetical (or laudable) that you will not entertain (or will favor) the embrace strategy.

With regard to circumstances, the second part of step 3, there are at least four relevant considerations.

Opportunity for advance coordination. Do you have—or can you create—an opportunity beforehand to coordinate strategy with your counterpart? If so, consider the joint strategies. If not, concentrate at the outset on feasible, unilateral strategies.

Time schedule. Time may also shape a negotiator's choice in that different strategies require different levels of effort and time. For the negotiator with moderate familiarity of the counterpart's culture but an inside track on a good agent, employing an agent may take less time than adapting to the counterpart's script. The time required to implement a strategy also depends on the counterpart's culture (e.g., negotiations based on the French script generally take longer than the American script). And time constrains the learning one can do to increase familiarity. Imagine the possibilities that open up for a diligent negotiator when discussions are scheduled as a series of weekly meetings over a twelve-month period instead of as one two-hour session.

Audiences. Consider whether you or the counterpart will be accompanied by other parties, such as interpreters, advisers, constituents, and mass media. Their presence or absence can affect the viability and effectiveness of a strategy. If no one else will attend the meeting, for instance, you have no one to defer to or involve as a mediator at critical junctures.

> During the early months of the ITT-CGE telecommunications negotiations in 1985 and 1986, fewer than ten individuals were aware of the talks. That permitted the parties to conduct discussions in ways not possible later, when over a hundred attorneys, not to mention other personnel, became involved. At the same time, that choice may have ruled out the initial use of some culturally responsive strategies.

Wild cards. Finally, you should assess your own and the counterpart's capacities to alter some relationship factors and circumstances. Parties may have extra-cultural capabilities such as financial resources, professional knowledge, or technical skills that expand their set of feasible options, bases for choice, or means of implementation.

> During the GM-Toyota joint venture negotiations in the early 1980s, Toyota could afford to and did hire three U.S. law firms simultaneously for a trial period in order to compare their advice and assess their compatibility with the company. After three months, the company retained one of the firms for the duration of the negotiations.

4. Predict or Influence the Counterpart's Approach

The last step before choosing a strategy is to attempt to determine the counterpart's approach to the negotiation, either by predicting it or by influencing its selection. For the effectiveness of a culturally responsive strategy in bringing about coherent interaction depends not only on the negotiator's ability to implement it but also on its complementarity with the counterpart's strategy. Embracing the counterpart's script makes little sense if the counterpart is embracing your script. Further, reliable prediction and successful influence narrow the scope of a negotiator's deliberations and reduce uncertainty. And the sooner the prediction, the greater the time available for preparation. While these concerns relate to the parties' relationship (step 3), they have a direct impact on interaction that merits a separate step.

Assuming that your counterpart will not ignore cultural backgrounds and that each of you would adopt only a unilateral strategy, you can use Figure 14.3 to preview all possible intersections of these strategies.[29] They fall into three categories: complementary, potentially but not inherently complementary, and conflicting. Thus the figure shows the coherence of each strategy pair.

Among these pairs, adapt-adapt and improvise-improvise might seem inherently complementary. The catch is that parties can adapt or improvise in conflicting ways. Of all the potentially complementary cells, the improvise-improvise interaction may, however, be the most likely to become coherent, given the nature of the improvise strategy and the capabilities it entails.

Not all of the strategies in Figure 14.3 will be available to you in every situation. Remember that in addition to potential coherence, your choice will be based on your familiarity with the counterpart's culture, the counterpart's familiarity with yours, appropriateness, and acceptability.

Prediction. Sometimes a counterpart will make this step easy by explicitly notifying you of his or her strategy in advance of your talks. If the counterpart does not do that, there may be telling clues in the counterpart's prenegotiation behavior, or other insiders (associates or subordinates) may disclose information.

Without direct and reliable information, you are left to predict the counterpart's strategy choice on the basis of his or her traits and motivations. Some counterparts will have a rational, task-directed orientation. Strategy research based on this perspective shows that counterparts seeking to coordinate their actions with a negotiator often select the course of action most prominent or salient to both parties (e.g., choosing a river as a property boundary).[30] Other counterparts will focus on what is socially proper.

FIGURE 14.3. The Inherent Coherence of Parties' Culturally Responsive Strategies

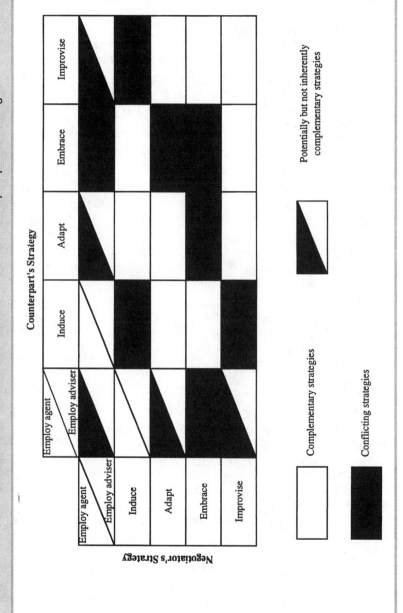

Indeed, whether a counterpart even responds to the cross-cultural nature of the interaction may vary with his or her cosmopolitanism. A cosmopolitan counterpart may lean toward adapt and improvise strategies, whereas a counterpart having little experience with other cultures may be motivated primarily by internal, cultural norms. In the latter case, the counterpart's negotiator profile may be used to predict some behavior. For example, the internally focused individual from a culture with high communication complexity (reliance on nonverbal and other contextual cues for meaning), which often correlates with low risk-taking propensity, would be more likely to involve a mediator than to coordinate adjustment (which is too explicit) or to embrace or improvise (which are too uncertain).[31]

Influence. Whether or not you can predict a counterpart's strategy choice, why not try to influence it? If you predict a strategy favorable to you, perhaps you can reinforce it; if unfavorable, change it; and if predicted without certainty, ensure it. Even if prediction proves elusive, it behooves you to try to influence the counterpart.

The first task in this process is to determine your own preferred strategy based on the criteria in step 5. This may appear to be jumping ahead, but choosing and influencing go hand in hand. They will go on throughout negotiation, for new information will come to light and necessitate reassessments.

Once you have chosen a strategy, use the matrix in Figure 14.3 to locate interaction targets. Your prime targets should be the coherent (complementary) combinations, followed by the potentially coherent ones. For example, if you intend to employ an agent, influence the counterpart to use the induce strategy.

Some negotiators may also contemplate targeting conflicting strategies. In this line of thinking, a conflict could bring out the parties' differences so dramatically as to provide valuable lessons and "working" material for both the negotiator and counterpart. Influencing the counterpart to pursue a strategy that conflicts with one's own (or selecting one by oneself if the counterpart has already set a strategy) might establish that one is not a negotiator who can be exploited. However, these effects lie outside of our main purposes of demonstrating responsiveness to cultural factors and establishing a coherent form of interaction. Furthermore, such conflict often confuses, causes delays, and provokes resentment. (Note also the other cautions in Table 14.4.)

With respect to means of influence, Americans sometimes preemptively take action, such as using English in conversation without inquiring about a non-American counterpart's wishes or capabilities, but there are other, often

---

TABLE 14.4 Cautions: Predicting or Influencing the Counterpart's Approach

- Try to discern whether the counterpart's culture categorically favors or disfavors certain strategies.
- Don't fixate on "what's typical" for someone from the counterpart's cultural group.
- Recognize the difficulty in accurately assessing the counterpart's familiarity with your culture's negotiating script.
- Heed the line, however fuzzy, between influencing and "meddling"—a U.S. diplomat was detained in Singapore in 1988 for interfering in internal affairs.*
- Track changes in the counterpart's strategic choices over time.
- Don't focus so obsessively on parties' strategies that you ignore the richness of the relationship or the context.

*F. Deyo, *Dependent Development and Industrial Order* (New York: Praeger, 1981), p. 89.

---

more mutually satisfactory, ways to influence a counterpart. They range from direct means, such as explicitly requesting a counterpart to choose a particular strategy, to tacit means, such as disclosing one's level of familiarity with the counterpart's culture, revealing one's own strategy choice, or designating a meeting site likely to elicit certain types of conduct. For example, in 1989, then U.S. Secretary of State James Baker hosted his Soviet counterpart Eduard Shevardnadze in Jackson Hole, Wyoming, instead of Washington, D.C. Prenegotiation communications may also be carried out by advance staff or through back channels. As you evaluate these options, bear in mind that their effectiveness will probably differ according to the counterpart's culture and personal attraction to you.[32]

5. Choose Your Strategy

When you have completed the previous steps, it is time to choose a strategy or a combination of strategies. Four selection criteria emerge from these steps. The strategy must be feasible given the counterpart and cultures involved; able to produce a coherent pattern of interaction, given the counterpart's likely approach; appropriate to the relationship and circumstances; and acceptable, ideally but not necessarily, to both parties. These criteria apply to the prenegotiation choice of strategy, but you may also use them to assess your strategy during negotiation.

A possible fifth criterion would be your degree of comfort with a strategy. Even negotiators highly familiar with two cultures' scripts favor one script over another in certain circumstances. So if the four criteria above do not direct you to only one right strategy, consider, at the end, which of the remaining strategies you would be most comfortable implementing.

Apply the four criteria in order, for their sequence is deliberate and designed for negotiators with a pragmatic orientation (e.g., Americans). Feasibility, after all, appears first. Acceptability appears later because the value judgment it involves impedes deliberation in cross-cultural situations when used too early.[33] (Note that counterparts from other cultural groups may prefer to use a list that begins with appropriateness or acceptability.)

Each criterion deserves attention. Feasibility and coherence considerations may narrow your choices down to one unilateral strategy, yet you should still check that choice for its appropriateness, given the relationship and circumstances, and its consonance with core beliefs and values. For a negotiation scheduled to take place over many years, for example, the negotiator might look at a strategy that is potentially but not inherently complementary to the counterpart's (see Figure 14.3) or at combinations or progressions of strategies. For a negotiation where the negotiator cannot narrow strategy options by reliably predicting the counterpart's strategy, the negotiator may actually have to rely on the last two criteria. And when a negotiator wishes to consider joint strategies, relationship factors and circumstances are essential to consult. In sum, the support of all four criteria for a particular strategy choice should give you confidence in it.

Occasionally, criteria may conflict. Feasibility and coherence point to an embrace strategy for a counterpart's induce strategy, but the negotiator may find aspects of the counterpart culture's script unacceptable (e.g., *fatwa*, Iran's death threat). Or the embrace-induce strategy pairing may have worked well in a cross-cultural relationship for years, but now you expect your counterpart to be at least moderately familiar with your culture. The resolution of such conflicts begs for further research. In the meantime, you may want to defer to your core beliefs and values. Values define the very existence of your home group and your membership in it; by ignoring or violating them you risk forfeiting your membership.[34]

As an example of strategy selection based on all four criteria, consider an American, Smith, who is preparing for a confidential, one-on-one meeting with a Frenchman he has never met before, Dupont.

> Smith once lived in France and, as the meeting is being held in Dupont's
> Paris office, his gut feeling is to speak in French and behave according to

> **TABLE 14.5** Cautions: Choosing a Strategy
>
> - Don't assume the counterpart will use the same criteria or order you do (e.g., efficiency is not a universal concern).
> - Watch out for parties' miscalculations and conflicting impressions (e.g., the counterpart's assessments of your respective levels of cultural familiarity may differ from yours).
> - Proceed carefully when criteria conflict; further research may help.
> - Don't treat an embrace strategy, by mere definition, as costly or a concession.

Dupont's culture—that is, to use an embrace strategy. However, he takes the time to evaluate his options. Smith realizes that he is no longer familiar enough with French language and culture to use an embrace strategy, and the short lead-time prevents him from increasing his familiarity. With a moderate level of familiarity, he has five feasible strategies: employ an agent or adviser, involve a mediator, induce Dupont to follow his script, adapt to Dupont's script, or coordinate adjustment by both parties. Smith does some research and learns that Dupont has only a moderate level of familiarity with American negotiation practices. That rules out the induce strategy. The relationship and circumstances made an agent or mediator appropriate. An adapt strategy would be hit-or-miss because Smith has no cues from previous face-to-face interaction and only one meeting is planned. Overall, the best strategy choice is to coordinate adjustment.

A complicated situation will require more complex considerations. (See also the cautions on choosing a strategy in Table 14.5.) But the five steps above—reflect, learn, consider, predict, and choose—constitute a sound and useful guide for strategy selection.

■ Implementing Your Strategy

The full value of the most carefully selected strategy rests on effective implementation, a formidable task in the general fluidity of negotiations and especially in the multifaceted process of most cross-cultural negotiations. It is here, in a negotiation's twists and turns, that a negotiator deals head on with distinctions between the counterpart's attributes as an individual and as a member of a cultural group. Simply adhering to one's own plan of action is difficult—and may become undesirable. For the negotiator must ensure that the strategy complements the counterpart's approach and enables the two of them to establish and maintain a coherent form of interaction.

Whatever the chosen culturally responsive strategy, a negotiator may enhance the effectiveness of first moves and ongoing efforts by generally respecting the counterpart and his or her group's culture and by demonstrating empathy (both of which may take different forms for different cultures). These qualities, among others, have been recommended in the literature on cross-cultural competence and are consistent with cultural responsiveness.[35] They do not necessitate lowering one's substantive negotiation goals.[36]

First Moves

The strategies of employ agent, embrace, and induce entail complete, existing scripts for negotiation. Pursuing one of these strategies essentially involves following the script associated with it. The adapt strategy involves modifications of your own script, at least some of which should be determined beforehand. With the improvise strategy, you ought to give some advance thought to a basic structure even if much of the path will emerge as you travel on it. Thus you have a starting point for each of the five unilateral strategies.

These strategies assume that when a counterpart recognizes your strategy, he or she will gravitate toward its corresponding script.[37] The counterpart wants to understand you and to be understood; that is what occurs in *coherent* interaction. If you have accurately assessed the counterpart's level of familiarity with your culture and ability to use a particular script, and if the counterpart recognizes the strategy you are using, you stand a better chance of achieving coherence.

Should you make the first strategic move or wait until the counterpart does? This decision affects the transition from preliminary "warm-up" discussions to negotiation of business matters. It depends, in part, on whether you need to gather more information about the counterpart's strategic intentions and abilities. This would matter when both parties have at least moderate familiarity with each other's cultures and have more than one unilateral strategy they can realistically choose, and when you have chosen a strategy (e.g., adapt, improvise) that relies on cues from the counterpart. The decision over timing also depends on whether you need to make the strategy you have chosen distinguishable from another one (e.g., improvise from adapt) and want to clearly establish this strategy at the outset. (Note that if a negotiator has chosen to employ an agent or has successfully influenced the counterpart, then timing should not be an issue.) In sum, to decide on timing, you should weigh the benefits of additional information against the costs of losing an opportunity to take leadership and set the tone of the interaction, a loss that includes being limited in your strategy options by the counterpart's strategy choice.

The three joint strategies are explicit and coordinated by definition. Once parties have decided to use a joint strategy, first moves consist of fleshing out particulars. Which mediator? What kinds of adjustments? What basic structure will underlie improvisation? These discussions may require the intermediate use of one of the five unilateral strategies.

Parties coordinating adjustment might consider trading off their respective priorities among the twelve cultural aspects in the negotiator profiles. If your counterpart values certain interpersonal conduct (protocol) more than the form of the agreement, for example, and you value the latter more than the former, the two of you could agree to adhere to a certain protocol and, on agreement, to draw up a comprehensive legal document. This pragmatic approach will probably appeal more to Western counterparts than to Asian ones, however, particularly if the Asian counterparts have only low or moderate cultural familiarity. So take this approach with caution rather than presuming that it will always work.

Whichever joint strategy you adopt, pursue it visibly in your first moves. Especially in first-time encounters, a counterpart reads these moves as indications of one's integrity ("sincerity," in Japan) and commitment to coordination.

Ongoing Efforts

A cross-cultural negotiator has myriad concerns and tasks, including vigilant attention to the cautions in the tables presented thus far. Still, as negotiation proceeds, one's most important task is concentrating on interaction with the counterpart. Parties' actions and reactions evidence adherence to and departures from a given negotiation script, fill out the incomplete scripts associated with some strategies (i.e., adapt, improvise, effect symphony), and determine the ultimate effectiveness of every one of the eight culturally responsive strategies. These interactions occur so quickly that analyzing them makes them seem fragmented and in "slow motion." Nevertheless, some analysis can have tremendous value.

As you negotiate, shift most of your attention from the counterpart's culture to the counterpart as an individual. Specifically, monitor feedback from him or her, be prepared to modify, shift, or change your strategy, and develop *this* relationship.

Monitor counterpart's feedback. A counterpart's reactions to your ideas and conduct provide critical information about the counterpart personally and about the effectiveness of your chosen strategy with this particular individual. As you use that information to make continual adjustments and to evaluate your strategy, you may want to return to the four criteria of feasibility, coherence, appropriateness, and acceptability.

Some verbal and nonverbal cues transcend cultures in signaling positive or negative reception to a negotiator's use of a certain script. They range from a counterpart's statements ("Things are going well," "We don't do things that way") to a tightening of the corner of the mouth and cocked head, which convey contempt.[38]

> In one film of the "Going International" series, an American manager urges his Saudi counterpart to expedite delivery of supplies from the docks to the hospital building site. He points out that the supplies have already sat at the dock for a week just because of paperwork, he personally is "in a crisis," "nobody works here" on Thursday and Friday (it is now Tuesday), and during the upcoming Ramadan observance "things really slow down." At various points during these remarks, the Saudi does not respond at all to a direct question, perfunctorily sets aside a written schedule he receives, and looks disparagingly at the American's shoes. In the end, the Saudi states, "Mr. Wilson, my people have been living for many years without a hospital. We can wait two more weeks."[39]

Admittedly, a counterpart's statements can be more or less honest or truthful, and the gradations are often fuzzy to an outsider. A number of cultures distinguish between saying what is socially acceptable (*tatemae* in Japanese) and saying what is truly on one's mind (*honne*). Other standards may also differ across cultures.

Many cues (e.g., silence) do not carry consistent meaning from culture to culture. Generally, individuals learn the culturally specific meanings as they become familiar with a culture. Negotiator profiles include some cues and imply others under dimensions such as "communication complexity" and "nature of persuasion." A negotiator can use these cues when he or she embraces the counterpart's culture.

Then again, some singularly powerful cues are very subtle. (See other cautions for strategy implementation in Table 14.6.)

> In the 1950s, an American couple—the lone foreigners—at a Japanese wedding banquet in Tokyo were socializing and dining like everyone else. All of a sudden, everyone else finished eating and left the reception. Residents of Japan for many years, the Americans concluded later that a signal had been sent at some point, and they had not even detected it.

TABLE 14.6   Cautions: Implementing Your Strategy

- Remember that cross-cultural interaction can be creative and satisfying, not always taxing.

- Stay motivated.

- Separate your observations of the counterpart's behavior from your interpretations and conclusions about his or her intentions.

- Notice the changes as well as the constants in the counterpart's behavior over time.

- Try to pick up even the subtle cues.

- Give some thought to whether the counterpart might be feigning low familiarity with your culture and language.

- Don't get in too deep; don't unwittingly lead the counterpart to think your familiarity with his or her culture is higher than it actually is.

- Accept some of the limitations that the counterpart's culture may impose on outsiders; not all limitations can be surmounted no matter how well or long you try.

- Balance your responsiveness to cultural factors with your other aspirations and needs as a negotiator.

In cross-cultural interactions that do not involve embracing or inducing, or when a negotiator cannot clearly decipher the counterpart's strategy, nonuniversal cues are disconcertingly difficult to detect and interpret correctly. You can handle ambiguous cues (e.g., the hesitation of a counterpart who has so far been loquacious) by keeping them in mind until additional cues and information convey and reinforce one message. Other ambiguous cues may be decoded only by asking the counterpart; alternatively, they remain unclear. Dealing with these cues is a very real and ongoing challenge.

Be prepared to modify, shift, or change. Even the well-prepared negotiator faces some surprises and some negative feedback in a negotiation. You want to be nimble enough to respond effectively. "Modifying" refers to refining implementation of a strategy without abandoning it; "shifting" refers to moving from one strategy to another within a previously planned combination of strategies; and "changing" refers to abandoning the strategy for another, unplanned one.

Making alterations is relatively easy with some counterparts.

> For the first round of the 1980-1981 Ford-Toyota talks, Ford negotia-
> tors employed a bilingual Japanese staffer from their Japan office. The
> Toyota team, apparently confident in their English language abilities,
> suggested that Ford not bring the interpreter to subsequent meetings, so
> that the negotiators could "talk directly." Ford negotiators obliged and
> changed their approach.

On other occasions, one may have to explain modifications, shifts, and
changes before they are made in order to minimize the odds of being perceived as unpredictable or deliberately disruptive. One may also deflect criticism by directly or indirectly associating these actions with changes in
circumstances, the subject on the agenda, phase of the discussion, or, when
negotiating as part of a team, personnel. For ideas about specific modifications to make, other than those prompted by your counterpart, review the
counterpart's negotiator profile. Changes in strategy should be shaped by
both a negotiator's culturally relevant capabilities and the strategy being
abandoned. You may go relatively smoothly from an adapt to a coordinate
adjustment strategy, for example, but not from inducing to embracing or
from involving a mediator to employing an agent.

Over time, some movement between strategies may occur naturally
(e.g., adapt to coordinate adjustment), but a shift as defined here involves a
preconceived combination, or sequence, of strategies (e.g., coordinate
adjustment, then effect symphony). A negotiator could plot a shift in strategies for certain types of counterpart feedback, variation in circumstances or
relationship factors, or, especially during a long negotiation, for a jump in his
or her level of cultural familiarity.

Develop this relationship. Pragmatic Americans may view the cultivation of a
relationship with the counterpart primarily as an instrument for strategy
implementation. Concentrating on coherent interaction and a satisfactory
relationship usually does enhance a culturally responsive strategy's effectiveness. But the strategy should also—even primarily—be seen as serving the
relationship.

> Riding describes the views of Mexican negotiators when they returned
> home from Washington after the negotiations over Mexico's insolvency
> in 1982: " 'We flew home relieved but strangely ungrateful,' one Mexi-
> can official recalled later. 'Washington had saved us from chaos, yet it did
> so in an uncharitable manner.' Even at such a critical moment, the sub-
> stance and style of the relationship seemed inseparable."[40]

Many of your non-American counterparts will be accustomed to an emphasis on relationships. Indeed, greater attention to relationship quality may be the most common distinction between negotiators from American and non-American cultures. Developing a relationship with a particular counterpart requires an attentiveness to its life and rhythms. The form of your interaction can evolve across different scripts and approaches, especially after many encounters. There is also the potential for culturally driven conflict, which you should be willing to try to resolve.

Clearly, such a relationship should be treated dynamically, whether time is measured in minutes or in months. In that light, you can continuously learn about the counterpart and the counterpart's culture and educate the counterpart about you and your culture. Over a long period, you may experiment with a counterpart's ways in noncritical areas (at low risk) to develop skills within and across culturally responsive strategies. In this way, you can expand the number of feasible strategies, giving both you and the counterpart more flexibility in the ways you relate to each other.

Toward Cross-Cultural Negotiating Expertise

A friend of mine, a third-generation American in Japan who was bilingual in Japanese and English, used to keep a file of items that one must know . . . to function in Japan. . . . [He] never stopped discovering new things; he added to the file almost every day.[41]

Over the years, many cross-cultural negotiators have essentially asked, "What happens when you're in Rome, but you're not Roman?" The most common advice available today was first offered 1,600 years ago: "Do as the Romans do." Yet these days, a non-Roman in Rome meets non-Romans as well as Romans and encounters Romans outside of Rome. The more we explore the value of parties' capabilities and circumstances and the more we question the feasibility, coherence, appropriateness, and acceptability of "doing as Romans do," the more apparent the need becomes for additional culturally responsive strategies.

The range of strategies presented here provides every negotiator, including one relatively unfamiliar with a counterpart's culture, with at least two feasible options. Combinations of strategies further broaden the options.

If there is "something for everyone" here, the value of developing and sustaining cross-cultural expertise should still be clear. That includes high familiarity with a "Roman" culture—knowing the cognitive and behavioral elements of a Roman negotiating script and being able to use the script competently. The negotiator at the high familiarity level enjoys the broadest possible strategic flexibility for negotiations with Romans and the highest probability that, for a particular negotiation, one strategy will solidly meet all four selection criteria.

A negotiator can also gain a great deal from learning about more than one other culture. For lack of space I have concentrated on negotiations between two individuals, each belonging to one cultural group, but most cross-cultural negotiations involve more than two cultures: most individuals belong to more than one group; negotiations often occur between teams that have their own team cultures in addition to the members' ethnic, national, and organizational backgrounds; and multiparty, multi-cultural negotiations occur as well. In short, the non-Roman highly familiar with culture A still encounters cultures B, C, and D. Even though a negotiator may need to focus only on the one culture that a counterpart deems predominant at any one point in time, there are several to explore and manage across time, occasions, and people.[42]

> As soon as he was assigned to GM's Zurich headquarters in the mid-1980s, Lou Hughes, one of GM's main representatives in the GM-Toyota negotiations of the early 1980s, began taking German lessons because GM's main European plant was located in Germany. Now president of GM Europe, Hughes' effectiveness as an executive has been attributed in part to his cultural sensitivity and learning.[43]

In the process of exploring other cultures, one may discover an idea or practice useful for all of one's negotiations.

> Another American negotiator in the GM-Toyota talks was so impressed with the Tokyo negotiators' template for comparing parties' proposals that he adopted it and has relied on it since for his negotiations with others.

It is in this spirit of continuous learning that this article has presented culturally responsive strategies, selection criteria, key steps in the choice process, and implementation ideas. If negotiators with a moderate amount of cross-cultural experience have the most to gain from these tools, first-time negotiators have before them a better sense of what lies ahead, and highly experienced negotiators can find some explanation for the previously unexplained and gain deeper understanding. In addition, the culture-individual considerations and ongoing challenges highlighted throughout the article will serve all cross-cultural negotiators. Perhaps we can all travel these paths more knowingly, exploring and building them as we go.

■ Notes and References

1. S.E. Weiss, "Negotiating with 'Romans' Part 1," *Sloan Management Review*, Winter 1994, pp. 51-61. All samples that are not referenced come from personal communication or the author's experiences.

2. See J.K. Murnighan, *Bargaining Games: A New Approach to Strategic Thinking in Negotiations* (New York: William Morrow and Co., 1992), p. 22.

3. G.T. Savage, J.D. Blair, and R.L. Sorenson, "Consider Both Relationships and Substance When Negotiating Strategically," *The Executive* 3 (1989): 37-47; and S.E. Weiss, "Analysis of Complex Negotiations in International Business: The RBC Perspective," *Organization Science* 4 (1989): 269-300.

4. Attending to both culture and the individual has also been supported by: S.H. Kale and J.W. Barnes, "Understanding the Domain of Cross-National Buyer-Seller Interactions," *Journal of International Business Studies* 23 (1992): 101-132.

5. To speak of an "American culture" is not to deny the existence of cultures within it that are based on ethnic, geographic, and other boundaries. In fact, the strategies described in Part 1 of this article and the five steps described here can be applied to these cross-cultural negotiations as well. These ideas deserve the attention of those, for example, who are concerned about diversity in the workplace.

6. G. C. Thubron, *Behind the Wall* (London: Penguin, 1987), pp. 158, 186-187.

7. See R. Keesing as quoted in: W.B. Gudykunst and S. Ting-Toomey, *Culture and Interpersonal Communication* (Newbury Park, California: Sage, 1988), p. 29.

8. H. Binnendijk, ed., *National Negotiating Styles* (Washington, D.C.: Foreign Service Institute, U.S. Department of State, 1987).

9. For a review of popular books, see: S. Weiss-Wik, "Enhancing Negotiator's Successfulness: Self-Help Books and Related Empirical Research," *Journal of Conflict Resolution* 27 (1983): 706-739. For a recent research review, see: P.J.D. Carnevale and D.G. Pruitt, "Negotiation and Mediation," *Annual Review of Psychology* 43 (1992): 531-582.

10. For self-examinations, see: G. Althen, *American Ways: A Guide for Foreigners in the United States* (Yarmouth, Maine: Intercultural Press, 1988); E.T. Hall and M.R. Hall, *Understanding Cultural Differences* (Yarmouth, Maine: Intercultural Press, 1990); and E.C. Stewart and M.J. Bennett, *American Cultural Patterns* (Yarmouth, Maine: Intercultural Press, 1991). The views of outsiders include: A. de Tocqueville, *Democracy in America, 1805-1859* (New York: Knopf, 1980); L. Barzini, *The Europeans* (Middlesex, England: Penguin, 1983), pp. 219-253; and Y. Losoto, "Observing Capitalists at Close Range," *World Press Review*, April 1990, pp. 38-42.

11. The original framework appeared in: S.E. Weiss with W. Stripp, "Negotiating with Foreign Business Persons: An Introduction for Americans with Propositions on Six Cultures" (New York: New York University Graduate School of Business Administration, Working Paper No. 85-6, 1985).

12. Although I am not certain, my recollection is that the clients relented, and the bank team made the trip to South Africa. The point, however, is that the banker took a stand on an issue that struck values dear to him. Other examples include whether or not to make "questionable payments" and how to handle social settings in France and in Japan when one is allergic to alcohol or cigarette smoke. On payments, see: T.N. Gladwin and I. Walter, *Multinationals under Fire* (New York: John Wiley & Sons, 1980), p. 306. On smoking, see: W.E. Schmidt, "Smoking Permitted: Americans in Europe Have Scant Protection," *New York Times,* 8 September 1991, p. 31. On the other hand, some customs, while different, may not be abhorrent or worth contesting. An American male unaccustomed to greeting other men with "kisses" (the translation itself projects a bias) might simply go along with an Arab counterpart who has initiated such a greeting.

13. Murnighan (1992), p. 28; and Kale and Barnes (1992), p. 122.

14. J.L. Barsoux and P. Lawrence, "The Making of a French Manager," *Harvard Business Review,* July-August 1991, p. 60.

15. For example, for each of the four categories respectively, see: D. Chalvin, *L'entreprise négociatrice* (Paris: Dunod, 1984) and C. Dupont, *La négociation: conduite, théorie, applications,* 3rd ed. (Paris: Dalloz, 1990); N.C.G. Campbell et al., "Marketing Negotiations in France, Germany, the United Kingdom, and the United States," *Journal of Marketing 52* (1988): 43-62 and G. Fisher, *International Negotiation: A Cross-Cultural Perspective* (Yarmouth, Maine: Intercultural Press, 1980); L. Bellenger, *La négociation* (Paris: Presses Universitaires de France, 1984) and A. Jolibert and M. Tixier, *La négociation commerciale* (Paris: Les editions ESF, 1988); and Hall and Hall (1990).

16. Nonfiction writings include: J. Ardagh, *France Today* (London: Penguin, 1987); L. Barzini, (1983); S. Miller, *Painted in Blood: Understanding Europeans* (New York: Atheneum, 1987); and T. Zeldin, *The French* (New York: Vintage, 1983). Fictional works include the classics by Jean-Paul Sartre and Andre Malraux and more recently, A. Jardin, *Le Zèbre* (Paris: Gallimard, 1988).

17. I will leave to others the debate over the effectiveness of training focused on "skills" versus other types of training. Somewhat surprisingly, some research on individuals' perceived need to adjust suggests that "interpersonal" and documentary training have comparable effects. See: P.C. Earley, "Intercultural Training for Managers," *Academy of Management Review* 30 (1987): 685-698. Note also that a number of negotiation seminars offered overseas do not directly increase familiarity with negotiation customs in those countries. These seminars import and rely on essentially American concepts and practices.

18. On cultural assimilator exercises, see: R.W. Brislin et al., *Intercultural Interactions: A Practical Guide* (Beverly Hills, California: Sage, 1986).

19. J. Watson and R. Lippitt, *Learning across Cultures* (Ann Arbor, Michigan: University of Michigan Press, 1955), as quoted in: A.T. Church, "Sojourner Adjustment," *Psychological Bulletin* 91 (1982): 544.

20. See Savage, Blair, and Sorenson (1989), p. 40. The following all include relationship factors (e.g. interest interdependence, relationship quality, concern for relationship) in their grids for strategic selection: R. Blake and J.S. Mouton, *The*

Managerial Grid (Houston, Texas: Gulf, 1964); Gladwin and Walter (1980); and K. W. Thomas and R.H. Kilmann, *Thomas-Kilmann Conflict Mode Instrument* (Tuxedo, New York: Xicom, Inc., 1974).

21. For more extensive lists, see: Weiss (1993).

22. D.G. Pruitt and J.Z. Rubin, *Social Conflict: Escalation, Stalemate, and Settlement* (New York: Random House, 1986), pp. 33-34.

23. Weiss with Stripp (1985); F. Gauthey et al., *Leaders sans frontèires* (Paris: McGraw-Hill, 1988), pp. 149-156, 158; and R. Moran and W. Stripp, *Dynamics of Successful International Business Negotiations* (Houston, Texas: Gulf, 1991).

24. P.H. Gulliver, *Disputes and Negotiations* (New York: Academic, 1979), pp. 186-190, 200-207.

25. G. Hofstede, *Culture's Consequences* (Beverly Hills: Sage, 1984).

26. The literature on women and negotiation includes: M. Gibb-Clark, "A Look at Gender and Negotiations," *The Globe and Mail*, 24 May 1993, p. B7; J. Ilich and B.S. Jones, *Successful Negotiating Skills for Women* (New York: Playboy Paperbacks, 1981); and C. Watson and B. Kasten, "Separate Strengths? How Men and Women Negotiate" (New Brunswick, New Jersey: Rutgers University Center for Negotiation and Conflict Resolution, Working Paper). On gender-based communication, see: D. Tannen, *You Just Don't Understand* (New York: William Morrow and Co., 1990).

27. N.J. Adler, "Pacific Basin Managers: Gaijin, Not a Woman," *Human Resource Management* 26 (1987): 169-191. This corresponds with the observation that "the different groups a person belongs to are not all equally important at a given moment." See: K. Lewin, *Resolving Social Conflicts* (New York: Harper & Row, 1948), p. 46, according to: Gudykunst and Ting-Toomey (1988), p. 201.

28. A. Riding, "Not Virile? The British Are Stung," *New York Times*, 20 June 1991, p. A3. See the disguises used by a female American reporter in: S. Mackey, *The Saudis: Inside the Desert Kingdom* (New York: Meridian, 1987). On the other hand, the all-woman New York City-based firm of Kamsky and Associates has been widely recognized for their business deals in the People's Republic of China. See also: C. Sims, "Mazda's Hard-driving Saleswoman," *New York Times*, 29 August 1993, Section 3, p. 6; and M.L. Rossman, *The International Business Woman* (New York: Praeger, 1987).

29. This interaction format draws on a game theoretic perspective and borrows more directly from: T.A. Warschaw, *Winning by Negotiation* (New York: McGraw-Hill, 1980), p. 79.

30. T.C. Schelling, *The Strategy of Conflict* (New York: Oxford University Press, 1960), pp. 53-58. The prominence of many courses of action would seem, however, to rest on assumptions that are culturally based and thus restricted rather than universal.

31. On risk-taking propensity, see: Gudykunst and Ting-Toomey (1988), pp. 153-160.

32. For discussions of similarity-attraction theory and research, see: K.R. Evans and R.F. Beltramini, "A Theoretical Model of Consumer Negotiated Pricing:

An Orientation Perspective," *Journal of Marketing* 51 (1987): 58-73; J.N.P. Francis, "When in Rome? The Effects of Cultural Adaptation on Intercultural Business Negotiations," *Journal of International Business Studies* 22 (1991): 403-428; and I.L. Graham and N.J. Adler, "Cross-Cultural Interaction: The International Comparison Fallacy," *Journal of International Business Studies* 20 (1989): 515-537.

33. N. Dinges, "Intercultural Competence," in *Handbook of Intercultural Training,* vol 1., D. Landis and R.W. Brislin, eds. (New York: Pergamon, 1983), pp. 176-202,

34. Individual members do instigate change and may, over time, cause a group to change some of its values. Still, at any given point, a group holds to certain values and beliefs.

35. See Dinges (1983), pp. 184-185, 197; and D.J. Kealey, *Cross-Cultural Effectiveness: A Study of Canadian Technical Advisors Overseas* (Hull, Quebec Canadian International Development Agency, 1990), pp. 53-54. At the same time, Church cautiously concluded in his extensive review of empirical research that effects of personality, interest, and value on performance in a foreign culture had not yet demonstrated strong relationships. See: Church (1982), p. 557.

36. This advice parallels the now widely supported solution for the classic negotiator's dilemma of needing to stand firm to achieve one's goals and needing to make concessions to sustain movement toward an agreement: namely, "be firm but conciliatory," firm with respect to goals, but conciliatory with respect to means. See: Pruitt and Rubin (1986), p. 153.

37. Sometimes counterparts do not actually desire an agreement but some side effect. Thus their behavior may differ from that described here. See: F.C. Ikle, *How Nations Negotiate* (Millwood, New York: Kraus Reprint, 1976), pp. 43-58.

38. See "Universal Look of Contempt," *New York Times,* 22 December 1986, p. C3.

39. "Going International" film series, Copeland Griggs Productions, San Francisco.

40. A. Riding, *Distant Neighbors: A Portrait of Mexicans* (New York: Vintage Books, 1984), p. 487.

41. E.T. Hall, *Beyond Culture* (Garden City, New York: Anchor Press, 1977), p. 109.

42. The assertion concerning the predominance of one culture at a time was made by: Lewin (1948).

43. A. Taylor, "Why GM Leads the Pack in Europe," *Fortune,* 17 May 1993, p. 84.

PART V

Metaphorical Applications

W̲e end this book with applications. Michael Agar begins with his fascinating treatment of language shock and the use of critical words and phrases that convey underlying values and attitudes. In this sense, such words and phrases are cultural metaphors that allow the outsider to gain an understanding of the culture. Agar uses the Austrian word *Schmäh* to illustrate his points, and the reader is invited to think of words and phrases reflective of his or her culture and to complete the exercises that Agar suggests.

William Newman then employs the well-known biological-stages metaphor of organizations, that is, organizations are living entities that are born, grow, mature, and ultimately die or fade away. Newman profiles a successful joint venture between an American and Chinese firm in which the joint venture was ultimately completed or symbolically died as the new Chinese entity took on a life of its own as an independent firm.

Next, we turn our attention to a heated point of difference between Asians and Westerners, namely, that the Western style of leadership is inappropriate in Asia, where the "headman" concept of village life still dominates the values of individuals and behavior expected in firms. The reader should probably review the research translations of Alan Fiske and Harry Triandis found in Part II before reading this article, for the headman concept is reflective of Authority Ranking or Vertical Collectivism.

Finally, Pearce and Osmond employ the concept of cultural metaphors created by Martin Gannon to explore the differences between British and American values and behavior. They have developed a change model (ALPs, or Access Leverage Points) that uses cultural metaphors as a basis for understanding and implementing organizational change when cross-cultural issues are involved.

CHAPTER 15

Language Shock

Understanding the
Culture of Conversation

MICHAEL AGAR

W hen you encounter differences, when you experience culture, some connections are fairly simple to find. Others, in contrast, are striking by their difficulty. The English verb "do" and the German second person pronoun *Du* are examples of contact points that catch an English speaker's attention just because they are problematic when trying to speak German. The concept I'm about to discuss, that of *Schmäh,* makes these earlier examples look easy. At the other extreme, many points of contact between English and German are no problem at all. An ashtray is an *Aschenbecher* and that's that.

The problem is Whorfian, with a simple twist. Unlike Whorf, the argument about differences is not a global one, that two languacultures, *in general,* constitute an insurmountable or difficult barrier, depending on which version of the Sapir-Whorf hypothesis you hold to.[1] Instead, the argument is that points of contact vary—some, perhaps most, are easy jumps, some are traversed only with difficulty, and a few are almost impossible to connect.

AUTHOR'S NOTE: Originally published in M. Agar, *Language Shock.* New York: William Morrow, pp. 99-107. Copyright © 1994 by Michael H. Agar. Reprinted by permission of the publisher.

Rather than a Whorfian wall, a Whorfian Alps would be a better image, a mountain range with plenty of valleys and trails and a few vertical cliffs.

When two languacultures come into contact, *yours* and *theirs,* the most interesting problems, the ones that attract your attention, are the vertical cliffs. These cliffs are difficult because—on one side of the barrier or another, or perhaps on both sides—the problematic bit of language is puttied thickly into far-reaching networks of association and many situations of use. When one grabs such a piece of language, the putty is so thick and so spread out that it's almost impossible to lift the piece of language out.

I need a name for this location, this Whorfian cliff, this particular place in one languaculture that makes it so difficult to connect with another. I'll call it *rich,* with the connotations of tasty, thick, and wealthy all intended. Interestingly enough, this word and the connotations I intend work pretty well with the German *reich* as well, not to mention the Spanish *rico.* Maybe some European, or perhaps even universal, patterns of connotation are around?

The *rich points* in a languaculture you encounter are relative to the one you brought with you. The juxtaposition of English and German highlight rich points that a juxtaposition of English and Hopi wouldn't. And a native speaker of Austrian German might be struck by different rich points than I would be if he or she set out to study how people talk in a Viennese neighborhood.

One rich point that grabbed my attention was the word *Schmäh*. It had registered when I was in Vienna three years earlier. I'd heard the term, but in the flow of language that flies by I'd tagged it with a rough gloss of "put-on"—a concept that in itself would take a while to analyze—and left it for a future date. But in rapid succession after my arrival, I heard it several times, saw it used in a book review and a newspaper article, looked it up in a couple of dictionaries, and read about it in a guidebook. It looked central, slippery, and interesting, and I had no idea what it really meant.

I was assigned a lecture course at the Linguistics Institute, and I decided to pick a rich point, show the students some of the ways an ethnographer would go about looking at it, and then turn them loose. I considered the concept of *Schmäh* as a candidate. I decided to try it out. At a lunch with some Austrian friends, I told them I was thinking about looking at *Schmäh* in my class. You can't imagine the laughter, which of course was the first sign that I'd made the right choice.

Everyone at the lunch said it was a good idea. I asked if they knew what *Schmäh* meant and they all looked at me like I'd asked if the sun rose in the morning. Of course they did. But then, as we discussed it, all kinds of disagreements followed. *Schmäh* was Viennese. No it wasn't, it was Austrian, or universal. It was something men did. No it wasn't. It was more characteristic of the lower classes. No it wasn't. It was telling jokes, picking up a woman in a bar, manipulating a situation, what politicians did, a way of life. No it wasn't. Yes it was.

I sat back and listened and realized that *Schmäh* was about as rich as a rich point could get. I learned that richness wasn't just reflected in the difficulties in connecting it with my native languaculture, but also in the disagreements among native speakers when they discussed it. Because the putty was so thick and broad, different native speakers would take different interpretive trails through it, and that meant that they would then disagree over what *Schmäh* meant. The confusion of the outsider signals a rich point, but so does immediate native-speaker recognition followed by wild disagreement.

I asked the students in my course to do three assignments (how would I translate "do" if I said that in German?). I'll describe them briefly. In general, they constitute an ethnographic approach to a rich point, one that mixes Whorf and Malinowski:

1. A systematic interview in the tradition of cognitive anthropology around the concept of *Schmäh*. Such interviews take some similarities, like a taxonomy or the sentence diagrams in the junkie example, place the concept in the center of them, and then pose questions that represent relationships and place the answers to those questions in the appropriate slots.

2. A collection of anecdotes of *Schmäh* use encountered in everyday life. The notes that result are like the field notes traditionally collected in participant observation.

3. An informal interview about *Schmäh*. Such interviews allow native speakers to discuss the concept in whatever way they choose. Methods of discourse analysis can be applied to such data to make explicit the underlying folk theory that contains the concept.

The students were beginners, and so was I, so I make no claims to a finished study. But from our discussions over the semester and the oral reports that the students delivered at the end, I'd like to summarize what we found out.

Schmäh is first of all a basic cultural premise, a Whorf-like way of looking at life, a general attitude; and it is in this sense, I think, that one talks about the Viennese *Schmäh*. A notion that repeatedly appeared in interviews and conversations was that *Schmäh* was a way of looking at things, often described by contrast with the expression that it was *nicht ernst,* not serious, but a not-seriousness of a particular kind. *Schmäh* as worldview rests on irony, on the fact that things are not as they appear, on the difference between dream and reality, to use another Austrian cliché. And reality is cruel, full of harmful events and ill-intentioned others.

Several interviewees mentioned that *Schmäh* was a way to deal with grisly reality, a way to convert this reality into humor, a release of hardship— real or imagined—through laughter. In this sense, *Schmäh* has something to do with *schwarzes Humor,* black humor, and several people mentioned this. But the difference is that, while a particular *Schmäh* attitude at a particular moment might also count as an example of black humor, black humor isn't used to describe a general orientation to life. *Schmäh* is.

At this general level, *Schmäh* isn't directly connected to particular bits of discourse. Rather, it labels a wide-ranging premise with implications for numerous situations that do connect in a more intimate way.

But the term doesn't just label the basic premise; it labels two specific situations as well. In the first kind of situation, *Schmäh* is a humorous comment or exchange that arises from the details of the moment. Many interviewees emphasized that not everyone can do a *Schmäh;* it is a skill requiring intelligence and wit. And several mentioned that it is not "telling jokes"—a description that people sometimes give at first—because jokes are prescripted and *Schmäh* is not.

Peter Nosbers, one of the students in my class, turned in several examples, and I'll copy one of them here just as he wrote it in his paper. A teacher walks into the room with a heavy purse.

Colleague 1: *Hast da Goldbarren drin?*
Teacher: *I oarbeit.*
Colleague 2: *Weißt eh, das is ihr Schminkkoffer.*
Teacher: *Das, was du brauchst, hätt ich gar nicht reinbekommen.*

Translated loosely, for humorous effect rather than accuracy:

Colleague 1: What you got in there, gold bars?
Teacher: I work for a living.
Colleague 2: I know, it's your makeup kit.
Teacher: The amount of makeup you'd need would never fit.

Here's a second example. I was talking to a colleague from another university. He told me a story about an American who taught in German. One day a student came up and said to the American, "You know, your English has gotten much better since you came to Vienna." I laughed and tried my new expertise by calling it a *Schmäh,* and my colleague laughed in return, surprised that I knew the term, and said that was exactly what it was. A *Schmäh* on that American, and probably a *Schmäh* on this one as well.

There were arguments in class and disagreements among interviewees as to whether the *Schmäh* is *bösartig* or *gut gemeint*, roughly, done with good or bad intentions. It is easy to understand why. The exchanges walk the line between the two. *Schmäh*, in this instance, reminds me of the verbal game my friends and I used to play in high school called "cut-lows." My impression is that *Schmäh* is more improvisational, that is, that *Schmäh* exchanges must be more tightly bound thematically, whereas cut-lows required less tightly linked statements, in part so that certain set pieces could be used and reused. But both *Schmäh* and cut-lows rest on the ability to form statements that attribute a negative reality to the other, and they all walk the line between humor and insult.

I can't resist an anecdote that is particularly appropriate for the recent two-hundredth anniversary of the French Revolution. Among the histories of *Schmäh* that interviewees offered, one mentioned the Austrian wife of the French king, Marie Antoinette. When told that the poor had no bread, she uttered her famous line, usually translated into English as "Let them eat cake." The interviewee pointed out that Maria Theresa's daughter had just uttered a *Schmäh*, but the French, as history has shown, didn't see it that way.

A second use of *Schmäh* is to label a lie, again with disagreement over whether it is ill or well intentioned, a lie that is linked to some personal, instrumental end. Again the folk history is interesting, since interviewees claimed that this version of *Schmäh* had roots in the monarchy—the same one that inspired Franz Kafka—where one often had to manipulate people with authority over them to get something done. This *Schmäh* is something different from the first type. Such a *Schmäh* may or may not be funny, and the listener may or may not know that a *Schmäh* is in progress. One student, for example, told stories about how she used *Schmäh* all the time to deal with the university bureaucracy.

Another example, one that is funny, obvious to the listener, and an illustration of how a *Schmäh* may be nonverbal, goes like this. A man pulls up and parks in a loading zone. A policeman tells him he can't park there. The man walks into the coffee house, brings a chair out, and puts it in the car, drives around the block, parks again, and carries the chair into the coffee house. In this case the policeman laughed and let him park. The lie was obvious and humorous, but the goal was achieved all the same.

A final example. In my other two classes at the Institute, seminars dealing with political argumentation and institutional discourse, we used the transcripts from some legislative hearings as data. The hearings centered on a political scandal in which several Austrian government officials were implicated in the cover-up of a case of insurance fraud. When I told friends and acquaintances outside the university that I was lecturing on *Schmäh* and studying the scandal in the seminars, the inevitable result was laughter and a suggestion that I had organized things well, since the scandal was a good example of *Schmäh*. In retrospect, I understand that they meant *Schmäh* in this second sense, the *Schmäh* as a lie told to achieve personal ends.

To sum it up, *Schmäh* is a view of the world that rests on the basic ironic premise that things aren't what they seem, what they are is much worse, and all you can do is laugh it off. Such an attitude is hardly unique to Vienna. What is unique to Vienna is that the premise, with all its complicated strands, is puttied into a single piece of language, and that rich piece of language is, in turn, used as a badge of identity.

The *Schmäh* worldview finds expression in at least two different situations that are both labeled *Schmäh:* one, a humorous exchange growing out of the moment that is based on a negative portrayal of the other; two, a deception designed to attain some instrumental end. Both specific examples fit the general philosophy—things are not what they seem, what they are is bad, but the fact that the difference exists is not to be taken seriously.

The reason this piece of language appeared so rich—in other words, appeared so problematic when brought into connection with my American English languaculture—becomes clear. Over the course of the semester the students and I played a game repeatedly, trying to link a specific example of *Schmäh* with an American English equivalent, or with other German-language varieties like the *Schnauze* from Berlin or the *Schmoos* from Cologne.

Such links are possible, on a situation-by-situation basis. Assume I equated one *Schmäh* example with my old high school verbal game, cut-lows, glossed another as a con, and then linked the worldview with New York City. (I tried to link it with Washington, but the "humor" part doesn't work; people in Washington take themselves too seriously, though since Clinton's election I'll have to admit things have loosened up.) Would I have understood the concept? No, I would have destroyed it.

The reason I would have destroyed it is what this book is all about. I would have destroyed it because I would have taken a rich point, cut the putty at different levels in different ways, and reputtied the different pieces I'd cut into another language in a way that not only was piecemeal, but didn't quite match, or didn't match very well at all. *Schmäh* isn't really like the cut-low game; *Schmäh* as con isn't the right fit either; and though New Yorkers may be *Schmäh*-like in their worldview at times, they don't encode it in a word and celebrate it as a badge of identity. The glosses might work to get by a single example, but in general they'd add up to confusion and distortion.

And that would only be the beginning of the damage. When *Schmäh* is lifted out of the language, the putty that comes with it drags along the raw material for a complicated but coherent set of meanings with links to history and culture. The ease with which it is used in Viennese discourse to characterize situations and persons and verbal and written expressions is a testament to its centrality and power, as are the disagreements when people discuss what it means. *Schmäh* is a laughing surface laid over an ugly world, a way of seeing and at least two different ways of talking within it.

To use an expression I learned, one that you now realize is ambiguous as to whether I am denying a lie or denying a joke, *Des is' ka' Schmäh*. "That ain't no *Schmäh*." Some of this, anyway, is both serious and true.

Rich points signal where the languacultural action is. Rich points don't *just* happen in language. The other night I ate dinner in a Japanese restaurant. A tour group from Japan partied in a separate room near my table. When they left, they filed out, and the owner and waitress stood near the door. The bows—I'm telling you, it was a symphony of bows, different in how much, how long, degree of head tilt, direction the bow was aimed. Richer points would be hard to find.

But I'm focused on language, and language is loaded with rich points, since language carries most of the rich and complicated symbolic freight that humans exchange.

Rich points are easy to find. They happen when, suddenly, you don't know what's going on. Several responses are possible. You can ignore it and hope that the next thing will make sense. You can number-one it to death, take it as evidence that the rich point only confirms that whoever produced it is deficient in some way.

Or you can wonder—wonder why you don't understand, wonder if some other languaculture isn't in play, wonder if how you thought the world worked isn't just one variation on countless themes. If you wonder, at that moment and later as well, you've taken on culture, not as something that "those people" have, but rather as a space between you and them, one that *you're* involved in as well, one that can be overcome.

Rich points aren't just the territory of professional students of languaculture. Rich points happen to all of us, all the time. The pro might take a well-worked-out academic framework for similarities and jump into the space within it. Similarities, to the extent that they work, save you a lot of time. But when most people encounter rich points, chances are they won't drag along a spectrum or a taxonomy. That doesn't mean there's nothing they can do.

Schmäh took me all over the Austrian German map. The most important data came from the informal interviews—translate that as talking with people about a rich point—and participant observation in daily life—translate that as going out into the world and actively engaging it. I do that more systematically than most people when I do a bit of research. And I write it up to make a convincing case to skeptical outsiders who weren't along for the ride. That's my professional job, to *document* and *report* in a credible way. But *any-*

one who stumbles across a rich point—inside or outside their native languaculture—can, in principle, do the same thing. All you have to do is talk and listen and engage a different world with languaculture in mind.

Talk to people who produced the rich point and go out and sample their world. Nothing mysterious about that. If you work, and continue to work, with the people who initially surprised you with a rich point, the understandings that you craft, with their help, will grow more and more complicated and interesting. And when you take that new understanding and try it out in another moment of talk, their reactions will telegraph, loud and clear, whether you're on the right trail or not. When you figure out rich points, the grades come back directly, right away. The people who produced the rich point are the judges, the ones you're learning to communicate with.

If what you're learning doesn't fit neat similarities, if you accept the principle but let the narrow frameworks go, what are you left with? What are you building, if not a taxonomy or a picture of a situation? You're building new knowledge born of personal experience, a new awareness, a new connection between you and them that can take any number of shapes. You're building *culture*.

Note

1. Note from editor: The strong version of the Sapir-Whorf hypothesis is that language is equivalent to culture, and there can be no culture without a specific language that needs to be understood by its members. The weak version of this hypothesis is that language is but one of the critical media through which culture is expressed.

CHAPTER 16

Stages in Cross Cultural Collaboration

WILLIAM H. NEWMAN

S kill in working together with strange neighbors will be a valuable strength in the 21st century. Increases in international trade, based on greatly improved communication and combined with more fluid political structures, will encourage cross cultural ventures. Alliances, consortiums, equity joint ventures, and other forms of merged effort will be common.

Despite a formal legal framework for each of these new organizations and a recognition of the cultural hurdles of such collective actions, there exists a critical gap in the knowledge of how to work together. Our existing knowledge is limited about when and why such collaboration runs smoothly,

AUTHOR'S NOTE: Originally published in *Journal of Asian Business*, *11*(4), pp. 69-94. Copyright © 1995 by the *Journal of Asian Business*. Reprinted by permission. Center for Chinese Business Studies, Graduate School of Business, Columbia University. Continuing support from the Center for Chinese Business Studies of Columbia University made this study possible. Hoke Simpson, Director of the Center, and Robert L Stultz, formerly with Hoechst/Celanese Corporation, were especially helpful in the field studies; and comments from Columbia colleagues added clarity to the presentation. Kristin Stucker was resourceful in helping to develop the eclectic set of references in Appendix B.

and when and why it so often falters. This deficiency arises, in part, from the wide variation in the roles that cross cultural collaboration is expected to play. We need frameworks to help sort and focus research attention.

This paper presents such a framework—an approach that distinguishes four stages of cooperative relationships which have distinct characteristics and call for different modes of behavior. The framework was observed in practice, and will be explained in the following sections:

Cross Cultural Field Study
1. Identifying and Committing to a Cross Cultural Win-win Strategy
2. Translating the Strategy into Viable Action Plans
3. Execution: Making the Cross Cultural Collaboration Happen
4. Self-initiation by the Emerging Organization

Executives Suited to Each Stage

Implications for Future Research

Cross Cultural Field Study

Rich Source of Data

Multinational joint ventures provide a ready-made laboratory. They require close collaboration of managers from two or more countries. Also, in developing countries the operations typically involve insertion of Western practices into unfamiliar cultures (Appendix B,1).

Two degrees of collaboration are often exposed in such ventures: a) interactions between organizations and individuals whose primary allegiance remains rooted in separate cultures, and b) merged behavior of individuals from different backgrounds into a hybrid organization.

Small joint ventures, such as the hundreds of labor intensive ventures that are fueling the current boom in southern China, often have their functions of technology and product design, marketing, and production sharply separated with each function performed in a different country. Here the cross cultural interaction is limited to a few boundary spanning individuals. (Newman, 1992a) In contrast, the Chrysler Jeep venture and the Otis Elevator operation in Tianjin are Chinese examples of cross cultural merging of individuals' behavior in several functions and at several levels. Clearly this second type of larger and more complex enterprise presents a richer array of cross cultural problems.

For more than a decade the author has been investigating foreign joint ventures in China—both small simple ones and large complex organizations. For larger joint ventures, data came directly from China based managers selected by companies listed in Appendix A; other local sources are described in publications listed in Appendix B,2. All this background is relevant to the "stages" issue. The present paper, however, focuses mainly on one high-tech, large joint venture for which in-depth information covering its entire life since 1984 has been obtained. Fortunately for our purposes, this venture has been highly successful—a distinction not yet shared by most of the large, complex joint ventures in China.

The NCFC (Nantong Cellulose Fibers Company) Example

This joint venture was formed by Celanese Corporation and China National Tobacco Corporation (CNTC) to produce "tow" (the fluffy fibers for cigarette filters).

Celanese Corporation (now merged with Hoechst A.G. of Germany) is a major U.S. chemical manufacturer with worldwide operations. For many years its Fibers Division has produced large quantities of synthetic yarns, composed of tiny fibers, for the textile industry. Tow is made by the same basic process; instead of being spun into yarn, the fibers are just loosely merged into filter material for cigarettes.

The Chinese partner, CNTC, is the operating arm of the tobacco monopoly in the People's Republic of China. In the early 1980s the central government placed all tobacco business in China under the direction of CNTC. These activities include the production and distribution in China of one and a half trillion cigarettes each year—roughly 30 percent of the world volume.

The experiences of the joint venture formed by these parent corporations illustrate many of the hurdles in cross cultural collaboration. Fortunately, as case writers we had full access to NCFC history from the start of negotiations in 1984 to the present. During this 1984-1994 period significant changes in the company environment have occurred. For example, domestic demand for tow and acetate flake has increased sharply, and this has intensified the shortage of foreign exchange for tow imports. Government regulations for foreign joint ventures have been altered frequently. Controls have been decentralized. China has started bold steps to get into the WTO. Each change has called for cross cultural adjustments in the terms for collaboration.

In fact, the first 5,000 ton/year tow plant located in Nantong, China, has produced world quality tow in quantities above its estimated capacity every year since its opening late in 1989. And since then the plant capacity has been expanded 150 percent and a $125 million raw material (acetate flake) plant opened in 1994. The significance of these figures for the present paper is that our primary example of "stages in cross cultural collaboration" is a successful operation.

The field study of NCFC is a joint effort by faculty members from the Graduate School of Business, Columbia University in New York, and from the Faculty of International Business Administration, University of International Business and Economics in Beijing. (For a descriptive report of this in-depth study see Newman 1992b.)

A "Stages" Model for Launching Joint Ventures

The record of starting large, foreign joint ventures provides ample evidence that launching is a complex task—especially so in China. Potential pitfalls are very diverse. So, seeking positive guidelines—what to do, rather than what not to do—may be more useful.

One positive approach is to view launching a joint venture as a series of distinct stages. Insofar as each sequential stage poses a different set of issues, a "Stages" model cuts a path through the complexity (Appendix B,3). While it is still exploratory, such a "Stages" model will be examined in this paper.

This "Stages" model is tersely sketched in Exhibit 16.1. To add descriptive content to the model, we will use the experiences in launching NCFC. Other collaborations will, of course, vary in their specific setting. Nevertheless, for purposes of describing the tentative model, NCFC is a propitious example. The ten year record enables us to observe differences in the Stages while also seeing the interdependence among the Stages.

In the following sections, for each Stage—1) negotiating a win-win strategy, 2) comprehensive planning, 3) executing the plans, 4) building local self initiative—we (a) describe the central activity, and then (b) note several hurdles created by cultural differences among the actors. With these features of the Stages in mind, next we note distinctive capabilities needed in managers for the different Stages. A final section calls attention to refinement and enlargements that researchers and managers should make in using the model.

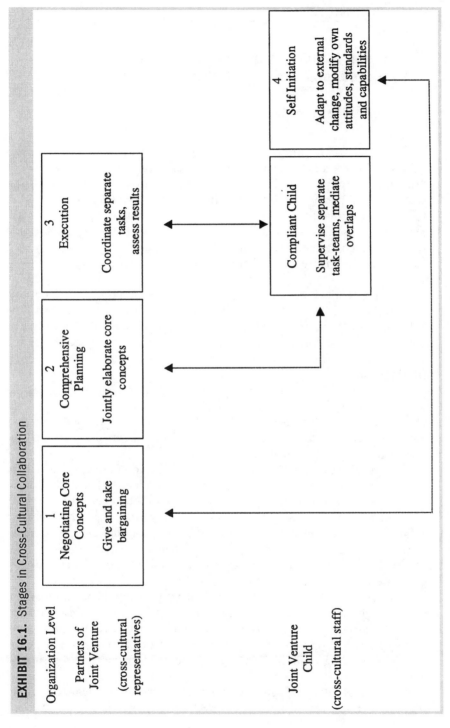

EXHIBIT 16.1. Stages in Cross-Cultural Collaboration

177

Stage 1: Identifying and Committing to a Cross Cultural Win-Win Strategy

Scope of Stage 1

A basic plan for merging partners' strengths to achieve a well defined goal is the heart, the sine qua non, of successful collaboration. This plan, or "strategy," is a way of ensuring continuing support from at least three parties: the two senior partners and the operating organization. Each partner agrees to provide a particular set of vital inputs of know-how, money, markets, materials, labor, or other resources. To maintain the flow of these inputs, the plan states that each partner is to receive recognized benefits. As viewed by each partner, its benefits are worth more than its inputs; each gains in the win-win strategy.

Also essential is a socially and economically sound operating company, sometimes called the "child" of the collaboration of the senior partners. The child receives the partners' inputs (and maybe mobilizes other inputs on its own initiative), and converts these into an array of benefits sought by the partners. Unless this conversion process generates a net gain, the collaboration will collapse.

The gain from conversion may arise, in part, simply from transferring an asset from one partner to another partner that can use that asset more beneficially. Or, the child may physically produce a different product or service. Especially when different cultures and different markets are involved, the conversion needs astute managing by the child.

A win-win strategy, then, is an agreement and commitment to a plan for collaboration covering the basic elements just identified—that is, the contributions and benefits of each partner, and the conversion role of the child. Win-win strategies are always tailor-made. Each partner has its own history, values and assets. The setting is dynamic and relationships among competitors and suppliers are deliberately being changed. Especially for CNTC (China National Tobacco Corporation), in the early 1980s its very existence was unsettled.

In 1982 CNTC had decided to raise sharply the number of Chinese cigarettes having filters; and this increased its need for tow. However, foreign exchange to increase its imports of tow was unavailable. All international suppliers of tow had refused to sell their production technology to China. So, CNTC was trying to interest an experienced producer of tow in forming a joint venture.

Celanese clearly was an attractive partner; it had excellent technology and ample resources. Moreover, in 1983 Celanese was facing a decreasing demand for its tow in the United States and Europe. The timing appeared to be right, so CNTC formally requested that Celanese enter into negotiation for a joint venture. Briefly, the position of each potential partner was:

CNTC's view

- Celanese would transfer its technology to a new tow plant in China, and would guarantee the volume and quality of the output.

- Celanese would provide all the hard currency needed to build the plant and start up the joint venture. CNTC would provide all the local currency needed.

- CNTC would ensure a local market for the tow output of the new plant.

- In accordance with recently issued foreign joint venture regulations, Celanese's share of the net profits would be paid in dollars. Also at the end of the contract (15 years) Celanese would be reimbursed in dollars for all its investment in the venture and the business would remain in China.

Celanese view

- Entry into potentially 30 percent of the world market would be very desirable but:

- Although Celanese would eventually recover its investment in dollars, the discounted cash flow would be low and uncertain.

- Chinese sale of tow in the international market would unsettle a market that already had more capacity than demand.

- Celanese could not guarantee the plant performance when labor and local services were under Chinese control.

These two viewpoints clashed. The Chinese government officials who had to approve any foreign joint venture felt that the assured market for tow plus guaranteed hard currency payment of dividends and full return of Celanese investment should be attractive to Celanese. However, the prevailing view within Celanese was that an unattractive cash flow plus possible destabilization of the international market were so serious that talking about a joint venture would be a waste of time and money.

In March, 1984, Celanese formally told CNTC that it was not interested even in starting to talk about a joint venture. After two years of arm's-length fencing Celanese would not even talk face-to-face about a possible venture. Each potential partner was thinking of a joint venture from its own perspective only.

At this point a senior manager from London Export Company asked for three months to help each potential partner reshape its view of a possible joint venture. London Export Company was well regarded in China for its help in other import and export deals; also London Export Company was Celanese's agent in China. Thus as an intermediary, the mediator was able to negotiate in a more frank manner than would have been possible in a face-to-face encounter.

As a result of this mediation, by July each potential partner had significantly expanded its view of the practical benefits of collaboration. Indeed, at a meeting that month each partner was prepared to accept the terms put on the table. The key additions and adaptations were:

- CNTC would make Celanese a preferred supplier of the tow that it expected to import before the new plant was finished and beyond. Celanese profit from these additional sales would provide cash flow up front.

- Within China the output of the new plant would be considered import substitution—just as helpful to conserving foreign exchange as exports. This removed the need for CNTC to enter the international market for tow.

- The guarantee of volume and quality of the new plant's output would be shared. CTNC would guarantee the power, steam, water and other local inputs. With that, Celanese would guarantee the processing within the plant.

- The "50/50" sharing of top management would be assured by each partner naming half of the members of the board of directors. In other words, the selection of directors would not be tied to supplying equity capital (which turned out to be about 70 percent CTNC and 30 percent Celanese).

Both potential partners promptly accepted these and related provisions for the strategy of a new joint venture. Each side got provisions that were important to it, and neither had to make costly concessions. It was a win-win strategy.

Within three months the basic agreement was endorsed by various supervisory agencies. At an October meeting ambiguous words were clarified and steps to develop a definitive contract were laid out. Significantly, at no time during this formative period was there resort to tricky bargaining, misleading exaggeration, catching the other party off guard, or the like. (Appendix B, 4) Instead, confidence building and openness prevailed. The agreement focused entirely on basic inputs and outcomes that one, or both, parties wanted assured; these were the foundation for continuing collaboration.

It was a statement of understanding, not a legal document nor inspiring oratory. Interestingly, the economic rationale of the joint venture and its strategic thrusts were implicit, not explicit, in this agreement. The implicit considerations were of crucial importance to both parties; but ground rules for working together through the child were the substance of this agreement.

Stage 1 Cultural Hurdles

Cross cultural settings usually add to the difficulty of devising a win-win strategy (see Exhibit 16.2). In the CNTC/Celanese situation, for example, *communication* hurdles almost stalled the discussions in 1984 before the potential partners even sat down at the same table. Differences in language, in business practices, and in legal institutions prevented each side from empathizing with the other—so that a workable collaboration could be conceived.

Also, culture interfered with needed *frankness.* A Chinese tradition of secrecy about business affairs coupled with politeness and avoiding open arguments was so different from Yankee blunt analysis that inaccurate stereotypes shaped expected behavior of a foreigner. Likewise, *mistrust* based on history led to impractical Chinese regulations on technology transfers, and to unwarranted risk assessments by the prevailing Celanese management.

Fortunately, London Export Company helped to surmount these barriers in our specific example. Lawyers did not confound these negotiations, and Celanese had more than usual U.S. patience. Nevertheless, dissimilarities in culture prolonged the negotiations and might have aborted them entirely.

Partners committing to a cross cultural win-win strategy may involve a bit of short-run bargaining about who will gain the most from the collaboration. Such quibbling over who gets the largest piece of pie, especially before trust between the partners has been established, adds to the cultural confusion in early negotiations. (Appendix B,5)

Vastly more important, however, is maximizing the rewards of cooperating. Recognizing an opportunity, structuring that opportunity in a way that is practical for both parties, and then getting mutual commitments on the contributions by each party—that is the vital task in Stage 1.

Achieving such an agreement between individuals from different countries and cultures encounters hurdles in communicating, in conceiving of unfamiliar operations, in understanding the institutional structures in which each partner lives, and in reconciling beliefs, fears, and values. Even with the aid of skilled boundary spanning, a lot of learning and adaptability by all parties to a genuine agreement is usually necessary.

EXHIBIT 16.2 Examples of Cross Cultural Hurdles at Different Stages of Collaboration[a]

Hurdles	Divisive Cultural Features
Negotiating core concept—stage 1	
Ability to communicate	Local meaning of a word; imputed meaning based on local practices and institutions, credibility of local financial data
Different manners in communicating	Establishing personal rapport and trust before discussing a deal; admitting own weaknesses publicly; agreeing on parts of a deal separately vs. insisting on holistic view
Resolving unpleasant, conflicting desires	Value attached to harmony vs. efficiency; belief in confronting problems bravely and promptly
Distinguishing between other party's stated desires and real needs	Prevailing attitude about personal privacy; acceptance of bluffing; encouragement of empathy
Doubt about negotiators' commitment to their principals	Role of lawyers, brokers, family members
Comprehensive planning—stage 2	
Technical description	Local terms, sizes, standards; what is considered important; what details are left to individual workers
Who is committed to what?	Estimates vs. intended actions; reviews, approvals, authorizations; compatibility and integration of proposed actions
Skill in anticipating the future	Punctuality; realistic vs. hopeful forecasts; normal span and scope of forecasting; tolerance for risk
Dependence on advisors	Who selects advisors, on what subjects; loyalties and values of the advisors; recognized "professional" conduct
Confidentiality	Legal protection of private knowledge; sale of "inside data"; disclosure requirements

EXHIBIT 16.2 Continued

Hurdles	Divisive Cultural Features
Execution—stage 3	
Motivating desired behavior	Attitudes toward risky incentives; comfort with group, not individual, accountability; workers' identification with employer's long-term success
Tailored measures of performance	Focus on performing activities vs. achieving specified results; unfamiliar measurements and prompt reporting of results; tight quality and on-time controls
Effective corrective action	Recognizing trouble without loss of face; expectation of changes and new learning
Avoiding conflicts of interest	Helping personal friends; building own *guan-xi*; acceptance of bribery or graft

Execution stage—added hurdles for "compliant child"	
Securing provincial support	Mistrust of foreigners; local priorities; political isolation
Effective delegation	Psychological acceptance of dictated targets; unobserved adherence to traditional behavior; resistance to control by foreigners

Self-initiation by local venture—stage 4	
Release from tight parental planning and control	Dependence of each parent on output of control child; expectation that child will grow and become adult
Social unity within operating unit	Identification with a parent vs. local organization; mutual respect among departments within organization
Achievement desire	Visualizing rewards from breaking with tradition; ready to take risks and sacrifices to make a change
Planning capability	Belief in self-determination; access to broad information affecting the future; familiarity with process of long-range planning

a. Based on interviews with general managers of Chinese/foreign joint ventures in China—see Appendix A.

Stage 2: Translating the Strategy Into Viable Action Plans

Stage 1 is heady stuff: creating new possibilities, assessing risks, gaining strengths, reaching an accord for new thrusts. In contrast, Stage 2 settles down to careful, firmly grounded action plans. The time for sparring is past. Now, with an accepted united goal, the focus shifts to spelling out the actions necessary to convert the basic agreement into a comprehensive plan for collaboration (Appendix B,6).

Scope of Stage 2

One important distinction between Stage 2 and Stage 1 is a shift from thinking about wide ranging alternatives to putting a selected mission into operation. "Feasibility studies" are no longer adequate. Instead, the viewpoint becomes, "We've decided, say, to go to the South Pole; what are our plans for getting there next January?"

These plans need to be comprehensive. For example, the key resources—people, money, equipment, government approvals, etc.—should be identified, interdependencies recognized, lead times set, responsibilities assigned. Of course, some detail may be postponed because necessary data are not yet available, or performance can easily be adjusted on the spot. But this waiver does not justify evading issues because they are unpleasant or tough.

Such comprehensive planning consumes effort and time—months or even years. In the NCFC example the elapsed time was over two years and the cost over a million dollars. Nevertheless, active participation by managerial personnel from all collaborating parties has significant advantages. Such diverse participants shape more practical specifications. The projected organization will be better understood and a cooperative "ownership" will be encouraged.

During this planning process temptations often arise to try to alter the Stage 1 agreement. The elaboration of the basic agreement, which is inherent in comprehensive planning, exposes costs or risks that may surprise a partner. The surprised partner may have failed to think through its role in the new venture, or especially in cross cultural deals the language may have been misunderstood. More serious, that partner may simply hope to squeeze out more favorable terms in a rerun of Stage 1 negotiations.

However, any repetition of the Stage 1 process after Stage 2 has started is quite disruptive. In addition to the time and effort of the rerun and damage to "trust" in respecting one's agreement, the comprehensive planning process is undermined. Instead of objectively seeking the best way, planning becomes a jockeying for personal advantage. As a consequence, the process is prolonged, the costs of outputs rise, and the project may be abandoned entirely.

The issue here is how to preserve the great benefits of adhering to a firm agreement, and yet adapt to genuine misunderstandings or unpredictable changes in the environment. Our stages model assumes that legitimate revisions of the Stage 1 agreement can be confined to a few relatively minor changes, and that the "trust" among the parties will facilitate such changes without undermining continuing commitments.

As Celanese and CNTC moved from the basic Stage 1 agreement to comprehensive planning they found that some features, such as importing tow, fitted easily into established procedures. The necessary documents, physical handling, insurance, cash transfers, and the like were all part of customary international behavior.

Planning for the construction of an unfamiliar plant and establishing a new business organization represented the opposite extreme. Almost nothing was standardized, at least for cross cultural ventures. China had regulations on technology transfers, feasibility studies, and joint ventures, most of which were poorly suited to the fledgling NCFC. Celanese thought in terms of free-enterprise practice. Both parties knew that large joint ventures in China had a record of heated squabbles and large losses.

The partners immediately agreed that, as far as possible, they would anticipate the needs of their new joint venture, and carefully plan before starting operations how these needs would be met. The assumption was that, especially in uncharted cross cultural collaboration, it would be easier to agree on how to deal with problems in the planning stage than waiting until they arose in operations.

Reflecting this belief, the comprehensive plan dealt with:

- Design and construction of the plant—including chemical processing, a large power plant, water processing, materials handling and storage, company offices, living quarters for foreign personnel, employee services, etc.

- Human resource practices—employment, training, compensation, housing, retirement plans, cafeteria, in-house recreation and services

- Purchasing of materials and supplies

- Finance and accounting credit terms, bank loans for working capital, taxes, required contributions to special funds, cash flow, accounting system

- Management structure—selection of directors and senior managers, powers of board of directors and senior managers, structure of major departments, liaison with governments

The preparation of these specific plans was shared by representatives of Celanese and of CNTC. The detail on various topics was assigned to small teams of Americans, of Chinese, or a mix who were experts in their topic. Their proposals were reviewed at formal meetings of the top representatives of Celanese and of CNTC held every four to six weeks. Over fifty different experts were involved at one time or another, with an almost continuous stream of travelers from Charlotte to Nantong.

The guidance and coordination of such an array of experts posed a management task quite different from guiding the Stage 1 negotiation of the basic agreement. The comprehensive plans emerging from this process were partners' commitments for specific action.

Stage 2 Cultural Hurdles

The process of developing comprehensive plans, always time consuming, is further complicated by cultural differences in the ways individuals interact. Significant hurdles arose early in our NCFC example.

The role of technical advisors in China, for instance, baffled Celanese planners. Following standard practice, CNTC selected an independent engineering institute as its representative in designing the Nantong plant. This institute was more concerned a) with protecting China from foreign exploitation than with the particular needs of the new joint venture, and b) with studiously conforming to standardized (and secret) instructions from Beijing. In contrast, Celanese believed that it had been selected as a potential partner because of its outstanding technology, and that the primary obligation of all technical advisors was to assist the joint venture. Five months were lost in getting the engineering institute to respect the joint venture agreement which had already been made.

Even where all individuals dealing with a particular feature, say, dormitories for unmarried workers or prevention of air pollution, had a common objective, frank and open discussion was difficult. The Americans quickly spotted differences in opinions, and opened a debate on these points. This practice startled the Chinese. For them, harmony and saving face of a respected colleague was a necessity. A senior CNTC manager said, "I had to learn that someone could argue with me and still be my friend."

Also considered brusque are sharp targets and firm commitments. When dealing with the future, most Chinese feel more comfortable being a bit vague, deferring hard decisions, and expressing optimism about completion dates. However, in the NCFC planning, the Americans sought to "think through to a doable outcome and then agree to make it happen."

At the start of the Stage 2 comprehensive planning, CNTC and Celanese recognized that their cultural differences might confuse the planning. So they agreed to inform each other when their interactions seemed to jumble an issue, and they asked London Export Company to provide "interpreters" who could not only translate but also mediate cultural hurdles. This open confrontation of troublesome problems such as the examples just cited prevented stalemates; it also permitted more penetrating understanding of problems.

Briefly, then, cultural differences had to be addressed, and this slowed down the process. Nevertheless, with patience and persistence a very comprehensive plan was completed without sharp conflict. The extensive friendly discussions led to learning and a high degree of trust on both sides.

Summary Comment

In Stage 2, by separating the shaping of strategy for collaboration from the careful planning for executing that strategy, both a) the strategy can be protected, and b) the planning can be more objective and practical.

An array of interdependent plans are needed to launch a joint venture, especially in a cross cultural setting. Processing technology, equipment, human resources, purchasing, marketing, financing, management structure, etc. all have to be thoughtfully designed so that they will reinforce each other. The effectiveness of this complex network leaves little room for piecemeal compromises reflecting partisan bargaining.

Extending the Stage 2 plans to a form suitable for execution squeezes out ambiguity and reduces the chances of distortion at the operating levels. But this degree of detail is unsuited for Stage 1 strategy formulation. Also, by separating strategy formulation from comprehensive planning, the inevitable difficulties of communication and commitment can be more openly addressed. The implications on executive selection of this separation of Stage 1 from Stage 2 activities will be considered later in this paper.

Stage 3: Execution: Making the Cross Cultural Collaboration Happen

Stage 2 plans, no matter how thorough, are hypothetical until they are acted out. And when plans coming from cross cultural discussions are applied to strange settings the outcome may include surprises. A common reason for such surprises is a failure to recognize how different the Stage 3 process is from that of Stage 2 planning.

Nature of Stage 3 Activity

The people who perform the operating activities, especially in foreign joint ventures, are a very different group from the planners. They run machines, talk to customers, pay bills, etc.—today and tomorrow. They are less contemplative; feedback comes from the real world; focus is on short term outcomes.

Execution also involves outside suppliers and subcontractors, another set of people with their own agendas largely dealing with short-run transactions. As with internal operations, a) working with outside suppliers has a real-world, prompt feedback nature not present in planning, and (b) the results are achieved primarily by influencing the behavior of local (Chinese) people.

Because these people who do the work come from the local culture, most of them are unfamiliar with risky incentives; group rather than individual accountability is normal; and, concern with overall plant results is low. For Western managers these attitudes make motivating workers difficult.

Ambiguous control standards typically further complicate execution of plans. Just acting busy is not enough. A Stage 2 comprehensive plan is built on dependable and promptly measured results, step by step; but in Stage 3 this sort of control is often shunned by the Chinese because it can lead to "loss of face." Indeed, for a Westerner corrective action starts with acknowledgement of unsatisfactory results, but in China flagging errors, especially when done by a foreigner, is regarded as a personal affront.

Nevertheless, to carry out Stage 2 plans, meeting the quality, time, and cost standards in a coordinated manner is critical. Such reliable behavior is necessary in service companies fully as much as in manufacturing. So, Stage 3 managers must try to guide activities of diverse sets of people into a synergistic package of activities that fits the plan. This, of course, calls for timely measurement of performance and adroit use of incentives. It is a make-happen task. Here in Stage 3, then, are an array of human supervisory problems unlike the technical and economic issues that dominate Stage 2 planning.

Stage 3 Cultural Hurdles

In the Nantong example cross cultural difficulties in execution arose mostly during the construction of the plant. The crews of the mechanical contractor, which came from Shanghai, just disappeared for days at a time.

Much more serious, they did only what they considered necessary and left the job even though the equipment was not ready to operate. (Local craftsmen under the direction of trainees who had just returned from the United States actually performed the start-up functions.)

Stated more broadly, these contracted workers defined "professional" performance as they pleased; they were indifferent to satisfactory completion of the project; and acceptance of suggestions by representatives of the foreign partner was considered as loss of face. At the same time, the U.S. representatives were surprised and baffled by such behavior. (Fortunately in the later plant expansion this kind of difficulty was largely ironed out during the negotiation of the job contract before work began.)

A potential hurdle continues in the current operating organization. The initial plans for the number of employees required were based on U.S. practice. And in departments supervised (temporarily) by expatriates these work loads are being observed. However in areas under Chinese supervisors work loads have been reduced and additional employees hired. As a result there is now a strong undercurrent that Yankees expect people to work harder. The foreign supervisors say, "In our country workers expect to work a full eight hours a day."

Note that this issue of sustained effort throughout the day exists in a fresh operation; here it is not a matter of changing a former slow pace in a state enterprise. (One impartial observer suggests that the Americans are driven more by the possibility of internal promotion.)

The particular features of the supervisory problems just noted may be unique to NCFC. These events are cited here only to support our underlying propositions that a) managing Stage 3 activities differs sharply from managing the other Stages, and b) cross cultural complexities increase the need to adapt to these differences.

Stage 4: Self-Initiation by the Emerging Organization

In Stage 3 the fledgling joint venture concentrates on becoming a viable organization. It is a "compliant child" relying on a comprehensive plan and other inputs from its parents; its differentiating strength comes from their collaboration. The joint venture is nourished by explicit plans for cooperation (Appendix B,7); and because this cross cultural cooperation has to be learned, the operating managers stress conformity to the agreed-upon protocols. Well conceived and planned joint ventures (such as NCFC) benefit greatly from such united, synchronized effort.

Nevertheless, joint ventures are fragile. The particular combination of advantages and drawbacks upon which even the most successful ventures are founded do change over time. Each founding partner is submerged in its own dynamic environment, strategy, and resources; and its interest in the joint venture is swayed by the twists and turns of its own major activities. The mutual interest between the two parent companies rarely remains stable, especially when their major activities are located in different countries. In addition, the child adapts to its competitive setting—often growing in unexpected ways or facing a new technology. So, sooner or later, the original charter is no longer viable (Appendix B,8). Stage 4 is concerned with how a joint venture deals with its unavoidable obsolescence.

Stage 4 Activity

Broadly, a mature joint venture has to choose between passive dissolution or active reorientation. Sometimes, as in a mining operation, the vein of ore is exhausted and the mine is simply abandoned. In a more likely dissolution, ongoing operations become attractive to only one of its partners; that partner buys out the other and fits the continuing activities into its larger structure. In these situations the joint venture never moves beyond the compliant child mode. The collaboration has served its purpose, perhaps brilliantly, and now shared effort is no longer needed.

An alternative response to obsolescence is self-initiative by the child itself. Because of its cross cultural experience, the child can take the initiative (with or without help from its parents) to transform itself into a distinctive competitor. The senior managers within the child study their evolving environment, assess the child strengths, and search for a new strategy. Perhaps with a new economic orientation, the child can forge an unprecedented competitive niche. (Appendix B,9)

Large or complex multinational ventures usually have a "going concern" value. The employees collectively have intimate knowledge of selling and supplying markets; they are sensitive to small variations in technology; they know the individuals who are important in communication networks. Moreover, their accumulated cross cultural skill and trust may be a unique strength in transnational transactions. Such background can make vital contributions to designing a new strategy suited to the changed environment. Also, jobs and careers are at stake, so the motivation to at least share in the new planning is high.

Note, however, the large shift in viewpoint that is necessary for the joint venture managers to turn from careful compliance with established plans to active participation in reorientation. The span of future predictions is greatly lengthened. The prospect of internal change is welcomed. Taking greater risks is accepted. Among the possible changes to be considered are new allies, altered government policy, different competitors, improved infrastructure, and other external forces—in addition to strengthened internal capabilities.

Stage 4 Cultural Hurdles

Support for Stage 4 initiative in a joint venture depends greatly on the *attitude of its parents*. For example, when NCFC was born the traditional attitudes about bottom-up participation clashed. In China centralized planning was still the norm whereas U.S. doctrine encouraged free enterprise even in subsidiaries. Currently the official position in China is exactly reversed; joint ventures are almost footloose, and spin-offs from state enterprises are expected to shape their own destiny. Now the tide is running strongly in favor of self-initiative, and the practical issue for parents is learning how to nourish entrepreneurial capabilities.

Within joint venture children, the cultural forces are also in flux. Most of the ventures are young, and many of their senior managers think of themselves as representatives of a parent. Their loyalty is to the parent and its needs, not to the local venture as a self-sustaining social organization. And this sort of ambiguous allegiance at least distracts from Stage 4 personal searching for a revised viable strategy for the joint venture.

Culture also affects an individual's ambitions. Widespread acceptance with one's lot in China undercuts Stage 4 restlessness.

A more temporary hurdle in China is the scarcity of reliable data for planning. Even a computer in every office will not overcome the dearth of good business statistics and insightful experience in using them.

The preceding abbreviated list of cultural hurdles that an enterprise faces when moving into a Stage 4 self-initiating mode is long enough to indicate the difficulties in making the transition from a Stage 3 compliant child status. Nevertheless international pressure is pushing in that direction.

The Chinese officials, like leaders in other developing countries, still talk in terms of a transfer of knowledge to their own indigenous personnel. This is a nationalistic view. Our Stages model leaves open the possibility that multi-culture management may have a distinct advantage in an internationalized economy.

■ Executives Suited to Each Stage

Two themes have been stressed in the preceding discussion: recognizing four distinct Stages—negotiation, comprehensive planning, execution, self-initiative in cross cultural collaboration—and separating the performance of each Stage because of inherent difficulties in cross cultural teamwork. A third theme helps to integrate these concepts into a more comprehensive theory of managing cross cultural collaboration. Each Stage calls for a different set of capabilities in the senior managers administering the joint effort.

Including this third theme in our model also helps in its *application* to active cross cultural ventures. It suggests guidelines for senior managers. More specifically, because desirable capabilities vary from Stage to Stage, the model helps to determine whether the same individual will be adept at managing two or more Stages. Or for already existing joint ventures having trouble, it provides a suggested set of characteristics that can be used in assessing present senior managers (Appendix B,10).

To amplify this third theme we will first illustrate vital characteristics of senior managers in each of the four Stages, and second note briefly some of the cross cultural problems in achieving a fit of managers to the optimum characteristics of each Stage.

Diversity of needed capabilities. Exhibit 16.3 illustrates the impact of the dominant function performed in the various Stages upon four vital qualities of an effective manager. This set of four personal capabilities—activity strength, essential knowledge, time-horizon effectiveness, and interpersonal skills—could be expanded or reshuffled.

Nevertheless, a reading of Exhibit 16.3 in its tentative form does emphasize that the temperament and skills needed in negotiating differ from those required in comprehensive planning; likewise, execution calls for localized interpersonal skills that are not critical for planning; and other capabilities have distinctive criticality in particular Stages.

Few individuals, from any culture, have the dexterity to be well qualified to perform in all Stages. So as a venture moves from Stage to Stage some turnover of senior managers is usually desirable though perhaps difficult to arrange. Of course, larger ventures have more than one senior manager, and the array of capabilities can be larger than those of a single individual. However, if the Stages of collaboration are separated sequentially—as proposed in previous pages of this article—the occasion for personnel turnover persists.

Added Cultural Hurdles

The task of matching managerial ability with the Stages of collaboration is further complicated when individuals from different cultures must work

EXHIBIT 16.3 Examples of Differences Among Stages in Vital Characteristics of General Managers

Characteristic	Negotiating Stage	Comprehensive Planning Stage	Executing Stage		Self-Initiating Stage
			Partner Level	Operating Level	
Activity strength	Getting agreement for new corporation	Laying out logistics of complex activity	Controlling performance of firm plans	Ensuring action according to standards	Plotting adaptation to future environment
Essential knowledge (possesses or has quick access)	Needs, power, and resources of both parties	Expertise in each key function	Performance benchmarks in the industry	Specific operating know-how	Outlook for market and resources Competitors' likely strategy Our future strength and weaknesses
Time-horizon effectiveness	Adjusts readily to main objective of partners	Focuses on start-up	Tied to steering controls 6 to 36 months	"Real-time" feedback controls 0 to 12 months	Long-term scenarios 1 to 5+ years
Interpersonal skills	Persuasive, stimulating	Stresses facts and analysis Rapport with "planners"	Gets scheduled work done Builds loyalty to company	Stresses disciplined behavior Considerate of other people	Welcomes change Inspiring Team leader

together. To be effective, a manager needs to recognize potential cultural pitfalls and find ways to overcome them. And, selecting a suitable person is difficult because these cultural hurdles vary from Stage to Stage. For example, common sources of friction arising in China include the following:

Negotiating Stage: Busy Yankees try to move abruptly into discussion of terms while Chinese take days establishing personal rapport. Chinese think and talk in a holistic framework, while Yankees isolate points of disagreement analytically. Unstated (and often unconscious) assumptions by either party lead to misunderstanding; for instance, what role will government agencies play? Where will reliable information come from? When has a firm commitment been made? How can a mutually trusted mediator be used?

Comprehensive Planning Stage: Chinese often place too much reliance on physical technology when operating "know-how" is even more critical. Yankees overlook local practice regarding taxes, personnel selection, obligations, and accountability. Third party roles are unexplored. Chinese have limited experience in making time estimates. To maintain harmony there is a temptation to postpone indefinitely the discussion of controversial issues. Vagueness or lack of commitment to the stated Stage 1 deal introduces haggling in place of mutual planning in Stage 2.

Execution Stage: The widespread use of objective measurements and access to resulting reports is much less common in China than in the United States. To save face of oneself or others, problems needing correction are not acknowledged. In China harmony is often considered more important than efficiency. The Chinese are loath to use direct incentives based on an individual's results. Yankees often fail to take time to understand local problems.

Self-Initiation Stage: Especially in state enterprises, local managers feel that their taking policy initiative is inappropriate; their freedom of thought and action is still ambiguous. Availability of reliable outside-company data is limited. Personal loyalties may interfere with bold changes. Incentives for initiating change are low. "Soft" communication with foreign partners is often weak.

In a cross cultural setting any attempt to match managerial competence with the Stage of collaboration may encounter the personal interaction hurdles just noted. Candidates for a management position need both substantive skills and cultural finesse suited to the Stage involved.

Two inputs are especially helpful in surmounting these hurdles: time and trust. All parties to the collective effort must take the time to empathetically agree on the terms describing their joint activities. Indeed, in the Nantong joint venture two and a half years passed between the date of the basic agreement to cooperate and the signing of a comprehensive plan, most of which was devoted to reaching clear and acceptable understanding. Much patience, persistence, and politeness was required at several levels to fully ensure agreement on the cooperative plan. "Trust" goes deeper. It is a belief that the other party is not intentionally evading or covering up significant features of an understanding. Trust also presumes that if unexpected facts do emerge the other party will be told and that the revised situation will be openly and jointly confronted. Fortunately the development of full understanding and trust does more than overcome the cross cultural aspects of filling managerial positions.

Another result of the time consuming process of exploring attitudes and unstated assumptions is improved ability to predict acceptance of other initiatives. The people involved in one successful collaboration project, as sketched in this article, have gone through a learning experience that prepares the way for successive projects.

Like the recognition of distinct Stages in cross cultural collaboration, the optimum qualifications of senior managers differ for each Stage. This shifting in desirable personal capabilities has been illustrated in Exhibit 16.3 in four dimensions—activity strengths, essential knowledge, time-horizon effectiveness, and interpersonal skills. As the central task changes from Stage to Stage, so also does the optimum managerial profile. Building a compatibility of competences with tasks, and a consistent focus, at each Stage calls for special time and effort.

Since few individuals are adaptable enough to excel in all roles, selecting managers who match the capabilities needed at each Stage implies turnover as the venture matures. So, a dilemma arises between close matches of personal capabilities and job needs versus maintaining continuity of employment and external contacts. In the Nantong venture during its early Stages this dilemma was partially met by continuity in the top representative of each partner but turnover of second tier managers.

Conclusions and Implications for Future Research

This paper focuses on a model for improving the effectiveness of cross cultural collaboration in purposeful organizations. The central thesis is that such collaboration will benefit greatly by recognizing distinctive Stages in the process and by fitting managerial effort to the needs of each Stage.

The major features of a proposed model for this approach are:

A) Four Stages—1) negotiation of the basic terms for collaboration; 2) comprehensive planning of the venture; 3) consistent and persistent execution of the agreed upon plans; and 4) self-initiative adapting to external changes. Each Stage has distinct functions, cultural hurdles, and managerial requirements. Each Stage calls for a different managerial process.

B) Especially in cross cultural ventures, maintaining the logical sequence of Stages and completing one Stage before starting the next avoids many of the conflicts that often plague international ventures.

C) The selection of senior managers for each Stage who have capabilities that match the needs of that Stage is also critical.

D) This Stages approach to managing is well suited for sharply focused ventures which provide prompt, recognizable benefits to the cooperating partners. Moving into new markets or industries can be done by a series of additional ventures, each of which has its own focused objectives.

Future research might well take two paths, a) elaborating the longitudinal model, and b) linking the longitudinal Stages concepts to more narrowly focused analyses of particular problems inherent in collaboration.

Since the model described in the present paper is based on a single body of data (foreign joint ventures in China), checking the usefulness of this model in other settings is an important next step. Current experience with joint ventures in East Europe, for example, is one inviting field. Likewise, it will be helpful to know how well the model suits alliances and coalitions which are more loosely structured than equity joint ventures. Another tack is to identify the critical contingencies which make a Stages approach viable.

Any longitudinal viewpoint covering a period of years inevitably crosses issue-centered paradigms such as the process of delegation, building trust, or headquarters control of foreign operations. These crossroads are stimulating opportunities to enrich both flows of thought. The historical stages analysis can latch onto the carefully crafted insights of the issue specialists, and the specialists gain a better appreciation of the context which often dominates the feasibility of some of their cherished prescriptions.

An exploration of such crossroads is far beyond the scope of this paper. Nevertheless, to encourage cross fertilization Appendix B does flag ten junctions where viewpoints overlap. And for each of these junctions we have listed a few references which suggest research possibilities. The aim is modest—only to provide a few links into other streams of research. We hope that this form of identifying other research possibilities will, in fact, encourage more insightful studies of cross cultural collaboration.

Parent Companies
of Chinese/U.S.
Joint Ventures Studied

Resident general managers and other top executives of these companies were
interviewed in China:

AT&T

Babcock and Wilcox

Business Week

Carrier Corporation

Coca Cola

DuPont

Foxboro

Hoechst Celanese

Ingersoll-Rand

McDonnell-Douglas

Merck

Schindler Elevator

Unisys

United Technologies

Westinghouse

W. R. Grace

Xerox

Bridges to Literature on
Topical Issues That Intersect Stages
in Cross Cultural Collaboration

1. Transnational Joint Ventures

Bartlett, C. A. & Ghoshal, S. 1989. *Managing across borders: the transnational solution*. Boston: Harvard Business School Press.

Collins, T. M. & Doorley, T. L. 1991. *Teaming UP for the 90's; a guide to international joint ventures and strategic alliances*. Illinois: Business One Irwin.

Eom, S. B. 1994. "Transnational management strategies: An emerging tool for global strategic management." *SAM Advanced Management Journal*. 59(2): 22-27.

Harrigan, K. R. 1986. *Managing for joint venture success*. Lexington, MA: Lexington Books.

Porter, M. 1986. *Competition in global industries*. Boston: Harvard Business School Press.

2. Managing Chinese/Foreign Joint Ventures

Newman, W. H. 1992a. "Focused joint ventures in transforming economies." *Academy of Management Executive*. 6:67-75.

Newman, W. H. 1992b. *Birth of a successful joint venture*. Lanham, MD: University Press of America.

Newman, W. H. 1992c. "Launching a viable joint venture." *California Management Review*. 35:68-80.

3. Longitudinal Analyses of Strategic Change

Adizes, A. 1988. *Corporate Lifecycles*. Englewood Cliffs, NJ: Prentice Hall.

Lamont, B. T., Marlin, D. & Hoffman, J. J. 1993. "Porter's generic strategies, discontinuous environments, and performance: A longitudinal study of strategies in the hospital industry." *Health Services Research.* 28: 623-640.

Shaw, S. M. & Meter, J. 1993. "Second generation MNCs in China." *The McKinsey Quarterly.* 4:3-16

Strelsen, S. C. & Mlot, S. 1992. "The art of strategic sales alignment." *Journal of Business Strategy.* 13(6): 41-47.

4. Negotiating the Terms for Joint Action

Fester, D. A. 1992. "Negotiating the mind meeting." *Directors and Boards.* 17: 52-54.

Grindsted, A. 1994. "The impact of cultural styles on negotiation: A case study of Spaniards and Danes." *IEEE Transactions on Professional Communications.* 37: 34-38.

Pinkley, R., Neale, M. A. & Bennett, R. J. 1994. "The impact of alternatives to settlement in dyadic negotiation." *Organizational Behavior and Human Decision Processes.* 57: 97-116.

Weiss, S. E. 1994. "Negotiating with "Romans" Part 2." *Sloan Management Review.* 35(3): 85-99.

5. Building Trust

Brunard, V. & Kleiner, B. H. 1994. "Developing trustful and cooperative relationships." *Leadership and Organizational Development Journal.* 15(2).

Gibbons, J. J. 1992. "Trust: The key to success for manufacturers and their agents." *Agency Sales Magazine.* 22(4): 22-25.

Horng, C. 1993. "Cultural differences, trust, and their relationships to business strategy and control." *Advances in International Comparative Management.* 8: 175-197.

Wolff, M. F. 1994. "Building trust in alliances." *Research Technology Management.* 37(3): 12-15.

6. Comprehensive Planning

Camillus, J. C. & Grant, J. H. 1980. "Operational planning: The integration of programming and budgeting." *Academy of Management Review.* 5: 369-379.

Lorange, P. 1980. *Corporate planning: An executive viewpoint.* Englewood Cliffs, NJ: Prentice Hall.

Mackey, W. A. & Carter, J. C. 1994. "Measure the steps to success." *IEEE Spectrum.* 31(6): 33-38.

Roman, D. D. 1985. *Managing projects: A systems approach.* New York: Elsevier Science Publishing Co.

Yavitz, B. & Newman, W. H. 1982. *Programming. Strategy in Action,* 113-128. New York: Free Press.

7. Headquarters Control of Foreign Operations

Bartlett, C. A. & Ghoshal, S. 1988. "Organizing for worldwide effectiveness: The transnational solution." *California Management Review.* 31: 54-74.

Egelhoff, W. G. 1988. *Organizing the multinational enterprise: an information-processing perspective.* Cambridge, MA: Ballinger Publishing Company.

Hedlund, G. 1980. "The role of foreign subsidiaries in strategic decision-making in Swedish multinational corporations." *Strategic Management Journal.* 1: 23-36.

Prahalad, C. K. & Doz, Y. L. 1981. "An approach to strategic control in MNC's." *Sloan Management Review.* Summer: 5-13

Roth, K. & Nigh, D. 1992. "The effectiveness of headquarters-subsidiary relationships: The role of coordination, control and conflict." *Journal of Business Research.* 25: 277-301.

8. Adapting Strategy to a Changing Environment

Glaister, K. & Thwaites, D. 1993. "Managerial perception and organizational strategy." *Journal of General Management.* 18(4): 15-33.

Miller, K. D. 1983. "Industry and country effects on managers' perceptions of environmental uncertainties." *Journal of International Business Studies.* 24: 693-714.

Schroder, B. & Mavado, F. 1994. "Strategy/performance/environmental linkage in agribusiness: Conceptual issues and a developing country example." *Agribusiness.* 10: 419-424.

Tan, J. J. & Litschert, R. J. 1994. "Environment-strategy relationship and its performance implications: An empirical study of the electronics industry." *Strategic Management Journal.* 15: 1-20.

9. Decentralizing Initiative to Operating Divisions

Kim, W. C. & Mauborgne, R. A 1993. "Making global strategies work." *Sloan Management Review.* 34(3): 11-27.

Nohria, N. & Ghoshal, S. 1994. "Differentiated fit and shared values: Alternatives for managing headquarters-subsidiary relations." *Strategic Management Journal.* 15: 491-502.

Prahalad, C. K. & Doz, Y. L. 1987. *The multinational mission; Balancing local demands and global vision.* New York: The Free Press.

Venetucci, R. 1992. "Benchmarking: A reality check for strategy and performance objectives." *Production and Inventory Management Journal.* 33(4): 32-36.

Yavitz, B. & Newman, W. H. 1982. *Organizing to execute strategy. Strategy in Action.* 142-161. New York: The Free Press.

10. Top-Managers' Fit With Strategy

Bantel, K. A. & Wiersema, M. F. 1992. "Top management team demography and corporate strategy change." *Academy of Management Journal.* 35: 91-121.

Buhler, P. 1994. "Strategic management: A process for supervisors organization-wide." *Supervision.* 55(3).

Miller, D. 1991. "Stale in the saddle: CEO tenure and the match between organization and environment." *Management Science.* 37: 3-52.

Wiersema, M. F. & Bird, A. 1993. "Organizational demography in Japanese firms: group heterogeneity, individual dissimilarity, and top management team turnover." *Academy of Management Journal.* 36: 996-1025.

CHAPTER 17

The Transferability of Leadership Training in the East Asian Context

R. I. WESTWOOD
ANDREW CHAN

Introduction

Management education, training and development have evolved into crucial elements of organizational strategies to build competitive advantage. In the US, such strategies are manifest in a variety of forms ranging from in-company training to consultant-led facilitation to university-based executive MBA programmes. They share a fundamental belief in the mutability of persons and systems. Managers can be changed through exposure to such activities and can in turn bring about a change in the organization and its members. Programmes purporting to effect such changes also rest on the presupposition that the knowledge and technology exists to bring it about. That is, it is presumed that the skills and competencies that managers need

AUTHORS' NOTE: Reprinted by permission from *Asia Pacific Business Review, Vol. 2, No. 1* published by Frank Cass & Company, 900 Eastern Avenue, Ilford, Essex, England. Copyright Frank Cass & Co. Ltd.

have been correctly identified and the means for inducing them are understood and technically implementable.

Leadership has long been taken as a requisite quality or skill for effective management. It is one of the battery of competencies which senior managers should develop and one deemed capable of being taught and learnt. Indeed, an analysis of training needs of corporate executives in a recent survey of Fortune International 500 companies (Anonymous, 1991) revealed shared assumptions about the core desired skills in a manager's profile. Respondents indicated leadership as the most prevalent in-company training programme topic and the highest ranked in terms of the relative importance to executive education's contribution to the future of their firms (Vicere and Freeman, 1990, p. 10-14). Numerous methodologies have been developed to effect such a process, including many full-blown training packages that have proven eminently marketable. Indeed, "leadership" has become something of an industry (Huey, 1994) especially through the commodification and popularization of leadership models and packages by certain management gurus (Huczynski, 1993).

Such assumptions about the nature of management and leadership and the capacity to effect change through training and education may not be universally shared. The notion that management is a phenomenon which can be theorized, researched, taught and practised in systematic, quasi-scientific ways was initially a peculiarly North American one.[1] However, there have been implicit—and at times explicit—assumptions of universality in North American theory and practice. This, together with American business success and international extension, plus the adoption of English as the international language of business, has led to a massive promulgation of such theory and practice around the world. The theories, concepts, research and practice of North American management have been exported extensively internationally, along with Coca-Cola and blue jeans. This has taken place by diffusion as American business has made its presence felt in overseas locations, and more explicitly through a massive management education and training industry that includes a dominant publishing activity and a whole array of other forms such as consultancy, seminars and conferences, courses, curricula and programmes (Huczynski, 1993; Huey, 1994).

These assumptions of universality have increasingly been questioned. The ready transference and applicability of North American management theory and practice, assumed to be non-problematical in the past, is now seen by many as untenable. In spite of this recognition, the take-up of American management education continues almost unabated. This can be witnessed by the continued success of American management publishing houses, journals, consultancy firms, and academic management institutions on a global scale. American MBAs are still proliferating, and even management educators outside of North America or Europe are more likely than not to possess an MBA or a Ph.D. from North American universities or colleges. This is nowhere more apparent than in parts of East Asia, particularly Southeast Asia.[2]

Leadership continues to be a core component of this exportable corpus. North American beliefs and values with respect to the importance of leadership and the capacity to train people in it have also led to assumptions about the feasibility of cross-national transference. Again East Asia has been a particularly fruitful location for promoting leadership material, especially in those areas with a strong Western influence such as Hong Kong, Singapore and the Philippines. The exposure ranges from assorted theoretical and conceptual accounts, and their attendant research in published media and courses, to specific training packages. Popular packages include those derived from the formulations of Likert (1967); Blake and Mouton's Managerial Grid (1964, 1978, 1985); Hersey and Blanchard's Situational Leadership (1982) and varieties of Path Goal theory (House, 1971). Attempts to introduce the more recent ideology of transformational and/or charismatic leadership (Bass, 1990; Conger and Kanungo, 1988; Tichy and Ulrich, 1984) are also becoming apparent.

North American expatriate managers, often already imbued with their own culturally informed conceptions of leadership, may by design or default, introduce and apply those orientations in their East Asian locations. They may not question the universality of their approaches to leadership and apply them in an untrammeled manner in the new context. Local East Asian managers, themselves increasingly exposed to North American leadership doctrine, may also activate it in their own organizations. This situation is compounded by the fact that some models and training packages expressly assert universality and culture-free applicability (for example Hersey and Blanchard, 1982).

As suggested, there has been some questioning of the plausibility of the successful transference of North American leadership conceptions across cultures (Hofstede, 1980a). There has also been recognition of the need for trainers and consultants to be sensitive to the cultural context in which the delivery of training takes place (see for example Chew, Tseng and Teo, 1990). Some of the difficulties of transferring management training and development into the East Asian context have been outlined (Kirkbride, Tang and Shae, 1989; Kirkbride and Tang, 1992).

These are important reminders, but we want to pose a more radical challenge to the promulgation of North American leadership training and education in East Asia. We question whether the general notion of leadership, as broadly conceived in North America, is an applicable one within the East Asian cultural context. We argue that the very concept of leadership is laden with North American cultural values such as individualism, assertiveness and independence. It reflects a particular ideology in which a tension between espoused democratic and participative principles, and inherent power inequalities is managed.

This article, then, addresses the issue of the transferability of Western leadership theories to the East Asian context. It is pointed out that the view of leadership, and particularly how it is legitimized, enacted and responded to, varies from one context to another. North American leadership models are ineluctably imbued with the value system of that culture. Furthermore, aspects of training facilitation based on North American leadership represents an unwarranted embodiment of the cultural-free assumption. Any such universalistic application in an unquestioning manner, especially in East Asia, may, at best, introduce significant ethnocentric bias and prove to be highly dysfunctional.

A more radical critique is provided by challenging the very concept of leadership itself. As an alternative to leadership, we suggest headship as a more encompassing and contextually meaningful term in East Asia. The notion of headship is explored in an idealized representation in which the "family model" is taken as paradigmatic for organizational forms and relationships in East Asia. Such a model draws upon the familistic and patrimonial traditions prevalent through most of East Asia. It has, as essential elements, two culturally informed requirements for functioning as a head in the East Asian context: the legitimized power of the patriarch together with the cultural requirements for harmony.

By comparing and contrasting the notion of headship with that of leadership, we challenge the universality and applicability of the latter and promote the former as a closer representation of the realities of organizational life in East Asia. The implications of this for providing cultural awareness/sensitization and leadership training for East Asian and expatriate managers in this region are also explored.

On the Culture-Boundedness of the North American Leadership Perspective

North American leadership theories and approaches have been overwhelmingly dominant in the literature. That tradition can be divided into four orientations: trait theories, behavioural or leadership-style theories, contingency/situational theories, and the more recent transformational/charismatic approaches. The fact that these various approaches are sufficiently well known (at least in broad and popularist terms), and not in need of extensive recapitulation here is, in itself, testament to the successful and extensive promulgation of them, as already noted. In the light of the emergence of transformational models it has become common to delineate extant leadership theories by the contrastive device of subsuming pre-transformational approaches under the label of transactional. Since we are making general points about the cultural values underpinning leadership in North America we will adopt that device as a convenience whilst recognizing that the generic label "transactional" is not wholly apposite as a broad rubric for the three, pre-transformational leadership theory perspectives. For the purposes of clarity a brief delineation of the transactional and transformational perspectives is offered.

The transformational perspective was first mooted by Burns (1978) and charismatic leadership by House (1977) but the approach has rapidly drawn wide support and a number of key champions (Bass, 1985; Conger, 1989; Conger and Kanungo, 1989; Shamir, House and Arthur, 1993; Tichy and Devanna, 1986). In essence, transformational leaders use charisma, vision and other non-contingent mechanisms to energize and motivate people to perform over and above their original expectations. They do so by raising employee awareness about certain key outcomes or processes, by getting them to place team or organizational goals and interests above their own, and by having employees adjust their need systems so that they have a stronger drive for responsibility, challenge, and personal growth (see Bass, 1985). Transactional leaders are depicted as relying upon their position power and authority and the provision of contingent rewards and punishments to influence followers. The emphasis has been on leader reinforcement behaviours, exchange relationships and positional influence. In summary, as House, Spangler and Woycke (1991, p. 364) put it, "Traditional leadership theory . . . focuses on leader control over such aspects of the followers' environment as rewards and punishments, job characteristics, authority relations, resources, training, and followers' perceptions of their environments."

Some writers have further suggested a kind of metacontingency view whereby leaders need to be adaptive to organizational change conditions (Beatty and Lee, 1992; Gibbons, 1992; Tushman and Romanelli, 1985). Two broad organizational states are related to the requirements for transactional and transformational leadership. The organizational state of convergence represents a situation in which the organization is seeking to operate in a steady state with clearly established goals and rather stable and predictable environments. Under these conditions the transactional leader functions by maintaining the system and only addressing incremental change within established parameters. The organizational state of divergence represents the situation where the organization needs to more radically address its goals, structuring and basic processes. Most typically such an orientation is generated by more dynamic, uncertain and competitive environmental conditions.

Under these circumstances the transformational leader functions as a challenger of the status quo and as a change agent. They seek to alter the goals, beliefs and behaviours of followers by mobilizing them behind a shared vision of a desirable alternative state for the organization. Thus, both leadership models become tenable depending upon the change conditions in the environment.

The differences in the approaches notwithstanding, each was constructed within the North American context, based on research and the perceived relevancies of the leadership situation therein. It would seem inescapable that they are strongly imbued by the values and sets of relevancies of the people and place in which they were developed. There is, in other words, a likely "culture-boundedness" in these diverse depictions of leadership.

It is suggested, thereby, that certain culturally informed values and assumptions lie behind the various leadership approaches developed in the US, although they are rarely made explicit. There is some difference in the articulation and assumptive base between the transformational approach and those other three captured under the rubric of the transactional approach. We will first explore the assumptive and value base common to the transactional perspective before briefly looking at the commonalities and differences in the transformational approach (the following analysis draws on Durcan and Kirkbride, 1994).

The US is strongly action-oriented and a high value is placed upon the achievement of specifiable performance outcomes. This entails strong achievement and performance values. The value of outcomes is most often judged in utilitarian or even narrowly materialistic terms. A prime requirement for any leader in the US is to demonstrate the capacity to generate such outcomes by extracting ever higher standards of performance from followers. This is the *raison d'être* of leadership. Leadership behaviours, traits and qualities are merely a means to this end, and have little value without this utility. The qualities of the leader and of the leader-led relationships are relatively unimportant and not really at issue in determining leader effectiveness. This strong utilitarian-achievement orientation is masked by a rhetoric of member satisfaction and morale in most models. However, we take the view that these are secondary goals relative to the primacy of performance and are really only part of the means to that end. Followers are "potential productives" and the job of the leader is to marshall that potential to achieve pragmatic outcomes.

This is the essence of the "transaction." Leadership is an exchange in which the leader provides appropriate behaviours and rewards, and the followers provide productive performance. There is little expected from the relationship other than that and no additional quality requirement is necessary.

North America has developed a strong ideology of equality and democracy. The resulting value base entails the second core assumption of leadership. The compliance of followers cannot be derived simply from the sheer exercise of the power and authority invested in the role and position of the leader. This would be too authoritarian and go against the egalitarian values of the culture. Entailed is a critical tension within US culture: a confrontation between equalitarian and democratic ideals with the realities of organizational power differences and hierarchy. The tension is apparent in the rather odd separation of the treatment of power and leadership in US management/organization theory. It seems that the raw exercise of power and frank confrontation of power distances is culturally unpalatable.

The Weberian legacy is of relevance here. That project sought to elide organizational power by displacing it with a rational, impersonal authority structure. Such a legal-rational system is the prime mechanism for organizational governance and power is a messy intrusion into that ordering. Leadership is something other than the exercise of authority and power. Followership needs to be based upon something else—on appropriate leadership qualities and behaviours. Furthermore, the ideology of leadership, eschewing the exercise of sheer power, assumes that the effective realization of follower performance can only really be effectively achieved via their voluntary consent and commitment. This cannot be attained through power and authority and thus it is incumbent upon leaders to furnish appropriate types of behaviour to elicit it.

A third value set forming the assumptive base of the conception of leadership in the US revolves around conceptions of human nature. US values strongly promote free-will doctrines and are broadly anti-determinist. The value set also gives people potent agency and asserts that they are capable of affecting and shaping events and outcomes. On Kluckhohn and Strodtbeck's (1961) classic formulation of dimensions of cultural variance, US cultural values resonate with the idea that people are inherently a mix of good and evil. A concomitant of such values is the belief that people are mutable and can change through learning.

It follows that education and training are seen as viable means for effecting change in people, including leadership behaviour. It also entails that followers can be affected by leaders, their productive potential activated, and that they can be made more "mature." But followers too are free-agents and their actions cannot be wholly determined by outside interventions. The ultimate assumption in US conceptions of leadership is the development of fully mature, autonomous individuals who will function effectively and appropriately without the need for external direction. In this sense, the logical extension of US conceptions of leadership is its self-effacement.

The latter relates to the final assumptive base, that of extreme individualism. In most models it is the individual qualities and behaviours of the leader and the one-to-one relationship between individual leaders and individual followers that is of paramount importance. Where contextual factors are taken into account (most notably in situational models) they are done so by the leader as necessary considerations in effectively aligning his/her style and behaviour. In addition, leaders are urged to recognize the unique individuality of their followers and seek ways of accommodating to that in the exercise of their leadership. Leader-group relationships are very much secondary to these sets of leader-led ones. This is necessary in the light of the individualistic values of US culture (Hofstede, 1980b).

Hofstede (1980a and 1980b) has been an acute critic of the culture-boundedness of US theories and practices and his work can usefully be employed to further explicate the value base of US leadership conceptions. The reported high individualism of the US supports the emphasis on the qualities of the individual leader and the salience of the one-to-one, leader-follower relationship. It also fosters the calculative engagement central to the transactional models in which individuals are presumed to rationally pursue their self-interests. This denigrates a more collectivist orientation in which the interests of the group and the quality of leader-group relationship are paramount. The low power distance orientation underpins the equalitarian/democratic values and supports the view that a naked exercise of power and authority is anathema to the conceptualization of effective leadership. It also supports the leadership rhetoric of inclusion, participation and empowerment. Hofstede also reports a weakish uncertainty avoidance value for the US. This further supports the latter inclinations by facilitating a low level relationship structuring which allows individuals (as followers) more autonomy and discretion. Finally, US culture is moderately "masculine." This would engender a strong performance and achievement orientation. Leaders under such a value system are judged in terms of their capacity to achieve high performance and materially-valued outcomes. Less instrumental and non-material outcomes, such as the quality of the relationships, are at the same time devalued.

Some of this assumptive value base would also apply to transformational models, but there are points of difference. Commonality lies in the retained presumption that the prime rationale for leadership is the instrumental one of delivering materially beneficial performance outcomes. The onus is still on the individual leader, but now the prerequisite for performance enhancement is the presence of more nebulous charismatic characteristics and the capacity to realign followers' needs and motives behind the leader's vision. Raw power is still deemed as inappropriate and ineffective, indeed, more so than under transactional models, and there is an even stronger rhetoric of empowerment and autonomy. The key assumptive difference lies in the eschewal of a calculative form of engagement and the demand for the sublimation of individual interest to a more collective one. There is also somewhat more of a group orientation with the quality of leader-group relations taking on greater significance. The approach depends, however, upon some other salient US values such as a belief in the openness and authenticity of communicative relationships.

Headship or Leadership?

The above discussion indicates the cultural-boundedness of US leadership theories and models. We have argued that they rest upon an assumptive base rooted in the values of individualism, equalitarianism, achievement, performance and instrumental materialism, as well as specific conceptions about the nature of power, structures and relationships. This value and ideological framework is far from universal. Differences in other cultural/national contexts may severely circumscribe the transferability and applicability of the US view of leadership and raise questions about the meaningfulness and value of its leadership education and training; both for US nationals doing business in those contexts and for locals exposed to such models. This may be particularly so in East Asian countries which are characterized as collectivist, high power distance cultures and display other significant value differences. Alternative values lead the issues of power, authority and leadership to be cast in a different light: both by those in a superior position and in a subordinate one.

The critique of the transferability of US conceptions of leadership also applies to some other "Western" cultures and a monolithic "Western" view of leadership is untenable. Hofstede (1980b) pointed out, for example, that the French have less concern with American-style participative management than about who has power. In other words, a leader has assumed a position which already has a *de facto* strong justification and legitimization for leadership. The capacity to gain compliance is assured by the occupancy of that position and his/her leadership qualities are unlikely to be "questioned."

We contend that a similar process operates in East Asian organizations. People show deference to the person who comes to occupy a superior status and authority position. Once that occupancy is achieved and taken as legitimate, there will be an assumed right to exercise power vis-à-vis subordinates. The position-holder's *qualities* as leader do not determine that right.

Furthermore, it has been noted that "leadership" is a fairly modern concept, only coming to prominence in Anglo-Saxon influenced countries since the 19th century (Bass and Stogdill, 1990). Prior to that—and, we would contend, still in other countries (especially East Asian)—the notion of "headship" was more prominent. Traditional forms of headship included monarchic or dynastic "heads," heads of state, clans or kinship groups, and chiefs. The power form, relationship structuring and values that accompany the notion of "headship" are still apparent in many locations. Under various forms of headship, the concern is less with the personality traits of the individual leader than with the legitimacy of the position and the status of the person in it. It appears that leadership, qua leadership, is a distinctly Western, primarily North American, conception, further fueling doubts about its culturally biased nature and transferability directly to other cultures.

As we have seen, the North American conception of leadership is concerned with the individual personality or behaviour of the leader-manager, largely in terms of what the leader needs to do or have in order to get compliance from subordinates and to accept, cooperate, and follow their lead. This implies that leadership is related to individual qualities and behaviours that are underpinned by certain cultural assumptions and values. Leadership is contingent upon the group members' spontaneous recognition of the individual's (leader's) contribution to group process and success.

However, headship has been described as being imposed on followers whereby the person who is head has "achieved" that status through some means outside of the leader-led relationship (for example, inheritance) (Holloman, 1986). According to Gibb (1969), the head's authority derives from some extra-group power which the person has over the members of the group, and as such they cannot meaningfully be called followers. That individual has a perceived right to "head" the group and determine its goals and objectives. There is no requirement for consensual agreement and often there is little sense of mutual interests or shared feelings in the pursuit of the given goals. Another distinctive feature, as Gibb (1969) points out, is the wide social gap between group members and the head, who "strives to maintain this social distance as an aid in the coercion of the group."

Superior-subordinate relationships in many organizational contexts in East Asia have a closer congruence with this description of headship than US notions of leadership style and behaviour. Many of East Asia's entrepreneurial owner-managers, in particular, function under regimes akin to the notion of headship as so far outlined. This has been documented, for example, in a participant-observation study of large-scale owner-managed enterprises in Taiwan (Silin, 1976), and in empirical studies of Korean companies established by self-made founders (see, for example, Yoo and Lee, 1987, p. 102). In Taiwan and Hong Kong, for example, an ethnic Chinese businessman's headship of an enterprise will be accepted and his rights as owner/founder will not be challenged. In the traditions of Malaysia, a person who is born into a "headship" position is expected to display leadership as a concomitant of that background and position occupancy. This is a reversal of the US regime whereby people who are seen to display leadership qualities are then elevated into positions of leadership.

Almost paradoxically, the US-based leadership literature invariably defines leadership in terms of the achievement of compliance (from subordinates) and the mechanisms of influence (present in definitions ranging from Moore's 1927 definition, Bass and Stogdill's 1990 version)—but this inherent basis in power relations is unattended to in subsequent elaborations of leadership theory. However, in East Asia, the clear and legitimized role of the "head" entails a natural and ready compliance, and the power dimension remains upfront and acknowledged.

Whilst this conception of "headship," derived as it is from Western sources, does not adequately describe and delineate the situation in East Asia, it more closely reflects the reality of that milieu than typical North American notions of leadership. We adopt it as a generating heuristic to drive an elaboration of an alternative East Asian model of headship/leadership in what follows. In so doing we construct an idealized model which extrapolates the values and assumptive base relating to the structures and processes of power, authority and leadership in East Asia to a plausible and coherent model. We also recognize that the familistic enterprise model is being taken as a paradigmatic case for other forms of organization and organizational relationships.

■ An East Asian Perspective on Headship/Leadership

A cautionary and explanatory note is required at this point. As we have already indicated, labels such as "East Asia" are not entirely satisfactory and we are using it only as a necessary and convenient device. We certainly do not intend to imply that East Asia is a culturally homogenous region and there are not likely to be differences in the approach to leadership within that geopolitical region. However, the idealized model we present below is held to derive from certain key socio-cultural values and social structures which have some commonality across much of East Asia. The strongest affinity is for those Chinese communities where Confucianism has had the strongest impact—particularly Hong Kong, Taiwan and Singapore—as well as South Korea. Both because of the presence of strong Chinese business communities and because of general cultural similarities, we also feel the model has some generalizability to other Southeast Asian countries such as Malaysia, Indonesia, Thailand, and to a lesser extent the Philippines.

However, we are explicitly excluding Japan for a number of reasons. Firstly, although it shares some cultural roots with other parts of East Asia (through Confucianism for example), it has other cultural elements that delineate it and mark it out as distinctive. Secondly, the features of Japanese management have already been more than adequately documented in the literature. Thirdly, and partly as a result of the cultural distinctiveness, Japanese industrial organization has developed in a very different manner from that of other economies in the region: most notably in the form of the large corporations that prevail there and the intimate and intricate inter-organizational relationships between these corporations and the banking institutions and government. The "family business" model (Redding, 1990; Wong, 1989), which has long historical traditions and remains a prevalent form among ASEAN countries as well as in Taiwan and Hong Kong (Putti, 1991), is no longer such a dominant feature in Japan's industrial organization. Given its pre-eminence in this region, we suggest that the family business phenomenon be taken as the "ideal" form for other organizational relationships—and it serves here as a framework for explicating an alternative leadership model for East Asia. It is in these forms of organization that the notion of "headship" has its clearest place and it is within that context, primarily, that we construct our idealized model of the leadership situation for East Asia. Figure 17.1 shows the basic model.

The model is constructed with three core components. It suggests that in any leadership/headship situation in East Asia there are dual elemental requirements. The first requirement is for the achievement of legitimized order and compliance. Headship/leadership requires that there is something which orders and structures the relationship between leader and followers. There must also be some legitimized basis upon which the head is able to assume that position and expect and achieve compliance from followers. This requirement can be held to be present in all leadership situations and is not unique to the East Asian context. The second requirement is for social harmony. This is deeply embedded in the cultural traditions of East Asia where there are widespread values associated with the notion of harmony—at the intrapersonal, interpersonal, group, societal and transcendent levels.

In general terms, the various ways by which these twin requirements are met in the East Asian context gives rise to a structured pattern of leadership/headship relations and behaviours that is distinctive vis-à-vis US models. This pattern has been most often referred to (in the Western literature) as paternalism—although the Western connotations around that term are misleading. "Paternalism" incorporates a number of significant facets such as personalism, moral leadership, harmony building, conflict diffusion and didactic leadership. These facets, and a range of associated strategies and tactics of "paternalistic headship/leadership," collectively represent the third component of the model.

FIGURE 17.1. A Model for East Asian Paternalistic Headship

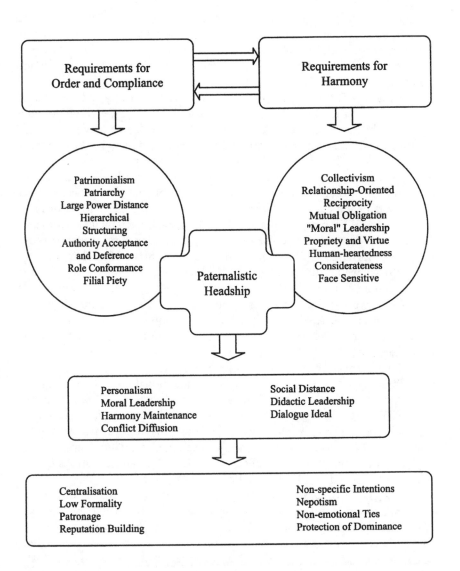

Meeting Requirements for Order and Compliance: Hierarchy, Patriarchy and Legitimized Power

The Oriental form of domination is characterized by patrimonialism (Weber, 1951) in which seemingly absolute power is vested in the patriarch, or family head. Such a power relationship is legitimized and accepted by others. The patriarch, however, is obligated to function as a protector and maintainer of the family and its interests. In return the patriarch can expect, and normally receives, respect, deference, obedience, loyalty and compliance from the rest of the family. A head need not actively seek this compliance; it is built into the nature of the relationship. East Asian cultures are characterized by high power distance and status hierarchies (Hofstede, 1980a; Redding and Wong, 1986), and there are strong social and cultural pressures to conform and comply. Conformance to the role associated with one's rank is seen as natural and morally correct. The cultural value of filial piety plays a key role in this and becomes a model for proper attitudes and behaviours in many relationships. Filial piety is based on the Confucian ethic which provides a set of social rules instructing people to abide by the duties of their assigned role. People are socialized to be conforming and deferential. Such characteristics tend to be viewed rather negatively in the West, where children are taught to be independent, questioning, and individualistic. In East Asia, however, they are part of the natural and necessary orientation for the maintenance of a complex and intricate social system whereby unequal distributions of power are seen as natural and proper, and there is a tendency to accept and not challenge authority.

These aspects of authority and hierarchy tend to extend beyond the natural family and are transferred into organizational contexts too. Such a high "power distance culture," according to Hofstede (1980a), implies a "hierarchical structuring" and an acceptance of authority in organizations within these cultures. A manifestation of this "hierarchical structuring" of interpersonal relations can be found, for example, in relationships between superior and subordinate as a reflection of the values and traditions of Chinese society (Bond and Hwang, 1986).

The extension of these kinds of structures and relationship into organizational contexts is especially apparent in those family-owned and managed enterprises prevalent in East Asia. The head of the organization assumes a role and position, and is able to function, in a manner analogous to the head of the family, with similar power and authority. Subordinates accept the "patriarchal right" and will be deferential and compliant to it. There is a natural acceptance of hierarchy and an inbuilt legitimacy for the superior-subordinate relationship (Redding, 1990, p. 7). Such naturally occurring deference, compliance, and dutiful fulfillment of role enables the East Asian manager to assume a headship role. He has less need of the leadership behaviours and characteristics seen as necessary to achieve compliance in the West. This is not confined to the Chinese case. Thompson (1989) suggests that Thais also accept an "authoritarian" style, deferring to authority and not challenging a manager's prerogative. However, this is not viewed as despotic or coerced but as the natural way of things. For the Philippines, Andres (1985) points out that firm family structures and the authority of the father-figure extend into the organization. In Indonesia, subordinates honour those of higher status in the organization because they are seen as occupying a father-like role (Widyahartono, 1991).

Thus, the cultural values and traditions within East Asia provide a legitimized set of structural arrangements and ways of behaving that enable the social construction of an environment in which the head can achieve the order and compliance necessary for the exercise of headship. But that, as the model indicates, is only half the story. Such an analysis may give the impression that the head has absolute power and a free hand to operate in a self-interestedly authoritarian and autocratic manner. This would be a very incomplete and misguided picture. The exercise of power by the head is not without its constraints nor is it unconditional. The apparent authoritarian "carte blanche" of the East Asian head is circumscribed and mediated by the second requirement in the model: the requirement for social harmony. The head must strive for and sustain harmony in the group and respond to the social pressures for considerate and proper behaviour. This is a subtle mixture, and significantly different from the conceptualization of the exercise of power/authority and leadership depicted in the US.

Meeting Requirements for Social Harmony: Reciprocity, Virtue and Human Heartedness

The rights of patriarchy and the apparent absolutism of the power invested in the role are, on their own, culturally inadequate to sustain a headship position effectively. The head must also fulfill an obligation to create and sustain social harmony. There are strong cultural pressures for harmonious relations between leader/led and in all relationships within the group. The two notions of deference to strong and clear authority and sustenance harmony are not at odds but in fact complement each other. The hierarchy and authority structures actually require a harmonious system to maintain them. From the other side of the coin, sticking to a proper role, and accepting the hierarchy and authority, helps to maintain harmony.

The roots of social harmony are again deep in the cultures of the region. East Asian cultures are collectivist and relationship-oriented (Bond and Hwang, 1986; Hofstede 1980a; Hui, 1992). China, the Chinese diaspora—in Taiwan, Hong Kong, Singapore, and around other parts of East Asia—and South Korea are influenced by Confucianism which stresses harmony as a core personal and social value. Thailand is influenced by Buddhism which also promotes a cultural value of harmony. In the Philippines and Indonesia, traditional values also lead to a strong relationship orientation and pressure to keep smooth and harmonious relations.

Thus, on the one hand, strong values and traditions legitimize patriarchy and the exercise of strong patriarchal power—and this is taken as legitimate, natural and proper by those within the system. But at the same time there is a strong set of cultural and social pressures that circumscribes and moderates the behaviour of the head and the manner in which that power is exercised.

Relationships may be unequal and hierarchical, but they are also reciprocal and contain mutual obligations. The head of a family may have strong patriarchal rights, but that power should be exercised for the benefit of the family and not for individual self interest. Properly, the family head should take care of, protect, nurture and expand the interests of the rest of the family. In the same vein, although heads of businesses expect loyalty and obedience from their staff, they must also reciprocate by taking care of and protecting the well-being of their employees. The rights of the patriarchal head are mediated by these responsibilities and obligations.

Heads must also exhibit a kind of "moral leadership" and function as an exemplar for others. This requirement stands in place of the Western legal-rational approach to ordering organizational relationships. In the East Asian context, improper behaviour on the part of leaders may be seen as an abuse of power and this may threaten their legitimacy in that position. This does not imply necessarily some high moral principledness, but rather the perceived conformance to widely held norms of proper behaviour and adherence to social etiquette.

General social and subordinate expectations, derived from shared cultural values, impinge upon the head and instill a set of behaviours and orientations that is deemed to be most desirable in promulgating harmonious leader-led relationships, and they constitute the profile of a successful and effective leader/head. This includes the rules of reciprocity and mutual obligation and moral leadership already noted. In addition, heads are expected to display human heartedness, considerateness, propriety, interpersonal sensitivity and respect for "face."

The concept of "human heartedness" is an essential element in East Asian headship. It is argued that the head's right to lead rests on this moral capacity. According to Confucian precept, a leader should be a morally superior person, striving for the ideals of "civilized" behaviour and conforming to the key virtues. In addition, the concept of "self" in East Asian philosophy tends to be highly relational, so that, simply put, one's personhood is a reflection of the sets of relationships in which one is embedded. In this light, one can only really be considered properly a person if one is able to take full account of the others with whom you are in a relation. This means that one's actions must be considered in terms of the effects upon oneself were the other person to be behaving towards you in the same manner. Such "human-heartedness" is considered to be the only true mark of the moral man (Silin, 1976, p. 35-36).

Considerateness and compliance with the rules of propriety are admired, respected, and expected from a leader/head. The rules of propriety are informal social rules for the guidance of behaviour. In the Chinese case they are again derived from Confucian traditions. People who display such behaviour will have their leadership positively responded to and receive legitimization. As indicated, the legitimacy reflexively allows for the acceptance of power differences, patriarchal authority and the achievement of compliance.

Another value and relationship mechanism—"face"—also guides the nature of the superior-subordinate relationship. This social code is most often discussed in the Chinese case, but variants are found in many parts of East Asia. "Face" must be maintained, protected and given in order to sustain social harmony. This is incumbent on all parties in a relationship—including relationships of power difference. The head must be sensitive to and not damage the face of others. In Malaysia, for example, the highest social value is the ability to get on with others. Individuals who are courteous, modest, sensitive to and respectful of others are considered as *halus* persons: one who displays proper Malay values. A leader should be a *halus* person and show those properties. Again, there is a reciprocal relationship. A Malay leader may be able to exercise authoritarian leadership provided the loyalty and deference of the subordinate is reciprocated with proper concern and respect.

In summary, the values of mutual obligation, human heartedness, considerateness, propriety and face are enabling conditions leading to the achievement of the requirement for harmony and this, together with the legitimized power of the patriarch, constitutes the dual conditions for headship. These are all transferable into the organization and leadership context. They create a common pattern throughout East Asia, and an alternative (to the US) model of leadership emerges from the structures, roles and social enactments embodied in these elements and their patterns.

Paternalism

We have explored the cultural ground upon which an alternative East Asian leadership approach is built in the preceding section and now turn to fleshing out some of the ways in which the style manifests itself in behavioural terms.

As already made clear, essentially this style reflects discipline, clear and strong authority, but is distinguishable from sheer autocratic leadership because of the requirements for benevolence, mutual obligation, responsibility to others, and moral leadership. It is most frequently referred to as a paternalistic style, or—using Western theoretical language—a benevolent autocratic style. These labels are inadequate since they represent a Western worldview with particular value and meaning connotations. Our intention is to avoid transducing the East Asian experience to Western leadership constructs since this runs the risk of doing violence to the reality and complexity of the East Asian form. We reiterate that although emphasis and illustration are being drawn from the Chinese case for the most part, it is suggested that the approach is not confined in that way, but is broadly generalizable throughout East Asia. Compelling and broadly similar depictions of a "paternalistic" style have been documented in Korea (Cho, 1991; Shin, 1984; Yoo and Lee, 1987), the Philippines (Andres, 1985), Singapore (Chong, 1987), Taiwan (Chen, 1991; Silin, 1976), Hong Kong (Kirkbride and Westwood, 1993; Redding, 1990; Redding and Wong, 1986), Thailand (Komin, 1990; Thompson, 1989), and Indonesia (Widyahartono, 1991).

In most East Asian cultures leaders are ideally expected to behave in ways that reflect the requirements set on both sides of the presented model. They are assumed to have clear and strong rights to determine goals and means, to exercise authority, and to expect loyalty, deference and obedience. But, they are also expected to be nurturing, benevolent, kind, sympathetic figures who inspire commitment and dedication. The US concept of the leader as being a commanding executive who is firm in decision-making, rational, impersonal and value neutral is less appreciated in Asia (Pye, 1985, p. 28).

The East Asian alternative rests on a shared assumption that those in headship positions do not solely use it to pursue their self-interests but have an obligation to take care of those over whom they have authority. This may be an ideal, but it is one with a lot of cultural force and sanction. A paternalistic style is further characterized by, in part, the following:

- A reliance upon and sensitivity towards *personalism*. In the Western bureaucratic tradition, organizational order, rule and authority are pursued on the basis of impersonalism. A logical, abstract rule system governs the relationship between formal positions. Relationships between persons are not at issue. In the East Asian context there is little reliance upon such legalistic or jurisdictive mechanisms. Personal relationships are *critical* and order is maintained through the subtleties of personalized systems of mutual obligation and reciprocity and informal rules of social behaviour within established status hierarchies. Loyalties are to the person not the institution and people will be subjectively assessed on personal grounds. Decision making and action are guided by personal criteria and relationship considerations cannot be separated from the person who produces them, and they need to be presented subjectively and personally—not distantly and abstractly.

- An endeavour by leaders/heads to exhibit *moral leadership,* observe the proprieties, and be seen to possess valued virtues such as human heartedness, integrity, compassion and humility. Their legitimacy rests upon a perception of these attributes and it is that which bolsters the head's position rather than an overt reliance upon formal structure and official sanction. The head, in this manner, also serves as a moral exemplar for organization members.

- An assurance and sustenance of an environment of *harmony*.

- A preparedness by the head to work to ensure *conflicts* do not erupt and to move in to diffuse any potential conflict situation. East Asian cultures are often depicted as conflict-avoiding. Certainly, open conflict between members is considered as a threat to harmoniousness. Within the East Asian system numerous mechanisms exist for preventing open conflict from surfacing which the head must be able to invoke. This contrasts with the US where conflict is viewed more positively and mechanisms have been developed for resolving emerged conflict.

- A general disposition of maintaining astute *aloofness and social distance* from subordinates. This reflects the father-like role and the firm hierarchical structuring of relationships. The heads are not amenable to challenge or input from the subordinates on their deliberations or decisions, and subordinates would not presume to interfere. "Superiors must convey an impression of aloofness . . . the boss is preferably a person of considerable stature, and reserved, taciturn deportment" (Silin, 1976, p. 66). This does not imply a dictatorial or unfriendly relationship.

- The use of *didactic leadership*—a term coined by Silin (1976) to apply to the Chinese case, but, again, extendable to other East Asian contexts. The notion appears to have a twofold meaning. On the one hand it denotes the head as teacher—meaning that the head functions as a (moral) model or exemplar for others. On the other hand it depicts a power tactic in which the head uses information, knowledge and expertise selectively and strategically. Much of the knowledge, expertise and information pertaining to the business naturally resides in the head. Playing the role of "master" in this regard, the head will selectively and strategically share and disperse knowledge and information to chosen subordinates. No individual member is given full access and this obviously serves to strengthen the power position of the head.

■ The head is expected to pursue what Thompson (1989) has termed the "dialogue ideal." The head cannot be seen merely as an uncaring autocrat, despite the legitimization of a strong power position, but must display care and concern for the subordinates. Heads must be seen to be sensitive to members' feelings and give recognition to their human dignity and "face." A somewhat ritualistic dialogue between head and member is sustained so that the head can remain aware of the sentiments and views of members and be in a position to show his concern and human heartedness. This is not a form of consultation since the substance of the dialogue is not concerned with work-related decisions and actions. The dialogue ideal also allows subordinates to get close enough to the head to be able to intuit his intentions and expectations. These are rarely made explicit, but it is taken as a mark of good followership to be able to intuit them and respond accordingly.

Leadership Strategies and Tactics

The broad features of a paternalistic style of headship in the East Asian context mapped out briefly above are typically complemented by a set of more specific behavioural strategies and tactics. These include the following:

■ It is not deemed appropriate for a head to share information and decisions relating to the general condition of the organization, its directions and strategies. The criteria, rules and methods by which decisions are made will not be available for scrutiny by other members (Bond, 1991, p. 85). Thus, a high level of centralization of decision making will characterize a paternalistic style (Pugh and Redding, 1985; Redding, 1990; Redding and Pugh, 1986).

■ A head relies on intuition and business acumen to determine strategic direction and to formulate loose, non-specific plans, which are also not explicitly revealed to others. By so doing, the head keeps options open and retains pragmatic flexibility by not being tied to a publicly declared line of action. This facet of the style also contributes to the maintenance of the power position of the head and entails that subordinates need to correctly intuit the head's non-specific intentions so as to demonstrate loyalty and good followership (Silin, 1976; Redding and Wong, 1986).

- There will be a lower level of formality in key areas of business functioning (with the exception of basic front line operating procedures) (Redding and Pugh, 1986; Redding, 1990). Heads rely upon personalism and reciprocity rather than formal rule. Formality is undesirable since it weakens centralization, makes things explicit, reduces the head's hold on knowledge and information, and limits flexibility.

- Unlike in the US, where *nepotism* is seen as inappropriate, in the collectivist cultures of East Asia, heads in business enterprises develop a trusted coterie and exercise better control by placing family and/or kinship members in key company positions.

- To put a subordinate in a bond of indebtedness and gratitude to the head, heads use their position to act like a father-like patron. Systems of *patronage* entail the use of personal power and resources at the head's disposal to do favours and provide things for others, thus locking them into a bond of gratitude and indebtedness.

- Heads seek to protect their dignity, mystery, and authority by maintaining a social distance with respect to their followers. This helps *prevent emotional ties* developing which may bring with them greater obligations for the head.

- *Reputation* in external relations is very important, and effort in building up good relationships and promoting reputation is a necessary part of the headship role. To fulfill this, the head needs to both be seen as successful in making correct business decisions and as possessing virtuous qualities and behaving with propriety and integrity.

- The personalism and the relative lack of a formal system means that heads need and have the opportunity to engage in a range of political tactics aimed at further sustaining their *position of dominance*. Didactic leadership and the strategic control and use of information and knowledge is one example. Centralization and lack of formality make it difficult for members to take the initiative, demonstrate their capability or mount a challenge to what the head is doing. The head also plays down or diminishes their contributions so that the part played by individuals is not experienced or seen as significant. The lack of specificity over roles, duties and responsibilities also weakens the position of subordinates and engenders dependency on the head, as does the personalistic and subjective evaluation of subordinates' performance. The head makes clear that alternative or challenging views and opinions are not welcome. Subordinates are obliged to correctly intuit what the head expects from them and failure to do so will be taken as a mark of disloyalty and poor followership. All this makes for a politicized environment in which the head engages in "divide and rule" and other disempowering tactics that serve to bolster his own power position. The style often gives rise to a good deal of politicking among members as they manoeuvre to get close to the head.

Implications for Leadership Training and Development in East Asia

Given the arguments advanced through this alternative perspective on headship in the East Asian context, there are some important implications for the conduct of leadership training for both expatriate and local managers in this region.

In general terms, the arguments mounted here pose a serious challenge to the veracity, portability and utility of leadership education and training based upon the US models for the East Asian region. Whilst it is true that the management systems of East Asia are in a very dynamic state and are increasingly exposed to US management theory, practice and education, more deep-seated and traditional values persist and impinge on matters such as leadership. An uncritical take-up of US-derived models and training packages on leadership is highly problematic and may not only be ineffective but could prove very dysfunctional in the long term.

All leadership/headship situations involve influencing subordinates/followers to comply with certain attitudinal and behavioural requirements in the pursuit of specifiable outcomes and goals. What those goals/outcomes are, who determines them and, most importantly, the warrant for the achievement and expectation of compliance are at issue. We contend that there are important differences across cultures that put the whole issue of leadership on a different footing.

In the East Asian context, the drive for performance enhancement of subordinates solely in order to achieve materially valuable outcomes does not have the same acuity as it does in the US, particularly when such a drive is at the expense of the quality of the relationship between the leader and the led. The East Asian leader expects followers to dutifully fulfill the requirements of their role positions and to accept and conform to the wishes of the leader. There is no necessary expectation that the leader seeks to enhance the performance of the subordinate beyond this. Indications of dutifulness, loyalty and obedience are more valued than initiative and performance improvement.

Under the US value system, leaders have the capacity to lead conferred upon them by their groups and this is contingent upon the expectation and maintenance of behaviours that a group feels are conducive to the accomplishment of desired outcomes. Compliance to the will of the leader is supposed to be voluntarily based on this assessment and cannot be achieved by the mere exercise of power and authority. In the East Asian case, subordinates expect individuals who have attained a leadership/headship position to exercise their authority as they will. The occupancy of that position is attained through mechanisms outside of the leader-led relationship and is often more ascribed than achieved. The sheer authority and power of the patriarchal head is more palatable, readily accepted and legitimized, and will be deferred to and complied with.

However, the East Asian head cannot sustain the power legitimacy if it is exercised in an untrammeled, self-interested, and socially and interpersonally insensitive manner. The emphasis on the quality of relationship and the requirement for harmony means that the East Asian head needs to reciprocate the ready compliance and deference of subordinates with displays of concern, consideration and human heartedness. The head must be a moral exemplar and exhibit qualities of propriety and virtue. The *manner* in which authority and power are exercised and the *quality* of the relationships created and sustained are of high significance. These elements sustain the harmony that is so essential to the maintenance of the whole system. These are not requirements confronting the US leader. Leaders/managers imbued with the US-based ethos (including Asians) who are not sensitive to these cultural imperatives will find it extremely difficult to function effectively.

US-based models also work on the value of a voluntaristic consent and commitment to the leader and the direction the leader constructs, by followers. Indeed, the rhetoric is towards autonomous, mature individuality. This is taken furthest in the transformational models' aspirations for empowerment. These values are antithetical to the East Asian scene. As should be clear from our presentation of the model, power distances are larger in the East Asian context and there are low expectations on the part of subordinates to engage with the head's decision-making activity. The notion of empowerment would be particularly anathema within the value system for headship articulated here. Again, US-influenced leaders would encounter severe difficulties if they adopt a leadership orientation that involves large measures of participativeness and empowerment.

As a consequence of these issues we urge that, as a minimum, due recognition be given to the differences cross-culturally in the conceptualization and enactment of leadership. Heads of training and development units particularly, should be sensitized to the culture-boundedness of US models and attuned to the traditions and expectations of the leadership situation in other cultures. The prescriptions given in current US-based leadership training programmes, packages and materials warrant critical evaluation to check their congruence with those conceptualizations and enactments that are culturally favoured and common in the East Asian context. This would apply to both local personnel and the trainers and developers of foreign companies responsible for overseas assignments.

Foreign companies who relocate staff to East Asia to occupy "leadership" positions should not assume the universality of the leadership models they more habitually have recourse to in their own environment. An effort should be made to alert relocating managers that their normal leadership style and preferences may not be fully effective in the new environment and to ensure that they are aware of and begin to develop a style more attuned to that cultural setting.

This can be facilitated, in the first instance, through cultural awareness/sensitivity training and then on to some more specific East Asian leadership awareness input and style development. Attention should be paid to proper selection and preassignment training as this is a key determinant of success for an overseas expatriation (Harris and Moran 1987; Phatak 1989). It is recommended that training be given before a manager sets off to a new overseas deployment. A "cosmopolitan" manager, according to Torrington (1994), should be sensitive to cultural differences, be able to appreciate a people's distinctiveness, and be prepared to make concessions and accommodation for such factors when working with and supervising foreign subordinates. Preassignment training should ideally prompt the managers to seek out ways to avoid ethnocentrism egocentrically imposing one's own cultural beliefs and values—including those that bear upon the leadership situation—upon staff and colleagues. The ready transferability of the expatriate manager's normal leadership orientation cannot be assumed.

Organizations contemplating leadership training in East Asia could make their training needs analysis more fundamental. A deeper and more systematic assessment of the values, preferences and expectations of both leaders and followers in the organization with respect to the leadership role should be undertaken. This would help to clarify the localized and prevailing conceptualization of leadership and facilitate the development of programmes more in tune with local conditions and values.

A more challenging solution would be to fully develop effective accounts and theories of leadership from an indigenously East Asian perspective and then to freshly develop training programmes and pedagogy from that base. More research on leadership in the East Asian context would be a prerequisite for that. A first step might be the development of case studies of effective headship/leadership. This would have the additional advantage of providing examples and models of successful practice outside of the US leadership orthodoxy and would help to legitimize and give credence to an East Asian alternative.

Conclusion

The main concern of this article has been to consider a distinctively East Asian approach to leadership. A critique of US-based approaches points to their cultural-boundedness and the universality and portability of them challenged. We show that US approaches to leadership represent a particular, and quite recent, view of "leadership," and one that reflects US cultural values, especially those of individualism, independence, voluntarism and participative involvement. The notion of "leadership" was contrasted with that of "headship," and it was felt the latter was a more meaningful term in the East Asian situation.

We contend, in the East Asian case, there are two basic requirements in any leader/headship situation: a legitimized warrant for securing order and compliance and the maintenance of social harmony. These two requirements structure a new ordering in management style—a "paternalistic headship." The model for headship/leadership is the patriarch, possessing strong and clear power but with a genuine and expected obligation to take care of subordinates. This style embodies the display of "proper" behaviour, mutual obligations, human heartedness, consideration and sensitivity to the "face" and dignity of the subordinates. To effect those ideals, a number of significant but practical facets of the style are elaborated.

Lastly, we point out that cross-cultural awareness training presents the local and expatriate managers, and their organizations, with new imperatives. Actions need to be taken to evaluate and to reconsider the appropriateness of ready-made leadership training packages available to expatriate managers as part of their pre-assignment training as well as to local managers as part of their exposure to contemporary management techniques. The alternative position outlined has opened up a seam which needs further research and elaboration and this article is offered as a first step in that direction.

▪ Notes

1. Here, we face the problem of geopolitical labels. We recognize that North America is a vague term and does not correspond to a homogenous culture; however, there is some validity in proposing a view of leadership that is shared across the North American continent. We will at times refer to the United States specifically where we feel that the clearer delineation is warranted.

2. Again, East Asia is not easily defined and certainly cannot be considered as a homogenous cultural region. However, we contend that the approach to leadership and the values and behaviours that accompany it has some commonality in much of East Asia. The greatest commonality exists in those societies influenced by Confucianism (except Japan) and other parts of Southeast Asia. Indeed, we would be comfortable with the notation "Southeast Asia" were it not for the need to include South Korea under the approach to leadership outlined in this article.

References

T.D. Andres, *Management by Filipino Values* (Quezon City: New Day Publishers, 1985).

Anonymous, "Trends in Leadership Training," *Leadership and Organisation Development Journal,* Vol. 12, No. 4 (1991), pp. vi-vii.

B.M. Bass, "From Transactional to Transformational Leadership: Learning to Share The Vision." *Organisational Dynamics,* Vol. 18, No. 3 (1990), pp. 19-31.

B.M. Bass and R.M. Stogdill, *Bass and Stogdill's Handbook of Leadership* 3rd. Edition (New York: Free Press, 1990).

C.A. Beatty and B.L. Lee, "Leadership Among Middle Managers—An Exploration in the Context of Technological Change," *Human Relations,* Vol. 45, (1992), pp. 957-989.

R.B. Blake and J.S. Mouton, *The Managerial Grid* (Houston, TX, Gulf Pub. 1964).

R.B. Blake and J.S. Mouton, *The New Managerial Grid* (Houston, TX, Gulf Pub. 1978).

R.B. Blake and J.S. Mouton, *The Managerial Grid III* (Houston, TX, Gulf Pub. 1985).

M.H. Bond and K.K. Hwang, "The Social Psychology of the Chinese People," in M.H. Bond (ed.), *The Psychology of the Chinese People* (Hong Kong, Oxford University Press, 1986), pp. 213-66.

J.M. Burns, *Leadership* (New York: Harper and Row, 1978).

C.H. Chen, "Confucian Style of Management in Taiwan," in J.M. Putti (ed.), *Management: Asian Context* (Singapore: McGraw-Hill, 1991), pp. 177-97.

I. Chew, A. Tseng and A. Teo, "The Role of Culture in Training in a Multinational Context." *Journal of Management Development,* Vol. 9, No. 5 (1990), pp.51-57.

D.S. Cho, "Managing by Patriarchal Authority in Korea," in J.M. Putti (ed.), *Management: Asian Context* (Singapore: McGraw-Hill, 1991), pp. 15-35.

L.C. Chong, "History and Managerial Culture in Singapore: 'Pragmatism', 'Openness' and 'Paternalism,' " *Asian Pacific Journal of Management,* Vol. 4, No. 3 (1987), pp. 133-43.

J.A. Conger, *The Charismatic Leader* (San Francisco, CA: Jossey-Bass, 1989).

J.A. Conger and R.N. Kanungo (eds.), *Charismatic Leadership: The Elusive Factor in Organisational Effectiveness* (San Francisco, CA: Jossey-Bass, 1989).

J. Durcan and P. Kirkbride, "Leadership in the European Context: Some Queries," in P. Kirkbride (ed.), *Human Resource Management in Europe* (London, 1994).

C.A. Gibb, "Leadership," in G. Lindzey and E. Aronson (eds.), *The Handbook of Social Psychology* (Reading, MA: Addison-Wesley, 1969).

P.T. Gibbons, "Impacts of Organisational Evolution on Leadership Roles and Behaviours," *Human Relations,* Vol. 45 (1992), pp. 1-18.

P.R. Harris and R.T. Moran, *Managing Cultural Differences* (Houston, TX: Gulf Pub., 1987).

P. Hersey and K.H. Blanchard, *Management of Organisational Behaviour* (Englewood Cliffs, NJ: Prentice-Hall, 1982).

G. Hofstede, *Culture's Consequences: International Differences in Work Related Values* (London: Sage, 1980a).

G. Hofstede, "Motivation, Leadership, and Organisation, Do American Theories Apply Abroad?" *Organisational Dynamics,* Vol. 9, No. 1 (1980b), pp. 42-63.

C.R. Holloman, "Headship vs. Leadership," *Business and Economic Review,* Vol. 32, No. 2 (1986), pp. 35-37.

R.J. House, "A Path-goal Theory of Leadership Effectiveness," *Administrative Science Quarterly,* Vol. 16, No. 5 (1971), pp. 321-38.

R.J. House, "A 1976 Theory of Charismatic Leadership," in J.G. Hunt and L.L. Larsen (Eds.), *Leadership: The Cutting Edge* (Carbondale: Southern Illinois University Press, 1977).

R.J. House, W.D. Spangler and J. Woycke, "Personality and Charisma in the US Presidency: A Psychological Theory of Leader Effectiveness," *Administrative Science Quarterly,* Vol. 36 (1991), pp. 364-396.

A. Huczynski, *Management Gurus* (London: Routledge, 1993).

J. Huey, "The Leadership Industry," *Fortune,* Vol. 129, No. 4 (1994), pp. 30-32.

C.H. Hui, "Values and Attitudes," in R.I. Westwood (ed.), *Organisational Behaviour: Southeast Asian Perspectives* (Hong Kong: Longman, 1992), pp. 63-90.

P. Kirkbride and S. Tang, "Management Development in the Nanyang Chinese Societies of South-east Asia," *Journal of Management Development,* Vol. 11, No. 2 (1992), pp. 54-66.

P. Kirkbride, S. Tang and W.C. Shae, "The Transferability of Management Training and Development: The Case of Hong Kong," *Asia Pacific Human Resource Management,* Vol. 27, No. 1 (1989), pp. 7-19.

P. Kirkbride and R.I. Westwood, "Hong Kong," in R.B. Peterson (ed.), *Managers and National Culture: A Global Perspective* (Westport, CT: Greenwood Pub., 1993).

F. Kluckhohn and F.L. Strodtbeck, *Variations in Value Orientations* (Evanston, Ill: Row, Peterson, 1961).

S. Komin, "Culture and Work-related Values in Thai Organisations," *International Journal of Psychology,* Vol. 25, (1990), pp. 681-704.

R. Likert, *The Human Organisation* (New York: McGraw-Hill, 1967).

B.V. Moore, "The May Conference on Leadership," *Personnel Journal,* Vol. 6 (1927), pp. 124-28.

A. Phatak, *International Dimensions of Management* (Boston: PWS Kent, 1989).

D.S. Pugh and S.G. Redding, "A Comparative Study of The Structure and Content of Chinese Businesses in Hong Kong," paper presented at the Association of Teachers of Management Research Conference, Ashridge, England, (January, 1985).

J.M. Putti, (ed.), *Management: Asian Context* (Singapore: McGraw-Hill, 1991).

L. Pye, *Asian Power and Politics* (Cambridge, MA: Harvard University Press, 1985).

G. Redding, *The Spirit of Chinese Capitalism* (Berlin: Walter de Gruyter, 1990).

G. Redding and D.S. Pugh, "The Formal and The Informal: Japanese and Chinese Organisation Structures," in S.R. Clegg, D.C. Dunphy and G. Redding (eds.), *The Enterprise and Management in East Asia* (Hong Kong: Center for Asian Studies, University of Hong Kong, 1986), pp. 153-67.

G. Redding and G.Y.Y. Wong, "The Psychology of Chinese Organisational Behaviour," in M.H. Bond (ed.), *The Psychology of the Chinese People* (Hong Kong: Oxford University Press, 1986), pp. 267-95.

B. Shamir, R.J. House and M.B. Arthur, "The Motivational Effects of Charismatic Leadership: A Self-Concept Based Theory," *Organisation Science,* Vol. 4, No. 4 (1993), pp. 577-594.

Y.K. Shin, *Characteristics and Tasks of Korean Enterprises* (Seoul: SNU Press, 1984).

R.H. Silin, *Leadership and Values: The Organisation of Large Scale Taiwanese Enterprises* (Cambridge, MA: Harvard University Press, 1976).

A.G. Thompson, "Cross-cultural Management of Labour in a Thai Environment," *Asia Pacific Journal of Management,* Vol. 6, No. 2 (1989), pp. 323-38.

N.M. Tichy and D.O. Ulrich, "The Leadership Challenge: A Call For the Transformational Leader," *Sloan Management Review,* Vol. 26, No. 1 (1984), pp. 59-68.

D. Torrington, *International Human Resource Management* (Hemel Hempstead, Hertfordshire: Prentice Hall, 1994).

M.L. Tushman and E. Romanelli, "Organisational Evolution: A Metamorphosis Model of Convergence and Reorientation," in B.M. Shaw and L.L. Cummings (eds.), *Research in Organisational Behaviour,* Vol. 7, (Greenwich, Conn.: JAI Press, 1985).

A.A. Vicere and V.T. Freeman, "Executive Education in Major Corporations: An International Survey," *Journal of Management Development,* Vol. 9, No. 1 (1990), pp. 5-16.

M. Weber, *The Religion of China* (Glencoe, IL: The Free Press, 1951).

R.I. Westwood and A. Chan, "Headship and Leadership." In R.I. Westwood, (ed.), *Organisational Behaviour: Southeast Asian Perspectives* (Hong Kong: Longman, 1992), pp. 118-43.

B. Widyahartono, "The Pancasila Way of Managing in Indonesia," in J.M. Putti, (ed.), *Management: Asian Context* (Singapore: McGraw-Hill, 1991), pp. 130-44.

S.L. Wong, "The Chinese Family Firm: A Model," *The British Journal of Sociology,* Vol. 36, No. 1 (1989), pp. 58-72.

S. Yoo and S.M. Lee, "Management, Style and Practice of Korean Chaebols," *California Management Review,* Vol. 29, No. 4 (1987), pp. 95-110.

Commentary

by MARTIN J. GANNON

This article is very critical of Western ideas of leadership, as the authors believe that the "headman" model of village life is more appropriate than all of the Western models that are supposedly more sophisticated. In fact, the Sampoerna Company in Indonesia, the most profitable maker of Indonesian clove-based cigarettes, uses this model very successfully to organize its factories (Blustein, 1994). Even though its president, Puter Sampoerna, was educated in the United States in modern business practices, he realized that village elders can have great influence in the modern firm. Hence he appoints such elders as supervisors and managers on his factory floors, and neither he nor other members of top management interfere at all in monitoring what occurs there. Top management's job is to set policies and to communicate with the "elders," who handle everything else.

However, this form of organization is based on Authority Ranking or Vertical Collectivism, as discussed in Part II. As national economies prosper and the middle class evolves, individuals have more choices in their lives and tend to react negatively to such a use of authority. Thus the "headman" model may simply be a stage of economic and social development and one that becomes progressively less important in developing economies.

Reference

Blustein, P. (1994, December 1). A spiced smoke makes Indonesian firm very hot. *Washington Post*, pp. B11, B14.

CHAPTER 18

Metaphors for Change

The ALPs Model
of Change Management

CRAIG L. PEARCE
CHARLES P. OSMOND

A s difficult as the term *organizational culture* may be to define, it is a very real force—one that any change agent ignores at great peril. The model presented here is designed to aid the change agent— whether a manager or a consultant—effectively implement complex organizational change by pinpointing Access Leverage Points (ALPs) within the culture where the change is to take place. These ALPs are critical aspects of the culture that can often aid, but sometimes impede, the introduction and management of organizational change efforts.

The model is not intended to help identify the types of change necessary in an organization. Rather, its use increases the change agent's cultural awareness, and enables the change agent to develop specific intervention strategies for the facilitation of change.

AUTHORS' NOTE: Reprinted by permission of the publisher, from *Organizational Dynamics*, Winter 1996. © 1996 by the American Management Association, New York. http://www.amanet.org. All rights reserved.

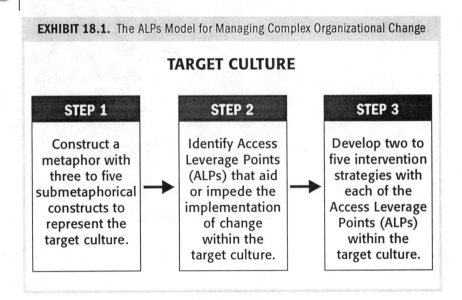

EXHIBIT 18.1. The ALPs Model for Managing Complex Organizational Change

TARGET CULTURE

STEP 1	STEP 2	STEP 3
Construct a metaphor with three to five submetaphorical constructs to represent the target culture.	Identify Access Leverage Points (ALPs) that aid or impede the implementation of change within the target culture.	Develop two to five intervention strategies with each of the Access Leverage Points (ALPs) within the target culture.

While other authors have identified particular "technical" aspects of organizational change, the underlying premise of the ALPs model is that organizational change is largely a "tactical" process, one where attention to key aspects of the culture can aid in managing the process. Thus, one important use for the model is to aid in planning change efforts. In different circumstances, this model can also be used to orient new managers or foreign nationals to the important aspects of their new culture.

The ALPs model for managing complex organizational change is a three-step process, as illustrated in Exhibit 18.1. The first step involves the development of a detailed metaphor to represent the target culture. The second step identifies the Access Leverage Points (ALPs) within that culture. The third step entails the development of intervention strategies to deal with each of the ALPs.

Culture can be conceptualized at a number of overlapping levels: national, organizational, departmental, and even at the work group level. The more specifically one can identify the target culture, the more the ALPs model approach can aid the organizational change effort. For illustration purposes, we have focused on national culture in this article because well developed metaphors at the national level already exist. By doing so, the specific intervention strategies we identify will have broader application than would strategies developed for a specific work group. However, it is important to realize that the same three-step process can be used as a tool in managing organizational change efforts at any level.

Dimensional Approaches to Culture

Many researchers have developed sets of dimensions to help define cultures. Florence Kluckhohn and Fred Strodtbeck, two pioneers in cross-cultural anthropology, proposed six dimensions to describe the assumptions of a society:

- Are people good or bad, or both?

- Do people subjugate nature or live in harmony with nature?

- Is the society oriented toward individualism or collectivism?

- Is the society a "being" or "doing" society?

- What are people's perceptions of public and private space?

- What is the society's temporal orientation toward the past, present, or future?

Another pioneer in cross-cultural research, Edward T. Hall, focused on communication patterns in his four dimensions:

- context and the level of explicit information required;

- space, especially personal space;

- time, in terms of monochronic versus polychronic orientation; and

- aspects of information flow related to the structure and speed of messages and communication.

Geert Hofstede, a prominent Dutch researcher, developed what is perhaps the most influential dimensional approach to the description of culture in international business. His empirically based study identified four dimensions, later expanded to five, to describe national cultures:

- *power distance:* the disparity of power distribution in a society;

- *uncertainty avoidance:* the degree of acceptance of uncertainty;

- *individualism-collectivism:* the degree of self- versus group-orientation;

- *masculinity-femininity:* the orientation toward aggressiveness; and

- *time orientation:* static tradition-oriented versus dynamic future-oriented.

All of these approaches have great value and offer significant insight into our understanding of broad national cultural similarities and differences.

However, as Martin Gannon, professor of international management at the University of Maryland-College Park and his associates demonstrate, by reducing cultures to just a few dimensions these approaches lack depth in describing cultural mind-sets used in daily activities, and ignore the institutional molding of these mind-sets. The limitations of the dimensional approach become especially problematic when we are interested in comparing a limited number of cultures, or more particularly when attempting to develop an in-depth understanding of a specific culture.

For example, Hofstede groups Great Britain and the United States very closely; our own, perhaps more sophisticated statistical analyses confirm this grouping. However, anyone who has worked in both countries knows there are very real differences that these comparisons simply do not reveal. These differences become especially noticeable under the conditions of major change efforts. Using the ALPs model provides a more descriptive and focused approach to culture representation for these situations.

Metaphorical Approaches to Culture

People frequently use metaphors in daily life to ease communication; researchers are increasingly employing them to represent and characterize cultures. Gareth Morgan, professor of administrative studies at York University, Toronto, developed several metaphors to describe organizations. His metaphors provide examples of organizational forms, but do not fulfill the requirements of the ALPs model. However, Clifford Geertz, a cross-cultural anthropologist who has written extensively on Indonesian cultures, and, particularly, Gannon and associates present several examples of the types of metaphors that we advocate developing for use in the ALPs model. They describe a single overarching metaphor with several submetaphorical constructs to represent the culture under consideration.

Some criticize the use of a single metaphor as too simple. However, the risk is not in simplification, since this is the deliberate intent of any representational model and certainly of the metaphor, but rather in oversimplification to the point of distortion or inaccuracy. To avoid this pitfall, and following the approach advocated by Gannon and his associates, the ALPs model requires a reasonable level of sophistication in the detail of the metaphor, appropriate to the situation. We offer examples, particularly in an international context, to illustrate the development of a metaphor.

Some also criticize the single metaphor as merely a pejorative stereotype. But consider the intent of the cultural metaphor. The ALPs model approach adheres to the five criteria specified by Nancy Adler, professor of organization behavior and cross-cultural management at McGill University, regarding the constructive use of stereotypes when describing the behavioral norms of a particular group. Adler states that stereotypes are useful only when "(1) consciously held, (2) descriptive and nonjudgmental, (3) accurate, (4) used as the first best guess, and (5) modified with experience." These criteria particularly apply to the use of a metaphor. The metaphor is not intended as a universal syllogism applicable to all individuals, but rather becomes a form of socio-typing, providing guidance in understanding the mind-set of a culture. Stereotyping is appropriate only at the group or community level of analysis and should be subject to limiting assumptions.

While Gannon and associates developed their approach at the national culture level, we advocate it for developing metaphors to represent culture at many levels: national, organizational, departmental, or even at the workgroup level. At whatever level of analysis, a rich metaphor aids in understanding the mind-set of the culture where change is planned.

The ALPs Model Approach

Step one. The change agent begins the ALPs model approach by selecting a single overarching metaphor to represent the target culture. The metaphor can either be developed in conjunction with people within the culture who will be affected by the change, or evaluated, and if necessary, modified as a result of input from the participants. Following the selection of the metaphor, the agent should develop three to five submetaphorical constructs as part of, and consistent with, the overarching metaphor. These subconstructs, along with the overarching metaphor, provide anchors, or benchmarks, from which to develop a rich and focused understanding of the cultural mind-set.

Step two. After choosing the metaphor and augmenting it with three to five subconstructs, the change agent must then isolate Access Leverage Points (ALPs) within the target culture. These ALPs are aspects of the culture that provide powerful opportunities to act as catalysts for change, or could present serious roadblocks or impediments to change. For example, if a culture values tradition then the implications for introducing and managing change are quite different from a culture where history is less central to social norms. However, the ALPs model does not present a complete cultural analysis, but rather narrows the focus of the change agent to the most salient aspects of the target culture relating to the management of change.

Step three. In the final step, the change agent specifies intervention strategies for dealing with each of the ALPs. We advocate specifying at least two but no more than five specific strategies for each ALP. Balance is the key, since too few strategies can leave the change agent without adequate flexibility, but too many strategies can lead to inadequate guidance and direction. To take advantage of the ALPs model, the change agent should use it as a tool to simplify and clarify the process of understanding the cultural mind-set, and to specify precise strategies to achieve the most effective results.

Let's Clarify—With a Metaphor

To summarize with a metaphor (one sure to bring a smile to anyone involved in change), introducing change in a culture is analogous to introducing a virus into an organic cell where there is resistance, but not immunity, to change. Much like a cell, a culture has semipermeable barriers that permit or block the introduction of the change (or virus). The ALPs identify key points of vulnerability or resistance in the culture (or cell wall). The successful management of ALPs facilitates the implementation of change. While many change efforts are successful without specifically identifying ALPs, we hope that by following a structured process the likelihood of successful change efforts will improve, especially if success is measured in the long-term acceptance of the changes (or infection). If a change agent is not attuned to the ALPs of a culture, then the group, much like a cell, will revert to its previous state upon removal of the change agent (or virus).

A Metaphor for Britain: The Traditional British House

To illustrate the use of the ALPs model, we will draw contrasts between the management of change in Great Britain and in the United States. For convenience, we will adapt "The Traditional British House," the cultural metaphor developed by Gannon and his associates to reflect the British culture in organizational settings, and extract ALPs as they relate to the management of change. Finally, we will offer specific intervention strategies that change agents can use when engaged in change efforts in Britain.

The traditional British house, as Gannon and his associates' metaphor suggests, is a durable, long-lived entity based on tried, tested and historically successful designs. Without wishing to sound like a real estate broker, homes in Britain are commonly many hundreds of years old, yet still wind- and water-tight and highly desirable. The British home design offers few surprises, and change is often evolutionary, what Gannon calls a "slow chipping away . . . over the years." Gannon and his associates provide three submetaphorical constructs for the British house, through which key aspects of the British culture can be better understood:

- *laying the foundations of the house:* strong ties to their history, and political and economic institutions;

- *building the brick house:* aspects of growing up British; and

- *living in the traditional brick house:* key elements of being British.

Each of these metaphorical constructs helps us understand the British organizational mind-set better.

Identifying the ALPs of Great Britain

Historical foundations of Britain. Britain's rich and powerful historical background can be likened to the foundations of the British house. The political, military, and economic influence of this nation once circumscribed the globe. Indeed, Christopher North aptly described the country as "His Majesties Dominions on which the sun never sets," a notion in which the British took great pride. Moreover, Charles Dickens wrote in *Great Expectations,* "We Britons had at that time particularly settled that it was treasonable to doubt our having and our being the best of everything." Although at times masked in severe cynicism, the pride in being British runs deep in the culture even today.

The first ALP related to introducing change in Britain is the *acceptance of tradition.* Though not necessarily a consciously held belief nor a preoccupation with tradition, the British desire to emphasize tradition and build on it is not surprising, considering their history of incredible achievement. Obvious illustrations abound: houses still standing strong after hundreds of years; one of the oldest Parliamentary systems in the world; one of the few remaining constitutional monarchies in the world that acts as a unifying force. The British seem to feel that if it still works and has lasted a long time, it must somehow be good. At the very least, tradition adds a feeling of stability in turbulent times.

Subtlely of language is the second British ALP relating to the management of change. Gannon and his associates observed that the British tend to be rather circumspect in their conversations; in all forms of communication, whether oral or written, subtlety is typical. Certainly the British commonly use language in a more subtle way than their American counterparts. This subtlety of language can be related back to the solid foundations of the British society, with conventions so long established and universally applied that everyone "knows the rules." The underlying assumption means that language needs be less explicit than in the United States, where a largely immigrant population has a greater requirement for specificity and precise language. This ALP has a great impact on the management of change in Britain.

Socialization in Britain. The British tend to prefer brick homes as opposed to wood frame ones, which are more prevalent in the United States. Many of the newer homes in Great Britain are built to resemble the older, brick-style housing. With their great sense of order and tradition, the British hold architects of the past in high esteem. This relates to the third ALP, *probity of position*. In British English, this term refers to openness and uprightness in the recognition of position.

For an example of probity of position, consider the major role that status conferred by membership in professional organizations has in the British work place. Business cards often not only have a formal job title following the name, but also a list of initials indicating honorary titles, earned degrees, and membership in professional institutes.

The bifurcation of management and labor hierarchies also emphasizes the importance of position. One of the authors of this article, a Fellow of the Royal Institution of Chartered Surveyors, found that he needed to communicate with lawyers on a number of simple matters. But he was routinely asked to deal with other chartered surveyors as opposed to negotiating with lawyers to settle issues. In many industries, the juxtaposition of managerial hierarchies and organized labor hierarchies leads to formal, often intractable, work place agreements. A gulf has developed that even Margaret Thatcher could not totally close.

Furthermore, building the brick house, or growing up in Britain, means that, compared with American children, British children are expected to behave, be controlled and not spoiled, and above all know their place and not be thought precocious—a clear precursor to fitting into society, and particularly into organizations.

British home-building follows what one might term a ceremonial procession, related to the fourth ALP, *use of ceremony*. In the United States homes are built in very short order. In Great Britain the process can take much longer. One of the authors observed a new office building under construction between Picadilly Circus and Leicester Square in London. Upon his first arrival in Britain, construction was well under way. However, more than three years later the four-story building was not yet completed. In the United States construction industry, a 40-story building would have been completed in the same time frame (although maybe not to the same specifications).

The other author experienced a similar trend while working for a development corporation in the Home Counties of London. Construction of just the infrastructure (roads, sewers, etc.), that in America might be completed within months, often took years to complete. This was not due to difficulties associated with the development, but rather the methodical procedures involved. The British seemed to take a certain comfort in things being done a particular way; the result was often that developments took many years from breaking ground to completion. Just as the construction industry uses ceremony, there is a role for it in all aspects of British life. This use of ceremony, while slowing the pace of life in Britain, also ties in to their history.

The Queen presiding over the ceremonial opening of Parliament each year to mark the beginning of a new legislative session may be termed an anachronism, but opening ceremonies are common. By comparison, in the United States ceremonies frequently mark the end of, and especially celebrate, accomplishments. Using ceremony to mark the beginning of new organizational initiatives clearly has a role in the management of change in Britain.

Awareness of traditions as a way of life in Britain. The fifth British ALP is *disposition toward following rules.* This willingness to follow rules manifests itself in many ways, often associated with aspects of privacy. The British home shows evidence of this in its division into many small rooms, each with a door. Further, because everyone is expected to know the rules, the average Briton obeys them with little fear that others will gain undue advantage through rule circumvention.

An example you will see on every street in Britain is the propensity to "queue up." People are more willing to wait patiently in line than in other countries. Where their American counterparts might form a "huddle" around a bus entrance, the British are more likely to form a nice orderly line and wait their turn. This behavior also takes place on highways where the British assiduously follow "lane discipline," with overtaking only on the right. The rules are clearly written down and followed. Compare this to the United States, where drivers interpret the overtaking rules more flexibly, and the idea of maintaining such lane discipline is an anathema. Yet because British society tends to obey rules more strictly, they can become a double-edged sword—both a convenience in efficient communication for those in the know, and yet an unquestioned barrier to change.

Case Illustrations: How Access Leverage Points Impact the Management of Change

Let's take a closer look at each of the previously identified ALPs. For each leverage point, we offer examples of organizational change efforts in Great Britain, along with examples of their counterpoints in the United States. The majority of examples are drawn from actual experience and consulting engagements in both countries: in Great Britain, from experiences at the reorganization of a major British firm, and in the United States, from many sources.

Acceptance of tradition (ALP 1). The British acceptance of tradition creates something of a dilemma for a change agent, placing the agent in a delicate role. Disregarding tradition is often tempting and convenient, or sometimes the agent fails to recognize its importance. But this can be fatal to organizational change efforts. To succeed, the change agent must work through the established traditions.

One of the major components of the British firm's reorganization effort was a strategy for managing product quality. Rather than merely introducing a cavalier approach to quality management, we designed an implementation plan that would build on the traditions already established in the firm. We took an existing "program" operating in only one area of the firm, kept the name largely unchanged, and transformed it into an organization-wide quality strategy "process." In an internal consulting report, the original program had been described as "lacking in focus, accountability and action." So although it was a long way from being a sound foundation, it had the powerful advantage of existing—a tradition.

Instead of viewing the program as an impediment to change, ALP 1 creates a fresh perspective. The program became a building block. By building on established tradition and introducing the quality strategy incrementally, we were able to introduce fundamental widespread change without the degree of resistance from incumbents that might otherwise have occurred. The strategic change's true nature was massive, establishing an integrated, cross-functional, multi-year time horizon for managing and introducing quality improvements across all product lines.

By contrast, the United States is much less concerned with preserving tradition. For example, while one might consider the U.S. Constitution the most fundamental tradition in the United States, the country is constantly eroding and reinterpreting the very fabric of the philosophy on which the document stands. Charles Hampden-Turner and Alfons Trompenaars, an English and Dutch scholar, respectively, in *The Seven Cultures of Capitalism,* represent the difference between the two cultures graphically, with managers' concepts of the role of past, present, and future represented by a series of circles. The British concepts were a sequence of circles, with the present overlapping with the past and a little apart from the future. The American concepts showed a similar sequential configuration, but the circle representing the present was clearly separate from the past, and touched the future.

Subtlety of language (ALP 2). While the new quality process at the British firm was ultimately a success, its implementation was not always certain. Several managers' subtle use of language nearly sidetracked the entire effort. In one particularly important instance, we chose to present the new strategy to key managers by staging a major presentation, designed to disseminate information about the new strategy, demonstrate the linkage to the past, and establish a framework for future efforts. In order to hold this event, we had to convince the "owner" of the existing program of both the need for the event, and the need for all of the top executives of the firm to attend.

Since the original program had several problems, the owner was naturally reluctant to hold such a public event with all of the top executives, and thus advertise its shortcomings. However, the language he used indicated anything but reluctance. He made such statements as "we are 99 percent together on this," in reference to the event's format, content, and audience. Yet when push came to shove and the timing for the event became critical, he dug in his heels. His one percent lack of support turned out to be 100 percent disagreement with the entire event. An appreciation for ALP 2 enabled us not only to anticipate potential problems, but also to develop an alternative approach in advance. The event went on as planned.

By contrast, during an organizational diagnosis at the departmental level of an American Fortune 500 company commissioned by its chief financial officer, the treasurer was not at all happy with the idea of some consultant "snooping around" his department. In unequivocal terms he made it clear, in a very loud voice with the door of his office wide open so that many of his staff could hear, that he intended to thwart the organizational diagnosis efforts. He did not use subtle language.

Probity of position (ALP 3). The "owner" of the original program at the British firm first aired his refusal to endorse the presentation in a meeting attended by all those directly reporting to him. Prior to this meeting, we had met with all of his direct reports on numerous occasions to plan the event. They had all, individually, indicated their support. Yet in this meeting, when the manager openly expressed his desire to stop the event and subsequently asked for input, all the direct reports supported the manager in his opposition.

The pressure was growing, and it looked as though the crucial presentation might be undermined. After the meeting, we met privately with the manager to discuss the future of the event. We informed him that his boss fully supported the event. Albeit a little late, by being cognizant of ALP 3 and meeting with him in private, we ensured that the probity of his position would not be disturbed; he would be able to inform his subordinates of the change in plan rather than have his views publicly overridden.

By contrast, a medium-sized American publishing firm had much less concern for the probity of position at the organizational level during the development of their five-year strategic business plan. To arrive at the final plan, they held a series of meetings and brainstorming sessions in which little to no regard for formal position was demonstrated. All individuals were encouraged to be mavericks and to push for their own agendas. However, when the final plan was pulled together, the total resources of the firm were focused on one mission, and they more than tripled in size during the next five-year period.

Use of ceremony (ALP 4). We designed the presentation of the new quality strategy process at the British firm to mark the beginning of the project, and to establish credibility for the course of action. The event had, in part, a ceremonial function with elements of ritual and drama. The top managers from all departments and product lines attended. To our knowledge, this firm had never held an event of this scope. It was designed to impress, and it was a great success. Subsequently, they commissioned us to conduct two additional events to ensure proper exposure to lower ranking individuals.

In our experience, ceremonies have a different emphasis in the United States. Clearly Americans lay great store in highly professional presentation proposals, but they are less ceremonial in nature. The emphasis is more on the celebration of success at the end of a project. For example, most companies and organizations have awards banquets. One year-end awards banquet attended by one of the authors at an American manufacturing facility recognized individuals for their efforts in bringing about significant improvements. However, a couple of months after the awards were presented, the organization slashed its work force dramatically, award winners and nonwinners alike.

Disposition toward rules (ALP 5). In certain industries where the division of management and organized labor is particularly important, the rigid application of rules negotiated in an attempt to alleviate confrontation (especially relating to job demarcation and procedural matters) can make change management difficult. Even with the strident efforts of Margaret Thatcher, obstacles remain; there is an ingrained reluctance to change established procedures.

At the British firm, our consulting team got bogged down in arcane rules so frequently that we coined a term to refer to this phenomenon. We called it "getting quagged," from the root "quagmire." One outstanding example had to do with computer printouts of parts lists. At an earlier stage in the implementation of the parts management computer system, someone decided that one standard report was needed, to be distributed to several people in each product area. This report consisted of somewhere in the neighborhood of 10,000 pages, and stood about three feet tall. It contained all of the data necessary for parts management, but not in a usable form. All those who received it thought it was wasteful, burdensome, and not very helpful. Each person only referred to a couple hundred of the pages with any regularity, and moreover, each would have preferred different formats. However, since this was the established procedure, none of the users challenged the format and pressed for change.

Yet, with an appreciation for ALP 5, this disposition toward rules can be advantageous. During the implementation of the quality strategy process, we built on the British propensity to follow procedures and established a set of written guidelines: the principles of the strategy, the information flow for the process, the organization structure required to support it, the job descriptions of key players in the process, and management tools to aid in the process. We enhanced the formality and credibility of the guidelines by getting senior managers to sign them prior to the organization-wide distribution. Following distribution, consulting staff worked with area management to ensure consistent application of the process to each of the product lines.

How might this approach work in the United States? Probably not so well. In America people often follow the dictum that "rules are made to be broken." People are in a hurry to get things done, whether that means double parking in order to run a quick errand or ignoring overly constrictive rules to get the product out the door. And others tolerate this attitude. People will accommodate the errant parker and drive around, or the boss will acknowledge the successful result and ignore the circumvention of rules.

One author worked for a multimillion dollar start-up company where the written work procedures were created after the event to reflect current practices, rather than ahead of time to dictate them. It was a question of seeing what worked and going with it. In another instance, one of the authors was commissioned to create an employee development program for a tightly knit work group of a non-profit organization. The management team of this group wanted an integrated system that would ensure that employees were developed to meet the emerging needs. We created a document complete with information flow, management tools, and clearly defined responsibili-

ties. The process outlined was very well received, but never fully imple-
mented because individuals were reluctant to follow the "rules"; they wished
to retain individual discretion.

ALPs in Perspective

Any culture has certain characteristics that create forces for or against
the management of change. We do not mean to imply, however, that the five
Access Leverage Points identified in this article fully define the British culture, or that they may not equally well apply in other cultures. Rather, we
expose those aspects of the culture to which one must pay special attention
when managing change. As our contrasting illustrations demonstrate, ALPs
can take on very different meanings in different cultures.

What is important, however, is that the identification of ALPs has very
practical implications for managing change in a given culture. Exhibit 18.2
summarizes the British cultural metaphor, the ALPs, and intervention strategies. Exhibit 18.3 provides recommendations on how these principles can be
applied for managing change in Britain.

Conclusion

We have not attempted to provide an in-depth understanding of the British
culture. Instead, our focus has been on specific components of the culture
that relate to the introduction and management of change. By examining a
major reorganization effort of one company in Great Britain, we demonstrated how each of the key cultural attributes we identified has an impact in
organizational life. By integrating this analysis, we provided several intervention strategies that individuals can adopt to deal effectively with each of the
ALPs.

Moreover, this article demonstrates a simple three-step process for
identifying the key aspects of a culture that must be attended to during the
process of implementing organizational change. This process can also be
applied at any level of culture. The organization level is perhaps where the
framework will become most powerful, provided that the underlying metaphor is carefully selected.

Additionally, the ALPs model can be useful as a management training
tool to familiarize new managers with the salient aspects of the culture they
are entering, or to assimilate foreign nationals as they enter a new country.

EXHIBIT 18.2 Summary of the British Cultural Metaphor (the Traditional British House), Access Leverage Points (ALPs), and Intervention Strategies

STEP 1 The Sub-Metaphorical Constructs	STEP 2 The Access Leverage Points	STEP 3 The Intervention Strategies
Historical Foundations of Great Britain	Acceptance of Tradition	Identify relevant tradition(s).
		Demonstrate how the change builds on tradition(s).
		Involve people in the change to enhance ownership.
	Subtlety of Language	Discount overt stimuli
		Pay strict attention to subtle clues.
		Engage in diplomatic behavior.
Socialization in Great Britain	Probity of position	Ensure contact at appropriate level.
		Demonstrate top management commitment.
		Involve key stakeholders.
	Use of Ceremony	Involve top managers in ceremonies.
		Use ceremonies to mark the beginning of change.
		Employ symbolism and ritual.
Awareness of Traditions as a Way of Life in Great Britain	Disposition Toward Rules	Specify rules precisely.
		Specify rules as guidelines.
		Build upon existing rules.

EXHIBIT 18.3 Recommendations for Managing Change in Britain

Acceptance of tradition (ALP 1). The British culture is built on solid traditions. Frequently an appreciation for the way things were previously done must be accommodated and incorporated in the change process. The intervention strategies for dealing with the British concern for tradition include:

- Identifying the tradition(s) associated with the desired change(s);
- Demonstrating how the change extends and reinforces the tradition(s); and
- Encouraging individuals to work through the change so that they develop ownership of the change.

Subtlety of language (ALP 2). The British use language in a subtle manner, perhaps because of their greater homogeneity and greater respect for tradition than exists in the United States. The strategies for dealing with the British use of subtle language include:

- Discounting overt stimuli;
- Paying strict attention to subtle clues, especially in conversation; and
- Engaging in diplomatic behavior as opposed to dictatorial behavior.

Probity of position (ALP 3). As opposed to their American counterparts, the British have much more awareness of formal position. Approaches for dealing with the probity of position in Britain include:

- Ensuring contact is made at the appropriate level within the organization;
- Ensuring top managers are sold before public commitment to a strategy with middle managers;
- Subtly demonstrating top management conviction to your course of action; and
- Careful identification of other key stakeholders, and ensuring their inclusion within the change process.

EXHIBIT 18.3 Continued

Use of ceremony (ALP 4). The British use of ceremony emphasizes marking the beginning of projects and courses of action. When using ceremonies in Britain it is important to focus on the following intervention strategies:

- Involving key managers in ceremonies, while being aware of the probity of position;

- Using ceremonies to mark the "psychological" beginning of a change to tie into traditional perspectives; and

- Incorporating symbolism and ritual, such as passing the keys over or signing the documents, making it an event of importance.

Disposition toward rules (ALP 5). As noted earlier, the British tend to follow rules once they are in place. This propensity should be exploited in organizational change efforts through the following key strategies:

- Defining rules precisely, otherwise disjointed efforts or reversion to tradition will result;

- Defining the rules as a set of guidelines, and not dictums to be followed; and

- Being aware of what has gone before to anticipate reactions to the new rules.

Perhaps other uses also exist. However, the important thing to note is that by following a structured process, one is more likely to identify the key aspects of a culture that relate to the introduction and management of change, thereby enabling greater likelihood of success.

Selected Bibliography

There have been several dimensional approaches to understanding national cultures, the most notable of which is Geert Hofstede, "Motivation, Leadership, and Organization: Do American Theories Apply Abroad?" (*Organizational Dynamics,* Summer 1980). For a more detailed description of this work, see Hofstede's *Culture's Consequences* (Sage, 1984). Nancy Adler also provides an excellent overview of the dimensional approach to culture and the ways culture can impact the management of organizations in her book *International Dimensions of Organizational Behavior* (PWS-Kent, 1991).

For a sophisticated statistical analysis of the grouping of countries according to work-related attitudes and values, readers are referred to Charles Osmond and Craig Pearce's working paper entitled "Workplace Attitudes and Values, and a Global Pattern of Nations: An Application of Latent Class Modeling" (CIBER working paper series, University of Maryland, 1995).

Recently there has been significant interest in the use of metaphors to understand the subtle differences between national cultures not captured by dimensional approaches. The most notable work in this area is Martin Gannon and Associates, *Understanding Global Cultures: Metaphorical Journeys Through 17 Countries* (Sage, 1994).

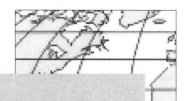

Author Index

Adler, N., 236-237
Alston, W. P., 18, 19
Andres, T. D., 217, 220
Arens, W., 97-98, 99
Aristotle, 9, 18
Arthur, M. B., 207

Bass, B. M., 205, 207, 211, 213
Beatty, C. A., 207
Black, M., 14
Blake, R. B., 205
Blanchard, K. H., 205
Blustein, P., 231
Bond, M., 43
Bond, M. H., 216, 218
Breal, M., 9, 10
Burns, J. M., 207

Carroll, R., 71, 73
Chen, C. H., 220
Chenery, H. B., 32
Chew, I., 205
Cho, D. S., 220
Chong, L. C., 220
Coleridge, S. T., 20
Conger, J. A., 205, 207
Crozier, M., 66

De Gramont, S., 66
Devanna, M., 207
Dickens, C., 239
Drozdiak, W., 75
Durcan, J., 208

The Economist, 72

Fang, T., 52
Fiske, A. P., 52, 56, 57, 125-126, 127
Fiske, S., 98, 99
Fleming, C., 73
Frank, R., 89
Freeman, V. T., 204

Gannon, M., 127, 130, 236, 237, 238, 239
Geertz, C., 93, 129-131, 236
Gelfand, M., 55
Gibb, C. A., 212
Gibbons, P. T., 207

Hall, E., 25, 26, 27-28, 64, 65, 67, 68, 235
Hall, M., 27, 64, 65, 67
Hampden-Turner, C., 242-243
Harris, P. R., 226
Hasenclever, A., 86
Henle, P., 18
Hersey, P., 205
Hofstede, G., 51, 69, 205, 210, 211, 216, 218, 235, 236
Holloman, C. R., 212
Hoppe, M. H., 51
House, R. J., 205, 207
Huczynski, A., 204
Huey, J., 204
Hui, C. H., 218
Huntington, S., 52, 83-86, 125, 127
Hwang, K. K., 216, 218

Johnson, H., 70, 72

Kahn, H., 33, 34
Kanungo, R. N., 205, 207
Kirkbride, P., 205, 208, 220

Kluckhohn, F., 209, 235
Komin, S., 220

Labov, W., 11
Lavin, D., 73
Lee, B. L., 207
Lee, S. M., 212, 220
Likert, R., 205
Locke, J., 15
Longfellow, H. W., 17-18

Matthews, J., 89
Mayer, P., 86
Moore, B. V., 213
Moran, R. T., 226
Morgan, G., 236
Mouton, J. S., 205
Myrdal, G., 31

Newman, W. H., 174, 176
North, C., 239

Olson, M., 121

Pennar, K., 89
Phatak, A., 226
Phillips, D., 51
Pozzo Di Borgo, P., 64, 69
Pugh, D. S., 222, 223
Putnam, R., 126
Putti, J. M., 214
Pye, L., 220

Redding, G., 214, 216, 220, 222, 223
Redding, S. G., 222
Richard, C., 126
Richards, I. A., 10, 18
Riding, A., 156
Rittberger, V., 86
Rokeach, M., 42

Romanelli, E., 207
Ronen, S., 29

Shae, W. C., 205
Shamir, B., 207
Shenkar, O., 29
Shin, Y. K., 220
Silin, R. H., 212, 219, 220, 221, 222
Spangler, W. D., 207
Stogdill, R. M., 211, 213
Stone, W. C., 96
Strodtbeck, F. L., 209, 235
Strout, A. M., 32
Swardson, A., 60, 67

Tang, S., 205
Taylor, S., 68, 71
Teo, A., 205
Thomas, D., 76
Thompson, A. G., 217, 220, 222
Tichy, N. M., 205, 207
Tocqueville, A. de, 109, 110
Torrington, D., 226
Triandis, H., 55
Trompenaars, A., 242-243
Tseng, A., 205
Tushman, M. L., 207

Ulrich, D. O., 205

Vedel, A., 62
Vicere, A. A., 204

Weber, M., 52, 216
Westwood, R. I., 220
Widyahartono, B., 217, 220
Wittgenstein, L., 11
Wong, G. Y. Y., 216, 220, 222
Wong, S. L., 214
Woycke, J., 207
Wuthnow, R., 115-116
Yoo, S., 212, 220

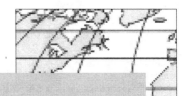

Subject Index

AARP. *See* American Association of Retired Persons

Access Leverage Points (ALPs) model:
application to Britain, 239-246
as management training tool, 246
cultural metaphors, 236-237
identifying ALPs, 237, 246
intervention strategies, 238, 247
steps, 237-238
use in organizational change efforts, 233-234, 237, 242-246

Advertising, French, 64

ALPs. *See* Access Leverage Points

American Association of Retired Persons (AARP), 115

American culture. *See* United States

Analogies, 19

AR. *See* Authority Ranking

Arguments:
in France, 69
metaphors, 4-6

Aristotle, 9-10, 18

Asia. *See* China; East Asia

Association membership, 110-111
church-related groups, 112, 113, 116
decline, 113-114, 116-117
explanations of decline, 118-120
new types of organization, 114-115
professional, 117
support groups, 115-116
types of organizations, 112-114
unions, 113, 116

AT&T, 140-141

Austria. *See* Schmäh

Authority Ranking (AR), 57, 126, 127

Baker, James, 149

Bali:
cockfights, 130-131
view of time, 129-130

Bible, 10

Bowie, David, 101, 102, 103, 104-105

Bowling, 114

Boy Scouts, 113

Britain:
Access Leverage Points (ALPs), 239-246
ceremonies, 240-241, 244
differences from United States, 242-243, 244, 245-246
historical foundations, 239-240
house as cultural metaphor, 238-241
socialization, 240-241
tradition, 239, 241, 242-243

Buddhism, 218

Bullfight, Spanish, 130

Capitalism, 52

Catholicism, 69, 95
See also Christianity

Celanese Corporation, 175, 178-181
See also Nantong Cellulose Fibers Company

CGE, 140-141, 145

Change:
catalysts for, 237
cultural, 127
metaphor for introducing, 238

use of ALPs model in organizational
change efforts, 233-234, 237, 242-246
Children, 34, 71, 73-74
China:
business environment, 175-176, 185, 191
Confucian values, 47, 218
decision-making processes, 28, 136
differences from American business
culture, 194
economic growth, 47
multinational joint ventures, 174-175
technical advisors, 186
workers and supervisors, 189
See also Nantong Cellulose Fibers
Company
China National Tobacco Corporation (CNTC),
175, 178-181
See also Nantong Cellulose Fibers
Company
Chinese diaspora, 213, 218
Chinese Value Survey (CVS), 43-44, 47, 50
Chirac, Jacques, 72-73, 75
Christianity, 48
Catholicism, 69, 95
Protestant Ethic, 52-53, 97
Protestantism, 95
traditional American model of social
universe, 94-96, 97
Chrysler Corporation, 174
Cigarette filters, tow used in, 175, 176, 178
Civic engagement:
costs, 120-121
efforts to increase in new democracies, 109,
121
in Italy, 126-127
in United States, 109-110
political participation and, 110-111, 117-
118
See also Association membership; Social
capital
Civic organizations, 113, 114
Civil society, 109-110, 121
Civilizations:
clash of, 83-84, 85-86
core states, 84
defining factors, 84, 87
See also Culture
Classes:
in French society, 63-65
See also Hierarchies

Clinton, Bill, 72, 85
CNTC. *See* China National Tobacco
Corporation
Cockfights, 129, 130-131
Collaboration, cross-cultural, 173-174
cultural hurdles, 181, 182-183, 186-187,
188-189, 191, 192-195
execution stage, 187-189, 192, 194
managers involved, 184, 192-195
mediators, 180, 187
model, 195-196
multinational joint ventures, 174-175
negotiation stage, 178-181, 192, 194
planning stage, 184-187, 192, 194
research needed, 196
self-initiation by emerging organization,
189-191, 192, 194
stages, 174, 176-177, 195-196
trust in, 195
Collective Sharing (CS), 56-57
Collectivism:
horizontal, 55, 56-57
in cultures, 37, 42, 51, 218
types, 55-56
vertical, 55-56, 57
Colombia, 32
Columbia University, Graduate School of
Business, 176
Communication:
cross-cultural, 25-26
cues, 154-155
emotional component, 28-29
gender differences, 144
high-context, 27-29, 30, 55, 67
low-context, 27-29, 30, 67-68
Compactness thesis, 10, 12-14, 15-16
Conceptual system, metaphorical, 3-5, 6, 7
Concorde, 77
Confucian Dynamism, 44, 48
economic growth and, 44-46
similarity to Protestant Ethic, 52-53
values, 46
Confucianism:
cultural influence in business, 213, 218
families, 34-35, 216
filial piety, 43, 216
neo-Confucian cultures, 33-34, 38
propriety, 219
teachings, 34-35
Confucius, 34

Corporations:
    football teams as model for, 98-99
    power, 90
    See also Joint ventures
Counterparts. *See* Negotiation
Creative model of success, 97, 101-106
Creativity, measuring, 103
Cresson, Edith, 144
Cross-cultural collaboration.
        See Collaboration, cross-cultural
Cross-cultural communication, 25-26
Cross-cultural management, 49-50
Cross-cultural negotiation. *See* Negotiation,
    cross-cultural
CS (Collective Sharing), 56-57
Cultural metaphors:
    Balinese cockfight, 130-131
    British house, 238-241
    distinction from stereotypes, 236-237
    Italian opera, 127
    Japanese garden, 127
    Spanish bullfight, 130
    subconstructs, 237, 239
    use in ALPs model, 236-237
    See also French wine metaphor; Metaphors
Culture:
    acquisition of, 34
    changes in, 127
    defining elements, 84, 87
    definitions, 25, 33-34
    East-West differences, 47-49, 87, 194, 212,
        224-225
    faith in ideology of, 93-94
    high- and low-context, 27-29, 30, 55, 67-68
    learning about others, 140-141
    levels, 234, 237
    power distribution and, 84-85, 86
    stability, 127-128
    See also Dimensional models of cultures
Culture measurement:
    Chinese Value Survey, 43-44, 47, 50
    etic and emic methods, 51-52
    IBM studies, 36-42, 43, 49, 51-52
    Rokeach Value Surveys, 42-43
    techniques, 35-36
Current Population Survey, 114
CVS. *See* Chinese Value Survey

De Gaulle, Charles, 67, 73, 76
Decision-making processes:

Chinese, 28, 136
    cultural differences, 28
    of headman, 222
Democracies:
    civil society, 109-110, 121
    election turnout, 111-112
    leadership in, 209
    See also Political participation
Deng Xiaoping, 47
Descartes, René, 65-66
Dialogue ideal, 222
Didactic leadership, 221-222, 223
Dimensional models of cultures, 235-236
    Chinese Value Survey, 43-44, 47, 50
    etic and emic, 51-52
    Fiske framework, 56-58, 125-126
    Hall's, 25-30, 235
    IBM culture measurement studies
        (Hofstede), 37-42, 43, 49, 51-52, 235
    influence of researchers' cultures, 47-49
    Triandis model, 55-56
Dylan, Bob, 101, 102, 104

East Asia:
    Confucian Dynamism, 44-46
    cultural differences from West, 47-49, 87,
        194, 212, 224-225
    economic growth, 31-32, 44-46, 47, 110
    expatriate managers, 225-226
    family business model, 214, 216-217
    headship, 206, 211-214, 231
    leadership training imported from North
        America, 205
    managers, 135-136, 205, 214
    neo-Confucian cultures, 33-34, 38
    See also China; Japan
Ecole Nationale d'Administration (ENA), 75
Economic growth:
    conditions for, 46-47
    Confucian Dynamism and, 44-46
    in East Asia, 31-32, 44-46, 47, 110
    individualism and, 42
    role of social networks, 110
    See also Trade
Economic integration, 84-85, 89
Education:
    French system, 73-75
    parent-teacher organizations, 113, 117, 118
    See also Management training
Elections, turnout, 111-112

EM (Equality Matching), 57
ENA. *See* Ecole Nationale d'Administration
English language, global use, 84
Entrepreneurship, 45-46, 51, 68
Environmental organizations, 115
Equality Matching (EM), 57
Ethnic conflicts, 85, 87
European Union, 84, 85, 89
Experience, continuous, 10-11, 15

Face, 35, 219, 222
Faith in ideology of society, 93-94
Families:
    as social capital, 117
    Confucian view of, 34-35, 216
    demographic changes, 119
    in French culture, 71
    nepotism, 223
Family business model, 214, 216-217
Federation of Women's Clubs, 113, 118
Feminine cultures, 37-38, 69
Feminist organizations, 115
Filial piety, 43, 216
Fiske framework, 56-58, 125-126
Football games:
    American culture reflected in, 97-98
    popularity in United States, 94, 97
    violence, 97-98
Football teams:
    as model for corporations, 98-99
    training, 99-100
Ford, 156
Foreign Affairs, 83
France:
    advertising, 64
    attitudes toward work, 68
    belief in cultural superiority, 61-62, 76-77
    centralization of businesses, 66-67, 69
    context dimension of culture, 67-68
    conversation, 69-71
    cultural metaphor. *See* French wine
        metaphor
    educational system, 73-75
    families, 71
    friendships, 70-71, 75
    health and fitness, 75-76
    history, 60, 62, 63
    immigrants, 77-78
    managers, 66, 140-141, 150-151, 211
    meals, 67, 71, 72

offices, 26, 66
political system, 72-73
regional identities, 61, 67
religion in, 69
small businesses, 68
social benefits system, 77
social classes, 63-65
technology, 77
vacations, 69
women, 71-72, 75, 144
Fraternal organizations, 113, 114, 116
Frederico, King, 126
French language, 70
French wine metaphor:
    classification, 63-68
    composition, 68
    elements, 60
    maturation process, 73-76
    pureness, 60-63
    suitability, 72-73

Game theory, 81-82, 86, 90
Garden, Japanese, 127
Gender:
    masculinity and femininity of cultures,
        37-38, 42
    of negotiators, 144
    See also Men; Women
General Motors, 145, 158
General Social Survey, 112, 113, 116, 117
German language, 166
    See also Schmäh
Germany, 26-27

Hall, Edward T., 25-30, 235
Headship:
    as stage of economic and social
        development, 231
    conflict avoidance, 221
    didactic leadership, 221-222, 223
    differences from Western leadership styles,
        212, 224-225
    family business model, 214, 216-217
    human heartedness, 218-219, 222
    in East Asia, 206, 211-214, 231
    legitimized order and compliance, 214,
        216-217, 224-225
    moral leadership, 218-219, 221
    nepotism, 223
    paternalism, 214, 220-222

power in, 213
relations with subordinates, 212, 214, 217,
    218-219, 221, 222, 223
social harmony, 214, 217-220, 221
strategies and tactics, 222-223
values, 211
vertical collectivism and, 55-56, 57
Hierarchies:
conflicts with egalitarian values, 209
in Britain, 240
in East Asian cultures, 216
in French culture, 63-65, 66
in headship, 216
High-context communication, 27-29, 30, 55, 67
Hofstede, Geert, 51-53, 235
Hong Kong:
business community, 213, 214
Confucian values, 218
economic performance, 31, 32
headship, 212, 220
House, British, 238-241
Hughes, Lou, 158
Human nature, differing views of, 209
Human relations, Fiske framework, 56-58, 125-
    126
Huntington, Samuel P., 83-87

IBM culture measurement studies, 36-42, 43,
    49, 51
Immigrants in France, 77-78
Individualism:
economic growth and, 42
effects on leadership styles, 210
horizontal, 56, 57
in cultures, 37, 42
in French culture, 69
types, 55, 56
vertical, 56, 57
Indonesia:
Bali, 129-131
headship, 217, 220, 231
social harmony as value, 218
Inexpressibility thesis, 10, 14-16
Intercultural communication, 25-26
Interval data, 56, 57
Islam, 48, 84, 85
Italy:
civic engagement, 126-127
history and economy, 126-127
northern, 126-127

opera as cultural metaphor, 127
political participation, 110, 126
southern, 126
ITT, 145

Jagger, Mick, 101, 102, 103, 104
Japan:
economic performance, 31
managers, 135-136, 214
Japanese culture:
bows, 171
changes in emperor's role, 127
communication, 154
differences from other East Asian
    cultures, 213-214
garden metaphor, 127
masculinity, 38
Joint ventures:
multinational, 174-175, 178-181
See also Collaboration, cross-cultural
Judaism, 48

Kong Fu Ze. *See* Confucius
Korea. *See* South Korea
Krueger, Phil, 98-99

Languages:
as defining element of culture, 165-166
as element of civilizations, 84, 87
conceptual system represented in, 4-5
English, 84
French, 70
German, 166
metaphorical expressions, 6
need for metaphors, 11, 14-16
points of contact between, 165-166
reconstructionist view, 12
rich points, 166-167, 170, 171-172
word meanings, 11
Leadership:
cultural differences and styles of, 38, 42,
    211
didactic, 221-222, 223
differences from headship, 212, 224-225
French view of, 211
legitimacy, 212
North American concept of, 205-211, 213
relationships with followers, 208-209, 210
theories, 206-208
training, 204, 205, 209, 224-226

transactional model, 207-210
transformational model, 207-208,
    210-211, 225
League of Women Voters (LWV), 113, 118
Leisure activities, 98-99, 119-120
Lennon, John, 101
Lewinsky, Monica, 72
Lichine, A., 68
Lombardi, Vince, 98
London Export Company, 180, 187
Louis XIV, King of France, 62, 63
Love:
    in creative success model, 97, 104-105
    in traditional American success model, 96,
        103
Low-context communication, 27-29, 30,
        67-68
LWV. *See* League of Women Voters

Mafia, 126
Malaysia:
    criticism of Western culture, 87
    headship, 212-213
    religious groups, 85
    social harmony, 219
Management:
    cross-cultural, 49-50
    expatriates in East Asia, 225-226
    in France, 66, 140-141, 211
    See also Headship; Leadership
Management training:
    in North America, 203-205
    use of ALPs model, 246
    See also Leadership, training
Managers:
    East Asian, 135-136, 214
    expatriate, 225-226
    French, 66, 140-141, 150-151, 211
    involved in cross-cultural
        collaboration, 184, 192-195
Marie Antoinette, Queen of France, 169
Market Pricing (MP), 57, 127
Masculine cultures, 37-38, 42
Memory, 11
Men:
    association membership, 114, 116-117, 119
    communication, 144
    roles, 96
    values of, 37-38
Metaphorical conceptual system, 3-5, 6, 7

Metaphors:
    "argument is war," 4, 5-6
    Aristotle on, 9-10
    change introduction, 238
    compactness thesis, 10, 12-14, 15-16
    distinction from analogies and similes,
        18-19
    educational utility, 10, 17-18, 19-20
    emotive force, 16-17
    etymology, 9
    failed, 15-16
    inexpressibility thesis, 10, 14-16
    knowledge needed, 12-14, 17, 18
    multiple characteristics, 12-14, 16
    need for, 11, 14-16
    pervasiveness, 3-5
    subconstructs, 7
    tension in, 13
    theory of, 10
    "time is money," 6-7
    vividness thesis, 10, 16-18
    See also Cultural metaphors
Minitel, 77
Mitterrand, François, 72-73
Money, metaphor for time, 6-7
Monochronic time, 27, 68
Morality, 96
MP (Market Pricing), 57, 127
Multinational corporations. *See* Joint
        ventures; Negotiation
Music. *See* Rock music
Muslim countries. *See* Islam

NAFTA (North American Free Trade
        Agreement), 85, 89
Namath, Joe, 99, 100
Nantong Cellulose Fibers Company (NCFC):
    construction of plant, 188-189
    formation, 175, 191
    negotiations, 178-181
    planning, 184, 185-187
    workers, 189
Napoleon Bonaparte, 62
Nations:
    declining power, 89-90
    torn or cleft, 85
NATO (North Atlantic Treaty
        Organization), 73
NCFC. *See* Nantong Cellulose Fibers
        Company

Negotiation, cross-cultural:
  balance of power, 143-144
  circumstances, 141-142, 144-145
  complementary strategies, 146-148
  counterpart's negotiation script, 139-141
  developing expertise, 157-158
  first moves, 152-153
  genders of negotiators, 144
  home culture negotiation script, 137-139
  implementation of strategies, 151-157
  influencing counterpart's strategy, 148-149
  joint strategies, 145, 150, 153
  joint venture formation, 178-181
  knowing counterparts, 135-136,
      139-141, 146-148
  negotiator profiles, 137, 138, 139-141, 143
  predicting counterpart's strategy,, 146-148
  process, 153-157
  relationships with counterparts, 135,
      141-144, 156-157
  selecting strategies, 135-136, 148, 149-151
  strategies, 133-135
  time schedule, 145
Neighborliness, 117
Neo-Confucian cultures:
  Collectivism, 38
  in East Asia, 33-34
  Masculinity/Feminity, 38
  Power Distance, 38
Nepotism, 223
NGOs. *See* Nongovernmental
      organizations
Nominal data, 56-57
Nongovernmental organizations (NGOs), 90
Nonprofit organizations, 113-114, 115
Non-zero-sum games, 81, 86, 90
North American Free Trade Agreement
      (NAFTA), 85, 89
Northern League, 127
Nosbers, Peter, 168
Numerical data, 56-57, 58

Offices:
  American, 26
  French, 26, 66
  German, 26-27
Opera, Italian, 127
Ordinal data, 56, 57
Organizations. *See* Association
      membership

Otis Elevator, 174

Parent-teacher organizations, 113, 117, 118
Past:
  views in different cultures, 26
  See also Time
Paternalism, 214, 220-222
Peguy, Charles, 63
People's Republic of China. *See* China
Performance appraisals, 28
Philippines, 217, 218, 220
Plato, 10
Political participation:
  civic engagement and, 110-111, 117-118
  in Italy, 110, 126
  trends in United States, 111-112, 117-118
Polychronic time, 27, 30, 68
Power Distance, 37, 38, 42, 69, 216, 225
Power shift, 89-90
Presley, Elvis, 101, 102
Protestant Ethic, 52-53, 97
Protestantism, 95

Ratio data, 56, 57
Reagan, Ronald, 31, 73
Reciprocity in relationships, 218, 219, 223
Red Cross, 113, 118
Relationships:
  Confucian view of, 34-35, 46, 216, 218,
      221
  dialogue, 222
  face, 35, 219, 222
  friendships in France, 70-71, 75
  nepotism, 223
  reciprocity, 218, 219, 223
Religions:
  as defining element of civilizations, 84, 87
  Buddhism, 218
  church-related organizations, 112, 113, 116
  Islam, 48, 84, 85
  Judaism, 48
  Western, 48
  See also Christianity
Residential mobility, 119
Reward systems:
  in creative success model, 103
  in traditional success model, 95,
      100-101
Rituals, 93, 99

Rock concerts, audience participation, 104-105
Rock music:
    lyrics, 102, 103-104
    popularity in United States, 94, 101
Rock stars, 101-102
    relationships with fans, 104-105
    sexuality, 102
    success models, 106-107
Rokeach Value Surveys, 42-43
Rolling Stones, 101, 102
Roper Organization, 112

Sampoerna Company, 231
Sampoerna, Puter, 231
Saudi Arabia, 154
Scandinavia, 57
Schmäh:
    as general attitude, 167-168, 170
    as humorous comment or exchange, 168-169
    as lie, 169-170
    disagreements about meanings, 166, 169
    examples, 168, 169-170
    importance to culture, 170-171
    lack of English equivalent, 170-171
    nonverbal examples, 169
Science, 48-49
Scientific-physicalist model of social universe, 94, 96, 97
Self-sacrifice, 96, 99
Shevardnadze, Eduard, 149
Similes, 13-14, 18-19
Singapore:
    Chinese business community, 213
    Confucian values, 218
    criticism of Western culture, 87
    economic performance, 31, 32
    headship, 220
Social capital:
    definition, 111
    explanations of decline, 118-120
    families, 117
    in other countries, 118
    influence of public policy, 121
    research needs, 120-121
    support groups, 116
    trends in United States, 111-114, 117-118
Social harmony, 35, 214, 217-220, 221
Social networks, 110-111

South Asia, 32
South Korea:
    Chinese business community, 213
    economic performance, 31, 32
    headship, 212, 220
Space, views in different cultures, 26-27
Spanish bullfight, 130
Status:
    in Authority Ranking cultures, 57
    in French culture, 65
    of headman, 212-213
    symbols, 95
    See also Hierarchies
Stereotypes, 236-237
Success models:
    creative, 97, 101-106
    traditional American, 94-96, 97, 99-101, 103-104, 105-106
Support groups, 115-116

Taiwan:
    business community, 213, 214
    Confucian values, 218
    economic performance, 31, 32
    headship, 212, 220
Television, 119-120
Terrorism, 85
TGV (Trains de grand vitesse), 77
Thailand, 217, 218, 220
Thatcher, Margaret, 240, 244
Time:
    American view of, 26
    as money, 6-7
    Balinese view, 129-130
    monochronic, 27, 68
    polychronic, 27, 30, 68
    views in different cultures, 26, 27
Tow, 175, 176, 178
Toyota, 145, 156, 158
Trade, 84-85, 86, 89, 90
Traditional American model of success, 94-96, 97, 99-101, 103-104, 105-106
Traditional model of social universe, 94-96, 97
Training:
    leadership, 204, 205, 209, 224-226
    management, 203-205, 246
Trains de grand vitesse (TGV), 77
Transactional model of leadership, 207-210

Transformational model of leadership,
207-208, 210-211, 225
Trilling, Lionel, 25
Trust, 117-118, 195
Truth, 38, 48-49
Turner, Ike, 102
Turner, Tina, 102

Uncertainty Avoidance, 38, 42, 48, 49, 69
Union membership, 113, 116
United States:
    Constitution, 242
    decision-making processes, 28
    differences from Britain, 242-243, 244,
      245-246
    individualism, 57
    management training, 203-205
    negotiation scripts, 137-139, 194
    political participation, 111-112, 117-118
    scientific-physicalist model of social uni-
      verse, 94, 96, 97
    social capital, 111-114, 117-118
    traditional model of social universe, 94-96,
      97
    view of time, 26
    violence, 94
    See also Football games; Rock concerts;
      Success models
U.S. Labor Department, 114
University of International Business and
    Economics (Beijing), 176

Vienna. *See Schmäh*
Violence:
    in football, 97-98
    in United States, 94
    terrorism, 85
    See also Ethnic conflict
Virtue, Confucian view of, 35, 218
Vividness thesis, 10, 16-18
Volunteers, 113-114, 118

War, metaphor for argument, 4, 5-6
Warriors, 13-14
Western cultures:
    criticism of, 87
    differences from Eastern, 47-49, 87, 194,
      212, 224-225
    See also Britain; France; United States
Wine:
    consumption in France, 76
    diseases of vines, 62
    high-quality, 66, 76
    making, 60-61, 78
    See also French wine metaphor
Women:
    association membership, 113
    communication, 144
    feminist organizations, 115
    French, 71-72, 75, 144
    in labor force, 118-119
    roles, 96
    values of, 37-38
Work group cultures, 234
World Values Survey, 118

Zero-sum games, 81-82, 86, 90

About the Editor

Martin J. **Gannon** (PhD, Columbia University) is Professor of Management and Director of the Center for Global Business, Robert H. Smith School of Business, University of Maryland at College Park. He is also the Founding Director of the College Park Scholars Program in Business, Society, and the Economy (an undergraduate living-learning community). Previous positions at Maryland include Associate Dean for Academic Affairs, Chair of the Faculty of Management and Organization, and Co-Founder/Co-Director of the Small Business Development Center. At Maryland, he teaches in the areas of international management and behavior and business strategy. He is the author or coauthor of 85 articles and 13 books, including *Dynamics of Competitive Strategy* (Sage, 1992); *Understanding Global Cultures: Metaphorical Journeys Through 17 Nations* (Sage, 1994, revised ed., 2001), *Managing Without Traditional Methods: International Innovations in Human Resource Management* (1996); and *Ethical Dimensions of International Management* (Sage, 1997).

Professor Gannon has been Senior Research Fulbright Professor at the Center for the Study of Work and Higher Education in Germany and the John F. Kennedy/Fulbright Professor at Thammasat University in Bangkok, as well as a visiting professor at several Asian and European universities. He has also been a consultant to many companies and government agencies. Currently he is the main consultant to GEICO Insurance Company on the design and delivery of its Senior Management Training Program, and the University of Maryland Director of the Nothrop-Grunman Managerial IMPACT Certificate Program designed to enhance international skills.